ETHICS AND COMMUNITY IN THE HEALTH CARE PROFESSIONS

Recently debate about the relationship between individual and community has become central to the making of social policy in Europe, the United States and elsewhere. Community approaches are particularly fashionable in discussion of health care. Philosophical treatment of medical ethics has also come to focus on the conflict between liberal forms of patient-centred medicine and communitarian values. How far do patients' rights need to be protected from community's imperatives and how far do communities themselves need to be protected?

This book is the first to explore the importance of these conflicting approaches to health care and examines the implications of these approaches both for medical ethics and for specific areas of health care practice. Among the topics discussed are:

- Liberal and communitarian views on the allocation of health care resources
- Young people and family care
- A European perspective on the role of IT in genetic counselling
- Health care decision-making for elderly patients

Ethics and Community in the Health Care Professions provides an accessible introduction to, and analysis of, a major debate in health care. It will be invaluable to both students and practitioners.

Michael Parker is Co-ordinator of a European Union research project on biomedical practitioners' ethics education. He is the author of *The Growth of Understanding* (1995).

D0363222

PROFESSIONAL ETHICS
Editor: Ruth Chadwick
Centre for Professional Ethics, University of Central Lancashire

Professionalism is a subject of interest to academics, the general public and would-be professional groups. Traditional ideas of professions and professional conduct have been challenged by recent social, political and technological changes. One result has been the development for almost every profession of an ethical code of conduct which attempts to formalise its values and standards. These codes of conduct raise a number of questions about the status of a 'profession' and the consequent moral implications for behaviour.

This series seeks to examine these questions both critically and constructively. Individual volumes will consider issues relevant to particular professions, including nursing, genetic counselling, journalism, business, the food industry and law. Other volumes will address issues relevant to all professional groups such as the function and value of a code of ethics and the demands of confidentiality.

Also available in this series:

ETHICS AND COMMUNITY IN THE HEALTH CARE PROFESSIONS

Edited by Michael Parker

London and New York

First published 1999
by Routledge
11 New Fetter Lane, London EC4P 4EE

Simultaneously published in the USA and Canada
by Routledge
29 West 35th Street, New York, NY 10001

Typeset in Times by Routledge
Printed and bound in Great Britain by Creative Print and Design
(Wales), Ebbw Vale

British Library Cataloguing in Publication Data
A catalogue record for this book is available from the British Library

Library of Congress Cataloguing in Publication Data
Ethics and community in the health care professions / edited by
Michael Parker. p. cm. – (Professional ethics)
Includes bibliographical references and index.
1. Medical ethics–Social aspects. 2. Communitarianism–Health aspects.
3. Medical personnel–Moral and ethical aspects.
4. Professional ethics. I. Parker, Michael, 1958– . II. Series.
R725.5.E87 1999 174'.2–dc21 98–35439

ISBN 0–415–15027–2 (hbk)
ISBN 0–415–15028–0 (pbk)

CONTENTS

CONTENTS

CONTRIBUTORS

Ruth Chadwick is Head of Centre and Professor of Moral Philosophy at the Centre for Professional Ethics at the University of Central Lancashire. Her publications include the four-volume edited collection, *Kant: Critical Assessments*; *Ethics, Reproduction and Genetic Control*; *The Encyclopaedia of Applied Ethics* and a large number of papers in learned journals. She is joint series editor of the Routledge series on Professional Ethics. She is Secretary of the International Association of Bioethics and a member of the National Committee for Philosophy.

Donna Dickenson is Leverhulme Senior Lecturer in Medical Ethics and Law at Imperial College, London. She is the author of *Property, Women and Politics: Subjects or Objects?*, Cambridge: Polity Press, 1997. She is also the author, with Michael Parker, of a series of ten workbooks on core themes in medical ethics.

Andrew Edgar is a Lecturer in Philosophy at the University of Wales, Cardiff, and Director of the Centre for Applied Ethics. He has published papers in a number of areas of philosophy and applied ethics and has directed a European Union funded research programme on the ethics of health-related quality of life studies.

Michael Hammond is a Lecturer in Philosophy at Lancaster University. He is the author of *Understanding Phenomenology*, Oxford: Blackwell, 1991.

Chris Heginbotham is the Chief Executive of East and North Hertfordshire Health Authority. Prior to this he was Chief Executive of Riverside Mental Health Trust, and for much of the 1980s was National Director of MIND, the National Association for Mental Health. He is Visiting Senior Fellow at the University of Birmingham Health Services Management Centre. His most recent book, co-authored with Professor Tom Campbell, is *Mental Illness: Prejudice Discrimination and Law*, Aldershot: Gower, 1991.

Sirkku Hellsten is a Research Fellow in Philosophy at the University of Helsinki, Finland and is also Visiting Fulbright Fellow at the Ethics Center, University of South Florida. She has published articles on applied ethics and social and political philosophy, particularly on the subjects of justice and the liberal–communitarian debate. She is the author of *In Defence of Moral Individualism*, North-Holland, 1997. She is currently working on a research project on the ethics of biotechnology.

J. Stuart Horner is a Visiting Professor in Medical Ethics at the University of Central Lancashire. He was previously a Director of Public Health in Croydon, Hillingdon, Preston and North West Lancashire. He now writes on medical ethics related to public health. Formerly the chair of its Medical Ethics Committee, Professor Horner is now a Vice-President of the British Medical Association.

Vivien Lindow is an independent consultant, trainer, researcher and writer on mental health issues in Bristol, England. She works from a critical perspective as someone who has received mental health services.

Michael Parker is a Lecturer in Medical Ethics at Imperial College School of Medicine, London. He co-ordinates a European Union research project on biomedical ethics practitioner education. He is the author of a number of papers and books on the liberalism–communitarianism debate including, *The Growth of Understanding: Beyond Individuals and Communities*, Aldershot: Avebury, 1995, and on medical ethics more generally. He is also the author, with Donna Dickenson, of a series of ten workbooks on core themes in medical ethics.

Kim Petrie is from Prince Edward Island, Canada and is currently a researcher at the Centre for Professional Ethics funded by the Canadian Society for International Health and the Canadian Department of Foreign Affairs and International Trade. She is currently carrying out research into the legal, social and ethical issues which arise in genetic research involving children.

Mark R. Wicclair is Professor of Philosophy and Adjunct Professor of Community Medicine at West Virginia University. He is also Visiting Professor of History and Philosophy of Science and Visiting Professor of Medicine at the University of Pittsburgh. He has published extensively in the areas of ethics and medical ethics and is the author of *Ethics and the Elderly*, New York and Oxford: Oxford University Press, 1993.

Hub Zwart is Director of the Centre for Ethics at the Catholic University of Nijmegen in the Netherlands. He has published several books and articles on philosophical, ethical and bioethical issues. He is editor in chief of the Dutch Journal for Medicine and Ethics. Recently he published *Ethical Consensus and the Truth of Laughter: The Structure of Moral Transformations*, Kampan: Kok Pharos, 1996.

SERIES EDITOR'S PREFACE

Professional ethics is now acknowledged as a field of study in its own right. Much of its recent development has resulted from rethinking traditional medical ethics in the light of new moral problems arising out of advances in medical science and technology. Applied philosophers, ethicists and lawyers have devoted considerable energy to exploring the dilemmas emerging from modern health care practices and their effects on the practitioner–relationship.

It is not only technological advance that has had an impact on ethical thinking about the practice of health care, however, but also the wider debates in moral and political philosophy about the contrasting perspectives of individualism and communitarianism. From the point of view of communitarian ethics the individual is regarded as essentially situated in relationships and communities which have shared values and which have a significant role to play in constructing the identity of the individual.

Michael Parker's volume explores the tensions between the two sets of values: individualistic values – which have informed to a considerable degree the development of medical ethics – and communitarian values, and their implications for the health care professions. Through its coverage both of theoretical issues in liberalism and communitarianism and of particular issues such as the imparting of genetic information, it makes a contribution to the wider ethical debate as well as to the practical applications of theory.

The Professional Ethics book series seeks to examine ethical issues in the professions and related areas both critically and constructively. Individual volumes address issues relevant to all professional groups, such as the applicability of theoretical frameworks, as in this volume, or the nature of the profession. Other volumes examine issues relevant to particular professions, including those which have hitherto received little attention, such as health care management and general practice.

INTRODUCTION

Health care ethics: liberty, community or participation?

Michael Parker

In their book *The Patient in the Family* Hilde and James Lindemann Nelson recount the case of a man whose daughter is suffering from kidney failure.[1] She is spending six hours, three times a week on a dialysis machine and the effects of this are becoming hard for her and her family to bear. She has already had one kidney transplant which her body rejected and her doctors are unsure whether a second would work but are willing to try if they can find a suitable donor. After some tests the paediatrician privately tells the father that he is indeed compatible.

It may seem inconceivable that a father would refuse to donate his kidney to his daughter under such circumstances. Yet he does refuse and justifies his decision not only on the basis that the outcome is uncertain but also on his concerns about the operation itself. He is frightened and worried about what would happen to him and his other children if his remaining kidney were to fail. He is ashamed to feel this way and cannot bear to refuse openly so he asks the paediatrician to tell the family that he is in fact not compatible. However, whilst having some sympathy she says she cannot lie for him. After a silence the father then says, 'OK then I'll do it. If they knew that I was compatible but wouldn't donate my kidney, it would wreck the family.'[2]

But why should this decision wreck the family? Does a father have a special obligation to donate his kidney to his daughter? What is it about families and the values which underpin them which leads to the expectation that parents will sacrifice themselves for their children (and in particular for the child who is ill)? What is it about medicine which intensifies such expectations? In order to understand such cases and the conflicts which characterise them it is

1

important to recognise the subtle differences and conflicts between the values in families and those found in medicine.

> The man who was afraid to donate his kidney thought he had failed his daughter because he wasn't willing to do everything he could to try to save her life; he thought he was being cowardly and a bad father. And perhaps he was. But another possibility he hadn't considered was that [with his consent] he was adopting the morality of medicine rather than honouring what's valuable about families. Both the father and the physician believed that the only legitimate question here was, 'What is in the best interest of the patient?' Yet families are made up of a number of people, all of whose interests have to be honoured. The single focus on one individual may be fine for medicine, but it's less fine for families, who have their own, very different, mechanisms for protecting their vulnerable members. In times of illness, families – anxious, needy and easily swayed – are drawn into medicine's overwhelming commitment to patient care. Family members lose sight of the value of family life at these times because, like a fish who takes water for granted, they generally live within such values without being explicitly aware of it.[3]

This example suggests that there is a conflict in health care between two sets of values; those individualistic values which the Lindemann Nelsons claim underlie patient-centred medicine and those which sustain families and communities. The Lindemann Nelsons argue that modern medicine's overriding focus on the good of the individual patient has distorted the ways in which family members interact with one another and in particular with those who are sick. They argue that at times of stress families often adopt the individualistic values of the medical world and this leads them unintentionally to trample on the values and concerns which sustain families. On the other hand, they argue that families in their adherence to values which are family-oriented have themselves sometimes created distortions in medicine. For couples who see their need to have a child and their subfertility as a medical problem, for example, and families who want their relatives kept alive no matter what the likelihood that there will be any life other than simply the organic, place demands upon medicine which it is impossible for it to meet.[4]

INTRODUCTION

The claim that there are important tensions between the values of patient-centred medicine and those which sustain families and communities reflects an ongoing and important contemporary debate in health care ethics and in ethics more widely between individualistic approaches and those which have come to be known as communitarian. It is the aim of this book both to reflect this debate and to explore its implications for the health care professions and vice versa. In the rest of this introduction I sketch the outline of this debate in order to provide a context for the chapters which follow, each of which engages with this debate with respect to a different issue in health care.

Liberty

For liberal individualists the human world is made up of individual people each with his or her own desires, interests and conception of the good, each with the ability to choose freely his or her own way of life. This means that they tend to explain moral problems such as that experienced by the father in the example above in terms of the competing needs and interests of such individuals and they have, as a consequence, a tendency to focus on the differences between people, the variety of their needs and values, and their separateness. That is, they concentrate rather less upon what people have in common; their similarities, shared values and projects, and rather more on their diversity.

The power of this emphasis on the needs and interests of individuals lies in its recognition that any workable understanding of the moral world must relate in a meaningful way to the actual decisions with which individual people are confronted in their everyday lives. That is, to the moral concerns of real people such as the father in the example. This leads naturally, argue liberal individualists, to a conception of morality which is concerned with how we are to live our lives in a world of competing conceptions of the good. Thus it is that liberal individualists interpret human relationships as the expression of individual needs and wishes and conceptualise moral problems in terms of and centred around the concepts of 'autonomy', 'rights', 'justice' and so on. And this leads to a model of health care ethics focused on 'patient-centred care', 'informed consent' and the 'best interests of the patient'.

In this sense the liberal individualist approach can be said to resonate with one of our most important moral intuitions, for as Berlin suggests,

I wish my life and my decisions to depend on myself, not on external forces of whatever kind. I wish to be the instrument of my own and not of other men's acts of will. I wish to be a subject, not an object, to be moved by reasons, by conscious purposes, which are my own, not by causes.[5]

Recently, however, liberal individualism and its focus on individuals has come under attack from several directions. For, despite the advantages of the liberal individualist conception of the subject it can in some ways be seen, as the example above shows, to create as many problems as it solves. Communitarians such as the Lindemann Nelsons argue that the problem with individualism as an approach to ethics is that its focus on the individual means that it inevitably undervalues the relationships between people, their shared interests and values and implies that families and other social entities can have no value other than that of the individuals of which they are constituted. That is, that the needs of families such as that of the father in the example above ought never to be put above those of individual family members; in this case the sick child. For, from a liberal individualist perspective it makes no sense, communitarians suggest, to attribute value to groups or to relationships.[6]

Communitarians argue that this inevitably leads to a one-dimensional view of the moral world. They claim moreover that from this individualist perspective the very possibility of us being the moral beings that we are in any sense at all is brought into question. For our understanding of questions as specifically moral is only made possible by virtue of the fact that we are engaged in a world with others and are *not* individuals in the liberal individualist sense. For, it is, communitarians suggest, only through such engagement that we come to understand the world and our relationships with others as ethical or moral; as a world which challenges us to both work out meaningful ways of living with others and to create a meaningful life for ourselves.

The case study described by the Lindemann Nelsons shows that the moral world in which we live is both more complex and more multi-layered than individualism would suggest. For whilst it is true to say that in an important sense moral problems such as the one facing the father are problems for us as individuals it is also true to say that they are understood as problems by us because of our engagement in shared ways of life with other people. Liberal individualism identifies an important dimension of the moral world in its concern for the protection of individuals and their rights, but it overlooks the extent to which morality is tied to the fact of our engagement in shared forms of life (such as families) with other people. Such considerations highlight the importance of a recognition of the value of the fundamental sociality of human beings and it is an implication of this that communitarians are right to argue against what they perceive to be the liberal attachment to the concept of an antecedently individuated subject. For in order to conceive of ourselves in this way we are called upon to deny the fact of our engagement in a world with others and of our social embeddedness and view such facts as simply, 'values we happen to espouse at any given time'.[7] And this is a significant cost indeed. For,

> we cannot regard ourselves as independent in this way without great cost to those loyalties and convictions whose moral force consists partly in the fact that living by them is inseparable from understanding ourselves as the particular persons we are as members of this family or community or nation or people, as bearers of this history, as sons or daughters of that revolution, as citizens of this republic.[8]

If we consider ethical problems from an individualistic perspective such a consideration is inevitably incomplete, for there are aspects of all moral problems which are not susceptible to analysis in terms of individuals. To see this is to perceive the importance for moral thinking of the other arm of the dilemma facing the father in the example above, that is, the value of the family or the community which communitarians claim is not expressible in individual terms.

Community

Avineri and de Shalit[9] argue that communitarianism has two aspects. The first of these is, as I have attempted to show above, a methodological critique of individualism, an argument to the effect that it is not possible to explain the moral world from an individualist perspective. The second aspect of communitarian thought which might be seen to complement this is a critique of the morally unsatisfactory *consequences* of individualism allied to a number of assertions about what constitutes the good society or community. These arguments clearly have important implications for health care, many of which are explored within the chapters of this book and, in this second sense, the case described by the Lindemann Nelsons is a good example of a communitarian argument about the morally unsatisfactory consequences of an overemphasis on the individual in medicine.

It is often suggested by communitarians that Western democracies are suffering from an overemphasis on individual rights and that this has led to the disintegration of the sense of social solidarity and responsibility which underpins social networks such as communities and families and has led to the breakdown of family and communal life. In response communitarians have begun to argue for a renewed emphasis on the *value* of communal life, social relationships, the family and of shared values. Amitai Etzioni for example has argued that,

> Communitarians [ought to] draw on interpersonal bonds to encourage members to abide by shared values, such as, 'do not throw your rubbish out of your window' and 'mind the children when you drive'. Communities gently chastise those who violate shared moral norms and express approbation for those who abide by them. They turn to the state only when all else fails. Hence, the more viable communities are, the *less* the need for policing.[10]

By such means communitarians argue that communities can come to be valued and a 'spirit of community' (re)built; acting as an antidote to the social disintegration caused by the growth of individualism.

Despite Etzioni's final emphasis however such arguments reveal something of a contradiction within communitarian thinking. For although they argue philosophically that our moral understanding arises naturally out of shared values, their political argument implies that such values must be enforced or encouraged. But if human beings are essentially and naturally embedded in shared values and shared ways of life why is it that they need to be reminded of them? Given the communitarian assumption that such shared values already feature in and are constitutive of our identity, it would appear that the political communitarian's point is that not just any shared values will do! Indeed communitarian thinking in relation to health care has tended to be manifested in the distinction, first discussed in this context by Daniel Callahan, between *eccentric* and *reasonable* demands,[11] which lends credence to the claim that for the communitarian not all communities or forms of life are of equal value. This is not a purely theoretical point. For this distinction is manifested increasingly frequently in health care decision-making. Recently in the United Kingdom for example it was alleged that a teenage woman was refused a liver transplant on the grounds that she had been a user of the drug ecstasy[12] and in his contribution to this volume Hub Zwart reports a debate in the Dutch media in which it was suggested that the desire of a post-menopausal woman to have a child is eccentric.

These and other examples in several of the chapters of this book, along with the communitarian emphasis on shared values and stable communities (given that we live in times of great change), suggest that communitarianism has an inbuilt tendency towards conservatism, a tendency to value traditional forms of social relationship (and life styles) as reasonable and to see social change as social disintegration and the call for individual rights as eccentric. A corollary to this, I have suggested, is the communitarian interpretation of the origin of contemporary social ills in terms of the breakdown of traditional modes of relationship i.e. marriage, the family and so on which communitarians tend to associate with the call for individual rights and freedom. For them, the liberal emphasis upon the individual and upon individual rights has gone too far and has encouraged us to forget the value of the life we share with others. In his contribution to this book Michael Hammond explores the extent to which individualistic values are compatible with 'community care' in its broadest sense.

This tendency to conservatism can be seen to originate in the communitarian account of moral reasoning, which is not character-ised as it is for the individualist by free rational choice and by the pursuit of one's goals and conceptions of the good, but as a search for an understanding of one's social identity or role, an understand-ing which can only be achieved through a grasp of one's constitutive attachments to particular communities and values. And this is in accord with the Lindemann Nelsons' consideration of the father's dilemma in the case previously mentioned where, when reflecting upon his situation, the father considers his moral options in terms of his relationships to the family as a whole, his role as a father, his responsibilities to his children and the likely effect of his choice upon his social identity.

I have suggested that communitarians blame the problems of contemporary liberal societies as they perceive them on the individualistic demand for more and more individual rights and the associated attempt to escape our attachments and responsibilities.

In her contribution to this book Donna Dickenson argues that far from seeing a burgeoning of individual rights in recent times we have in fact witnessed their gradual erosion. Nevertheless, communitarians such as Daniel Bell go on to argue that the (ultimately futile) attempt to escape one's constitutive attachments and one's social identity is profoundly damaging not only for communities but also for *individuals themselves.* [13] [For the communitarian] 'any attempt to "escape the grip" of our constitutive identities results in becoming a "disturbed" or "damaged" person.'[14]

But to what extent is it possible to argue that membership of a community and adherence to community norms is always good and escape from it harmful? A common difficulty faced by accounts of ethics which are based on notions of 'community' is that they tend to have difficulty explaining just what would be wrong with, say sexual abuse or female circumcision, were a particular community to approve of it. Communitarians tend to assume that membership of a community is always positive and the escape from community always harmful, focusing on the benefits of community at the expense of the damage communities may cause. In this sense it is undeniable that at the very least communitarians are guilty of underplaying the conflicts of values within existing communities and families.

Such conflicts and the existence of disadvantage and discrimination in real communities are problematic for the communitarian because they bring to the fore the fact that whilst describing powerfully the damage which can occur when people attempt to escape their constitutive attachments, communitarians are incapable of explaining the damage which is caused by *not* escaping such attachments. Some of the crucial dimensions of our moral life, notably the need to uphold the rights of individuals and minority groups against the community at large seem not to be explicable within a communitarian framework. As a consequence, Chris Heginbotham is right to argue in his contribution to this volume that communitarianism says little for those who feel themselves to be excluded from or at the fringes of communities. This is because it fails to see that the convergence of ideas with our deepest sense of self-image is in itself no guarantee of justice. The question of justice does not relate to the origin of our beliefs but to how to evaluate them and how to make moral judgements. For, as Will Kymlicka has argued,

No matter how deep a certain practice or belief is, we can still question its justice. Depth does not make something right. It is possible that something relatively shallow in our culture is more just, and should replace the deeper practice or belief.[15]

The communitarian emphasis on shared values, constitutive attachments and the value of community combined with their insensitivity to the damage which can be caused by communities leaves open the possibility, as Sirkku Hellsten's chapter shows, of the justification at least sometimes of the actual *oppression* of individuals by their communities. It is true that Etzioni says, 'A community does not have the right to burn books.'[16] And it is also true that Daniel Callahan specifically argues against the oppressive use of the concept of the natural life span in his book *Setting Limits*.[17] But this need not follow from a communitarian moral view. For, as Kymlicka argues,

> I agree that [the state] *can* act in less coercive ways, but why *should* it avoid coercion? If [communitarians] think that people are damaged by leaving their communities without adequate reason, why not protect them from damaging themselves? Why rely on the notoriously unreliable mechanism of the individual's own assessment of their best interests? We know that some people will be tempted into harming themselves if they are exposed to proselytisers, so why not prohibit proselytisation and apostasy?...[Communitarian] practical recommendations are plausible, but [their] ontological claim justifies far greater restrictions on personal liberty, and [they] have given no reason why we should respect certain commonly accepted civil liberties.[18]

Whilst Etzioni, Callahan and other communitarians vehemently deny that it is their intention to return to what they agree are oppressive ways of life, and whilst they argue that their real aim is a renewed and healthy balance between rights and responsibilities, communitarian moral theory is *capable* at least of justifying the oppression of individuals in favour of communities and shared values. For while communitarianism helps us to see the extent to which the possibility of morality and of moral thinking depends upon our embeddedness in ways of life with other people and helps us to see that 'identity' is a key moral concept, the communitarians' emphasis upon the social at the expense of the individual means that they are incapable of explaining the need to be able to uphold, at least sometimes, the rights of individuals against their community or family. Any workable theory of morality and of health care ethics must be capable of accommodating both our social embeddedness *and* of recognising the moral significance of the individual and in this sense it can clearly be neither wholly communitarian nor wholly individualist.

Participation: a resolution?

Whether or not it is in fact true that we are witnessing the breakdown of community and of unified traditions as communitarians suggest, such a possibility inevitably brings into question the viability of the communitarian project itself. For, it might be said that when we look around us there are few if any candidates for the shared values upon which a communitarian New World might be built. We live in a world characterised by diversity, a world in which candidates for the role of paradigmatic communities are revealed to be as often the sites of conflict and violence as of mutual support;[19] a world in which, as Jürgen Habermas suggests, it is not possible to identify the kind of shared values or traditions upon which a communitarian morality might be founded.

> Under modern conditions of life none of the various rival traditions can claim prima facie general validity any longer. Even in answering questions of direct practical relevance, convincing reasons can no longer appeal to the authority of unquestioned traditions.[20]

If appeal is no longer possible either to the kind of detached, individual, rational decision-making called for by liberal individualists nor to communitarian shared values and traditions as the basis of ethical decision-making in health care, how are we to reach even local consensus in the making of ethical decisions of the kind confronting the father at the beginning of this introduction?

What seems clear is that any resolution of this problem would have to be one capable of capturing the insights of both communitarianism and individualism whilst avoiding their weaknesses and pitfalls. And what this means is that it must be capable of capturing both the value of the individual voice and the moral status of the individual whilst at the same time recognising the intersubjective and social context of morality and the value of social relationships and their various manifestations.

These features of our moral world are *together* only explicable in terms of the actual relations between people in the intersubjective contexts which constitute their everyday lives with others.[21] For it is only here, in the relations between people, that the community meets the individual and vice versa. This is to suggest, following Harre and Gillett, that the primary social reality is neither the individual nor the community but *people in conversation.*[22] For it is through such 'conversations' that we negotiate our identity and our moral concerns. It is also here that we discover the ethical voice with which we reflect upon and change the nature of our relations to our community and other people. Any workable ethics must take as its starting point the centrality of the negotiation of ethical questions by real people in 'conversation'. For only within a moral framework of this kind is it possible to capture both the value of communal life and the moral significance of the individual ethical voice. This is a question which is explored further by Andrew Edgar in chapter 1.

From this perspective it is possible to begin to recognise the particular value of the engagement of people in the negotiation of the meaning of their own lives and the nature of their relations with those around them, with those who constitute their communities or families. This suggests that rather than adopting the now traditional top-down principalist approach to health care ethics, the subtlety and the significance of ethical dilemmas in medicine can only be fully grasped and resolved by an approach which is resolutely *bottom-up.* And from this perspective it is possible to recognise the importance of a wider involvement in health care decision-making as is demanded by both Vivien Lindow in chapter 9 and Hub Zwart, in chapter 2 who call for the establishment of an ongoing inclusive public debate about ethical issues relating to health care. Indeed, this book is intended to provide both a forum and a focus for just such a debate.

It is only by our engagement in such questions that the world can be said to have a moral dimension and in this sense the ethical and the moral can be seen to be closely linked to the epistemological. For the working out of ethical ways of going on and living with others is intrinsically related to the question of what it means to be human. From such a perspective the focus of ethics shifts significantly. Both liberal individualism and communitarianism *begin* with a conception of what it is to be human and move on from there to questions of ethics. To do so however is to overlook what I take to be the fundamental question of ethics. For it is our *engagement* in the questions of what it is to be human and what it is to live a life with others which gives our world a moral dimension. This is surely what Callahan had in mind as the kind of context of public negotiation of meaning in which the possibility of *Setting Limits* might be seen as one which enhances the meaning of old age rather than demeaning it.[23] By ruling out such questions in advance of ethics individualists and communitarians rule out the possibility of health care ethics itself. The centrality of the question of what it means to be human in medical ethics is witnessed most forcefully in relation to the recent and ongoing developments in genetics explored in this volume by Ruth Chadwick and Kim Petrie in chapter 6.

What then are the implications of this discursive perspective for health care ethics and for the making of ethical judgements in situations such as that facing the father in the example at the start of this introduction? First, it is clear that this is an ethical approach which is as I have suggested resolutely bottom-up and which prioritises a consideration of what constitutes *ethical decision-making practice*. In the case of the father who has to decide whether or not to donate his kidney this means that the ethical focus ought to be one which begins with a consideration of the meaning of the situation both within the family and between the family and the doctor along with a consideration of how decisions of this kind *ought* to be made. Considered more widely, this emphasis implies that ethical practice is that in which the question of what it means to be human, and what it means to live and work meaningfully with others in this particular kind of situation is *negotiated* in public debate, which, whilst focusing on the achievement of agreement about particular cases, is also framed by principles designed to ensure respect for the discursive and intersubjective nature of human relationships. In the case of ethical dilemmas of the kind faced by the father at the beginning of this introduction the implication is that an ethical resolution is only possible via the creation of fora in which such questions can be addressed and negotiation can take place among all those who have a legitimate interest in the case at hand. This would seem to depend to some extent upon the establishment of fora which place an emphasis upon *participation*, *subsidiarity* and *openness* and which might take a range of different forms from the establishing of public consensus conferences about ethical issues of widespread public concern, to conversations between doctors, patients and families or within families themselves about the ethical questions raised by a particular case or treatment option. In his chapter Stuart Horner argues that there is currently a need for just such a debate both within and between the health care professions.

Finally, this approach, whilst intersubjective, has the advantage of providing as communitarianism does not, space for a critique of accepted values on the basis of a respect for the discursive nature of human experience. For respect of this kind is capable of capturing both our social embeddedness *and also* of recognising that individuals have a right to be protected from their community. Indeed, a discursive approach might lead to the elaboration of a constellation of pragmatic rights and duties within health care: the right to participate; to engage; to have one's voice heard; the duty to listen; to include and so on and such rights would apply to all those with a legitimate interest in a particular case or issue where the question of legitimate interest might be determined according to a principle of 'subsidiarity'.

NOTES

1 Lindemann Nelson, H. and L., *The Patient in the Family*, New York: Routledge, 1995.
2 This story is a variant on one found in Beauchamp, T. and Childress, J., *Principles of Biomedical Ethics*, second edition, New York: Oxford University Press, 1983, p. 285.
3 Lindemann Nelson, *The Patient in the Family*, p. 3.
4 See also, Callahan, D., *Setting Limits: Medical Goals in an Ageing Society*, New York and London: Simon and Schuster, 1987.
5 Berlin, I., 'Two Concepts of Liberty', in *Four Essays on Liberty*, London: Oxford University Press, 1969, p. 131.
6 Kymlicka, W., *Liberalism, Community and Culture*, Oxford: Clarendon Press, 1989, is an important exception.
7 Mendus, S., 'Strangers and Brothers', in Milligan, D. and Watts-Miller, W., *Liberalism, Citizenship and Autonomy*, Aldershot: Avebury, 1992, p. 4.
8 Sandel, M., *Liberalism and the Limits of Justice*, Cambridge: Cambridge University Press, 1982, p. 179.
9 Avineri, S. and de Shalit, A. (eds), *Communitarianism and Individualism*, Oxford: Oxford University Press, 1992, p. 2.
10 Etzioni, A., *The Times*, London, 20 February 1995.
11 Callahan, D., *Setting Limits*.
12 *The Guardian*, Leader, London, 25 January 1997.
13 Bell, D., *Communitarianism and its Critics*, Oxford: Oxford University Press, 1993.
14 Ibid, p. 210.
15 Kymlicka, W., 'Some Questions about Justice and Community', in Bell, D. *Communitarianism and its Critics*, p. 217. Here Kymlicka is para-

phrasing Ronald Dworkin's argument in Dworkin, R., *Taking Rights Seriously*, London: Duckworth, 1977.

16 Etzioni, A., *The Guardian*, London, 13 March 1995.
17 Callahan, D., *Setting Limits*.
18 Kymlicka, W., 'Some Questions about Justice and Community'.
19 Campbell, B., *The Independent*, London, 16 March 1995.
20 Habermas, J., *Justification and Application: Remarks on Discourse Ethics*, Oxford: Polity, 1993, p. 151.
21 Parker, M., *The Growth of Understanding*, Aldershot: Avebury, 1995.
22 Harre, R. and Gillett, G., *The Discursive Mind*, London: Sage, 1994.
23 Callahan, D., *The Troubled Dream of Life*, New York: Simon and Schuster, 1993.

1

THE HEALTH SERVICE AS CIVIL ASSOCIATION

Andrew Edgar

The purpose of this chapter is to explore the possibility of developing a model of justice in health care that is appropriate to the European welfare states, and thereby to challenge the predominance of liberal social contract models. Crucially, the paper will seek to challenge the assumption that patients are to be conceptualised as autonomous agents, freely entering into a relationship with health care providers. It will be suggested, rather, that (at least within the European context) the patient may be understood as always already embedded within a particular community, and further as always already a member of a system of state health care provision, with at best limited scope for a partial withdrawal from that service. The justice of any such state system will be suggested to rest, not in rules of fair resource allocation, but rather in public subscription to, and negotiation of, the moral conditions under which health care is to be pursued.[1]

Michael Oakeshott's concepts of 'enterprise association' and 'civil association' will be used to explicate two possible models of health care provision, typified by Health Maintenance Organisations and the UK National Health Service respectively. Clarifying the distinction between these two types of organisation serves to raise questions as to the relevant conceptions of justice in each case.

Enterprise association

Oakeshott seeks to provide a series of models of the 'modes of association' within which relationships between human beings may be organised. The least ambiguous of these modes is that of enterprise association. In such a relationship, human agents come together, through their own free will, in pursuit of mutual benefit or a common purpose. Two or more agents may seek satisfaction of their distinct current wants, as in the relationship of giver and receiver, buyer and seller, busker and audience, or they may co-operate in order to secure a common goal, by forming fellowships, pressure groups, charitable bodies, commercial companies, and so on (Oakeshott, 1983, 121–125). In such associations, agents will be aware of, and will actively pursue, a substantive purpose. Indeed, as far as the association is concerned, all that is of interest about agents is their commitment to the chosen objective, and the 'power' (including time, energy, resources, skills) that they can bring to the project. An association can only be judged, as an enterprise association, in terms of its effectiveness in achieving its purpose, and will ideally be managed in order to maximise its efficiency. Management, through the organisation and co-ordination of the power of each member, responds to a changing environment, modifying the rules of the association after prudential considera-tion of the most appropriate means necessary to realise the objective. Such associations can be dissolved, should the objective be achieved or cease to be desirable, or should alternative methods be found to pursue the objective. Similarly, members are free to leave, should their interests no longer coincide with those of the association. (In practice there may be restraints upon foundation and dissolution, and upon the entry and exit of members, due for example to legal and financial regulations. Certain prospective members may equally be refused entry, on the grounds that they could not contribute adequately to the achievement of the objective.)

If the rules that serve to organise such associations, and thereby to distribute burdens, responsibilities, risks and rewards between members, can only be assessed in terms of the efficiency with which they serve to secure the desired end, then, for Oakeshott, the question of the 'justice' or 'fairness' of such rules cannot arise, for 'fairness' is defined in terms of the rules. A member of an association may complain that he or she has not received his or her due, as defined by the rules of the association, but cannot complain that the rules are unfair as such. Such a complaint only makes sense if the complainant is saying that the rules, as they stand and are accurately interpreted, do not serve the pursuit of his or her personal objective. As such, the objectives of the complainant and the association no longer coincide, and the complainant has every right to leave. The complainant has no right to demand a change in the rules against the will of other members.

Leonard M. Fleck has outlined a model of a national system of Health Maintenance Organisations (HMO) that may be interpreted in terms of Oakeshott's mode of enterprise association (Fleck, 1990). Following Enthoven's definition, an HMO may be understood as a system 'that accepts responsibility for providing comprehensive health care services to a voluntarily enrolled population for a fixed periodic payment set in advance (i.e. a "capitation payment" that is independent of the number of services actually used). Subscribers have an annual choice of health care plans and agree to get all insured services through the HMO of their choice' (Enthoven, 1985, 43). Fleck places a number of further qualifications on this model. Crucially, informed choice of membership and policy is ensured through potential members of the HMOs being made fully aware of what treatment is available, and what will be unavailable. (If necessary, substantial documents would be provided, detailing the rationing protocols that are part of any possible plan (Fleck, 1990, 116).) A national system of HMOs with different policies would allow any individual a more or less free choice of insurance that would suit him or her. Thus Fleck offers the slightly flippant examples of a 'sanctity of life' HMO (providing an 'extensive range of life-prolonging options'), a 'quality of life' HMO (without such life saving options) and Eldercare HMOs (variously specialising in life-prolongation, long-term care, home care, day care and the like) (Ibid., 114). Free entry and exit into an HMO is thereby facilitated. Further, and in accord with an enterprise association, ultimately the HMOs are to be judged upon their cost efficiency in providing health care (and Fleck takes particular note of the degree to which the provision of expensive treatment for marginal benefit is inhibited).

Such a system culminates in the following scenario: an HMO member has a life threatening disease that is expensive to treat, and that is not covered by his or her insurance. For Fleck, the HMO has no obligation to pay for the treatment, and no injustice occurs should the member die. As Fleck summarises this: 'Patients would have no right to that care, for this is *care that they have denied themselves.*' This is a system of 'constructive rationing...that all would have agreed to, openly and freely and knowingly' (Fleck, 1990, 114; original italics). In sum, as with any enterprise association, justice and fairness are seen as matters of abiding by explicit, fully understood and agreed rules, that have been entered into by autonomous ('rational economic') persons (Ibid., 113).

This model leads to predictable problems. On the one hand, there will be agents who are incapable of autonomous, rational economic action, due to incompetence or lack of finance. On the other hand, there are those who would be a liability to the efficient running of the HMO, and will therefore be denied membership. In response to these problems, Fleck is required to advocate a series of *ad hoc* amendments, typically in the form of a state subsidy or regulation (Fleck, 1990, 117–118). If HMOs are understood as enterprise associations, then there is no injustice in refusing entry to those who are unable to contribute to the pursuit of the members' objective. Insofar as an enterprise association assumes that its members (or those applying for membership) are competent (and if necessary, economically viable) agents, there is no reason why the association should deploy resources to facilitate that competency. Similarly, while an HMO may be a non-profit organisation (at least in Fleck's model), it is not a charitable organisation. Members are encouraged to join on the grounds that the risks of disease and costs of health care are distributed evenly about the membership. Should a potential member be predicted to make excessive demands upon the common resources of the HMO, then the existing members have the right to refuse him or her membership. Again, 'justice' is defined in terms of the rules of the HMO. 'Cherry picking' is, in consideration of the pure type of an enterprise association, not an injustice.

A further point may be made concerning the theorisation of HMOs (and of health care provision in general) in terms of enterprise associations. An enterprise association has a substantive objective. As is indicated by Fleck's advocating of the provision of detailed protocols to members, those who join an association may be expected to have a clear and precise idea of the objectives of the association. The member of an HMO is, in consequence, not pursuing health care *per se*. He or she is pursuing a more or less extensive, but still finite, set of treatments. These treatments may be defined in various forms (including the form of treatment, costs of treatment, conditions to be treated, and even cost-utility ratios), as is indicated by Fleck's suggestions for different HMO policies. This corresponds closely to Seedhouse's definition of 'health' as a commodity (Seedhouse, 1986, 34–35). It is assumed that a person is normally healthy, but that health can be lost, as one might lose any other item of property. Health can be restored, in a piecemeal fashion, by purchasing the appropriate medical care. Health is understood as something separate from the individual, thereby reproducing the conception of the autonomous and disembodied agent, being as free to choose his or her health as he or she is free to choose objectives (and thus membership of enterprise associations). The prospective member of an HMO thereby attempts to anticipate a series of medical interventions that he or she may require, and will be able to afford. The choice is, in consequence, between a more or less extensive list of medical interventions, and the alternative commodities that could be purchased with the insurance premium.

Civil association

Fleck's national system of HMOs, and indeed a state-funded national health service, may be seen as conglomerations of enterprise associations. Not just the HMOs themselves, but hospitals, hospital departments, ambulance units, and even individual consultations may be seen as enterprise associations. Each has a specific objective (or set of objectives), and there is substantial freedom of entry for both those who work for the units (be they medical staff, administrators or other support workers), and for those seeking treatment (albeit to a lesser and more variable degree). But if these systems were nothing more than conglomerations of enterprise associations, such that the system itself has no properties over and above those of its component parts, then the system would be inherently unstable. This may be demonstrated by comparing enterprise associations to social contracts.

Within an enterprise association individuals contract with each other, formally or informally, in order to pursue their objectives. Such contracts are unstable because they are relationships between self-interested bargainers, and the association can only continue if the various members keep to their bargains. To break one's promise at worst dissolves the association, and at best hampers the collective pursuit of the objective. (While there may, in practice, be penalties imposed upon those who break the rules to which they have subscribed, in principle, an associate may exploit the trust bestowed on him or her by others, in order to pursue his or her own objectives. Such cheating is wrong, only because it violates the rules of the enterprise association. The cheat has, however, placed him or herself outside of that association, and exploits the gullibility of the association as he or she might exploit any other resource.) If human beings are to be understood as solitary, self-interested and rational creatures (as is the liberal conceit), then neither a society, nor the system of health care within it, can be composed only of such contracts, for they will be perpetually threatened by what might be understood as a Hobbesian state of war.

Oakeshott's own analysis develops from his reading of Hobbes (Oakeshott, 1991). The inherent instability of enterprise association suggests to Oakeshott that its conceptualisation cannot provide an exhaustive account of the possible modes of human association. Oakeshott's concept of 'civil association' is thus introduced, in order to characterise a further aspect or mode of association. Civil association characterises a stabilising context of moral considerations, an ethical life, within which instrumental activities are pursued. While responding to the problem posed by Hobbes, Oakeshott seeks to break out of Hobbes's purely contractual model of human association. Thus, Oakeshott sees Hobbes as overcoming the instability of mundane social contracts (and thereby averting the threat of war,) by positing a unique contract between subject and sovereign. In such a contract the subjects abandon their unconditional freedom to pursue their self-chosen goals. In mundane contracts, and thus in pure enterprise associations, the associates retain their 'natural right' to pursue their objectives under conditions of their own choice. (As such, the potential associate may permit him or herself to cheat. He or she is under no obligation to subscribe to any more exacting moral rules.) In a Hobbesian commonwealth, the agent has transferred this unconditional right to the sovereign, so that the sovereign sets what Oakeshott terms the 'adverbial' conditions under which the agent continues to pursue his or her chosen objectives (Oakeshott, 1991, 259–263 and 1975, 58n). Mundane social contracts thereby come into existence within a broader, and prior, civil order. It is this civil order in which Oakeshott finds a rudimentary understanding of civil association.

Fleck's *ad hoc* amendments to his system of HMOs, in the form of state regulations, intuit something of this civil order. Regardless of the insurance policy an individual chooses, he or she is required to accept a set of core services that will be provided in all policies, and to submit to a system of top slicing, that will equitably impose additional burdens upon all HMOs, in order to ensure that provision is made for the economically incompetent. One may thereby pursue whatever health policy one likes, but only within certain boundaries. The state seemingly acts as the sovereign, dictating appropriate boundaries. Fleck thereby continues to work with the conceptual tools of a social contract. The amendments suggested are prudential, which is to say that they are designed to bring about some substantive purpose (complementary to those of the HMOs themselves). The system is designed to ensure that all, including the economically incompetent, receive a specific minimal health package. It remains unclear why the disembedded liberal agents should tolerate these amendments (for they will increase the cost of policies, at no obvious personal benefit). Should the agents so choose, they will presumably be able to remove these amendments at the next state elections. Three responses to this problem may be suggested. First, the amendments may be shown to be in the ultimate self-interest of the economically competent, if they serve to defuse the (political and physical) threat posed by those who would otherwise be denied health care, and to police those who would seek to cheat. On the condition that all believe that the economically incompetent are satisfied and that cheats are detected and punished, the amendments serve to stabilise an otherwise unstable system. Second, a rational defence of the justice and equity of the amendments may be given. This, however, begs the question of how readily swayed even rational liberal agents are by reasoned argument.[2] Third, Fleck may presuppose a prior moral sentiment prevalent amongst the economically competent that entails their acknowledgement of some obligation for assistance of the economically incompetent.

Hobbes's commonwealth, and by derivation Oakeshott's civil association, are more subtle responses to these problems. While Hobbes's sovereign has the authority to establish the manner in which its subjects pursue any chosen objectives, it cannot dictate the objectives that its subjects must pursue. Subjects are thereby left free to form whatever enterprise associations they may wish. Because the sovereign recognises no substantive interest as paramount, and requires no objective to be shared by all its subjects, the commonwealth is non-instrumental. The sovereign does not attempt to mediate or negotiate the various conceptions of the ultimate good held by its subjects. (Indeed, Hobbes suggests that there is no ultimate good for humans, precisely because the human condition is such that human satisfactions are transitory.) This is already at odds with Fleck's recommendation of a set of core services that all (including the poor) must accept. The only purpose that can be attributed to the commonwealth is that of maintaining a state of peace (and thus stability). This, for Oakeshott, is not a substantive purpose. Peace cannot be chosen in preference to any other objective, for peace is the precondition of achieving any substantive objective whatsoever (Oakeshott, 1975, 61–62). One cannot be motivated to pursue peace *per se*, for peace is only of value insofar as it facilitates the pursuit of other objectives. (As Oakeshott expresses this general principle, developing upon the nominalism that he identifies in Hobbes, a person does not want to be happy, but 'to idle in Avignon or to hear Caruso sing' (Oakeshott, 1975, 53).) The commonwealth is of value, not because peace is a consequence of this particular mode of organising human conduct, but rather because peace is inherent to it (Oakeshott, 1983, 161). The rules that compose a commonwealth, and which elucidate the adverbial conditions of all conduct, cannot then be assessed in terms of their efficacy for realising any substantive objectives, either of the commonwealth as a whole, or of factions within the commonwealth.

Oakeshott borrows from Hobbes's diagnosis of the civil condition the insight that any enterprise association needs to be supplemented by broader regulative conditions, and that these conditions must lie outside the choice of the individual agents themselves. The setting up of a Hobbesian commonwealth *ex nihilo* is, however, dismissed as an absurdity (Oakeshott, 1983, 150). Oakeshott turns to seek these moral conditions not in a contract, but rather in the socially embedded existence of all human beings. For Oakeshott, the human being does not pre-exist society, as it appears to for Hobbes and in liberal theory, but is rather, to use Heidegger's metaphor, thrown into a particular society upon birth, and is constituted, in its particularity, by that society. As such, the individual has no choice about his or her entry into (or exit from) a civil association. Civil association need not therefore be invented, for it always already exists. Civil association remains an artefact, insofar as it is a product of wilful, conscious human agency. But, while Hobbes's commonwealth is the product of a single creative initiative, Oakeshott's civil association is the outcome of a prolonged and continuing tradition of moral conduct and reflection. Civil association will thereby lack the coherence of Hobbes's vision, being rather 'a manifold of rules, many of unknown origin, subject to deliberate innovation, continuously amplified...not infrequently neglected without penalty, often inconvenient...and never more than a very imperfect reflection of what are currently believed to be "just" conditions of conduct' (Oakeshott, 1975, 154). Yet, as for Hobbes, all that binds society together is a common acknowledgement of the authority of this manifold.

Oakeshott's concept of a civil association rests upon a richer understanding of what it is to be human than the Hobbesian model.

He observes that the agent 'comes to consciousness in a world illuminated by a moral practice and as a relatively helpless subject of it' (Oakeshott, 1975, 63). Central to his account, and what distinguishes it from Hobbes's, is the role that morality, and thus civil association itself, plays in illuminating, or more precisely, in giving meaning to, the world. For Oakeshott, the human agent is not merely a rational, self-interested Hobbesian, but rather a creature that is continually struggling to make sense of itself, of its community and of its environment. Akin to Hobbes's commonwealth, the civil association is composed of the conditions that agents subscribe to in the pursuit of any substantial objective. Such conditions are the substance of moral sentiments. For Oakeshott, these 'conditions may be somewhat indefinite uses or customs, they may even be no more than general maxims of conduct, or they may have the marginally less indeterminate character of rules or regulations' (Ibid., 120). They are moral conditions precisely because they are not prudential. While an agent freely takes account of these conditions in carrying out any purposive action, they do not determine the purpose to be pursued. Rather, they characterise the manner of that pursuit, and thus do they characterise the agent. Oakeshott clarifies this thesis by drawing an analogy between morality and language. Morality is 'an instrument of understanding and a medium of intercourse', and has 'a vocabulary and a syntax of its own', and may be 'spoken well or ill' (Ibid., 62). Individuals are thus bound together in a civil association, again, not because they share common purposes, but because they share a common moral language (albeit that each may speak in a different idiom and with a different degree of competence). It is in this language that the community articulates, to itself, the sort of people it is. Morality is ultimately treated as a resource, through which we disclose ourselves to others, and enact ourselves (Ibid., 120). Oakeshott thereby subtly transforms the relationship that Hobbes establishes between subject and sovereign. For Hobbes, the subject transfers to the sovereign his or her right to specify the conditions under which objectives are pursued. For Oakeshott, individuals are always already subject to the judgement of others in the interpretation of what their actions mean (and thus in how they should be evaluated). If Hobbes's sovereign fails to provide peace, it can be replaced (as can Fleck's system of HMOs). At best, Oakeshott's civil association, and thus perhaps a national health service, can be reinterpreted.

In summary, a civil association is characterised by a lack of any substantive objectives (and thus by the contingent emergence of an understanding as to what it is about, as opposed to the execution of a pre-existing plan); by a lack of freedom of entry or exit for its associates; and in consequence, all that the associates have in common is an acknowledgement of the authority of the moral conditions to which they are obliged to subscribe.

This initial outline of civil association may begin to suggest something of the nature of a national health service, in contrast to a system of HMOs (and more importantly, begins to suggest what is lost if a national health service is understood and managed as a system of HMOs). Fleck's agents remain fundamentally Hobbesian. First, typically they have a choice to enter an HMO or not. In contrast, associates within a national health service do not, obviously, have this choice.[3] One may withdraw, by purchasing private health care (or insurance), but such a withdrawal will be complete only if one no longer makes any financial contribution to the national health service. Further, one would then relinquish all claims upon those services. Most significantly, one would also relinquish all rights to any say in the development of the health service. (One would have no more say than the member of one HMO has over the running of a rival HMO.) Yet, if the national health service is part of one's cultural and moral identity, for one comes to consciousness within the health service, then even this may not entail a complete break, for one would still, to a greater or lesser degree, be shaped by the experience of living within and adjacent to such a service.

Second, the stability that is a desirable characteristic of Fleck's system is akin to Hobbesian peace, and should the state fail to provide that stability its incumbent administration may be changed. In contrast, while a national health service may be the result of government policy, and may have a specific date of inception, it will undergo both formal and (more importantly) informal change. (While governments have frequently attempted to impose designs upon the NHS in the UK, the negotiation and political debate of such designs reflect diverse public understandings of the nature of the NHS and its place in the community.) It does not thus remain as a relatively simple, coherent system of regulations and offices, tailored to realise a specific set of objectives, but becomes something more defuse. Crucially, the idea that a national health service has a substantive objective can be questioned. It has been noted above that a national health service is a conglomeration of enterprise associations. It may therefore appear to be primarily concerned with the management and allocation of scarce resources within those component associations, and thus to be a purposive organisation. HMOs and indeed the system of HMOs (at least as suggested by Fleck), were shown to have substantive, precisely defined objectives. If the objective of a national health service is to sustain the health of a population (or to provide health care to that population), then the specificity of its objectives at once collapses.[4] It has been suggested that HMOs define their objectives in terms of precise lists and protocols, specifying the treatments they are able (and unable) to provide. If national health services manage to avoid such lists, then the health (or health care) that they offer must be defined in some other manner. More precisely, it may be suggested that, without precise protocols, final definition of the objectives of a national health service are permanently deferred. In effect, they are subsumed into a permanent process of negotiation, as the relationship of the health service to the community as a whole is continually reinterpreted. This is to suggest that the struggle to give the health service substantive objectives is deflected, and absorbed into a more profound attempt to articulate the conditions (and thus the moral language) within which associates pursue health. As a civil association, a national health service is thereby understood primarily as a forum within which health (and the moral framework of health care provision) is negotiated. This is to suggest that it becomes a part of the lives (and self-understanding) of its associates in a way that the system of HMOs, grounded as it is in Hobbesian self-interest and a commodified model of health, cannot be.

Justice within a system of HMOs lies in the fair application of the rules of the associations, so that agreed objectives are achieved. Justice within a national health service, as a civil association, must be otherwise. While a civil association has rules, these cannot be mere means to the achievement of an objective, but serve rather to articulate the conditions to which associates subscribe in all their purposive actions. They define the conditions of self-disclosure of 'a man like me' (Oakeshott, 1975, 129). Justice thereby emerges out of the concrete civil association, for, in acknowledging the authority of the civil association, each member, in self-disclosure, puts him or herself to the judgement of his or her peers (which is to say, all the other associates). Members of a civil association are metaphorical suitors before a judicial court (Ibid., 131). Such an initial account implies the repressive conservatism (and indeed relativism) of which communitarians are frequently accused. While Oakeshott may have been happier with this accusation than most, it is not wholly fair. Crucially, a civil association is dynamic, as any living language will

25

be, and the positive account of justice that Oakeshott offers articulates the motivation behind such a dynamic. As a legal suitor, the associate is not passive before an overwhelming authority. At any time, he or she may be accused of acting wrongly, and of violating the adverbial conditions of the association. As suitors, they can defend themselves, and such a defence is not the mere mechanical observation that their actions did in fact observe appropriate conditions, but is rather the hermeneutic process that demands the interpretation of both actions and conditions to demonstrate that they coincide. As Oakeshott notes, there 'is no "plain case" in the sense of a dispute which settles itself' (Ibid., 133). A judgement thereby amplifies the law, by clarifying and extending its meaning. The suitor seeks to vindicate (or justify) his or her act (and thus to demonstrate its justice), by demonstrating that it makes sense within the readily accepted terms of the moral community (see ibid., 69). Any such vindication will be creative, for while it may not create new rules, it will extend the accepted interpretation to encompass new experiences and circumstances.

Vindication is rarely simple or unambiguous. Having developed contingently over many generations, the rules of a civil association are unlikely to demonstrate any great consistency or transparency. Similarly, while all associates may acknowledge their authority, not all will understand them in the same way. A series of distinctive idioms exist, within which the moral language is spoken. The meaning of the civil association (and in consequence, the meaning of 'justice' itself) will be continually under negotiation. Such negotiation entails a particular form of moral discourse, culminating in the 'moral-legal self-understanding of the associates' (Oakeshott, 1983, 160). That is to suggest that if civil association provides the associates with the resource for moral self-disclosure and self-enactment, then not merely an action, but a rule (or the adverbial conditions it prescribes) may be judged to be unjust if it inhibits that self-disclosure. The moral discourse of justice thus culminates in a negotiation of the community's self-understanding.

The justice of a national health service may lie in the vindication of the manner in which individuals pursue health. This depends not merely upon the further articulation and amplification of the adverbial conditions, but possibly more crucially, upon the degree to which 'health' itself is understood as a concept within the moral language of the community. In a system of HMOs, the individual is under no obligation to consider others in his or her purchase of health care (as is the case for any commodity). Similarly, the health care provider has no grounds for refusing to fulfil a valid contract. (The agents need not be regarded as acting in a moral vacuum. Rather, the moral conditions that are subscribed to are those of any commercial transaction. That the commodity transacted is health care makes no substantial difference.) In contrast, in a health service, the request for health care is not the exercise of a contractual right. The associate of a national health service is an embedded, Oakeshottian agent. To request health care is then not the act of an autonomous agent, seeking recompense for something lost. It is rather, to disclose oneself to the moral community, by speaking the common moral language in the idiom of the ill. (This moral idiom may be a particularly lax one, for the ill are typically granted concessions as to their moral conduct that the healthy are denied.) That is to say, that the potential patient attempts to understand him or herself, and his or her social and natural environment, through the culturally available resources that serve to articulate health and illness. He or she will act as an ill person, and have the self-understanding of an ill person, and as such will cope better with the challenges posed by that body and environment than he or she would if considered healthy. If this disclosure is accepted by the community, which is to say, if it is vindicated, the moral conditions to which the agent is obliged to subscribe will be modified. However, there is no *prima facie* reason why the disclosure must be vindicated. A general practitioner's judgement that a patient does not need treatment or further tests will not be a purely clinical decision. It will be mediated by a culturally relative understanding of what health and disease are, and of the part that they play in mundane life (and possibly by a judgement of the sincerity with which the idiom of illness has been adopted).

The individual agents who negotiate the provision of health care (be it general practitioner and patient, consultant and patient, or hospital managers and accountants) each act in public. If the general practitioner denies a patient a requested treatment, the patient can appeal. If a child with a poor prognosis is denied a life saving treatment, the child and his or her parents can appeal. If a national health service hospital transfers elderly patients into social service or private nursing homes, the patients, their families and advisors can appeal. This is to suggest that key decisions about the allocation of health care resources rest, not upon the application and articulation of abstract principles of justice (albeit that these principles, alongside other information such as cost-utility measures, may be of relevance to the cases of both sides), but rather upon public perception and negotiation of particular cases. Ideally, this moral discourse occurs within the national health service as civil association, and between agents who acknowledge themselves, as associates, to be equal within and before that association. (While the national health service will have a managerial role, and complex managerial offices, it can, on this account, never be reduced to the management of an enterprise association.) The national health service is not then run in the interests of any particular faction (physicians, patients, managers, tax payers, or whoever), but is rather the focus of the self-interpretation and self-disclosure of its associates, of their community, and of the health of that community. A just health service is thus a health service that is open and responsive (and indeed a stimulant) to the development of the moral sentiments of its associates.

NOTES

1   Grounding this enquiry is a deeper concern, reflected in the nature of political philosophy itself. Political philosophy has been defined as reflection on 'the relation of political life...to the entire conception of the world that belongs to a civilisation' (Oakeshott, 1991, 224). Further, Oakeshott suggests, political philosophers tend to take a sombre view of the human predicament, and political philosophy is in consequence an advocating of a political order that will deliver humanity from that predicament (Ibid., 225). Reflection on the justice of health care provision falls within this problematic. At the heart of any such reflection is a concern with human mortality and morbidity, and thus with the darkest of human predicaments. At some level, to reflect upon the justice of a health service is not merely to advocate certain rules for the allocation of resources, or for access to treatment, but to engage with human mortality itself, and thereby to advocate a political order that, if it cannot deliver us from death itself, at least mitigates and makes sense of that threat.

2   While Oakeshott does acknowledge that the rules of a civil association should obey certain principles of any legal order (being not secret or retrospective, recognising no arbitrary exceptions, and no inequality before the law, and so on) (Oakeshott, 1983, 140), he rejects the appeal to the rational justification of these rules (which for Oakeshott follows from the natural law tradition). Such an approach confuses the justice of the rules with their authority. That is to say that the approach is concerned to ground laws, as binding upon agents, through appeal to reason. For Oakeshott, this is not an issue. Rules are binding because agents acknowledge them as such (not because there is a rational account of why they should be binding). The moral education of the agent is then of far greater significance than any rationalisation (Ibid., 135–136).

3   Oakeshott characterises modern political states as civil associations. Therefore, the system of HMOs, precisely insofar as it is state regulated, may acquire certain properties of the civil association.
4   In practice, UK governments and agencies have been remarkably poor at articulating the objectives of the NHS.

2

ALL YOU NEED IS HEALTH

Liberal and communitarian views on the allocation of health care resources

Hub Zwart

Introduction

At first glance the term community seems to emphasise what is *in*cluded, what 'we' (those who are included) have in common. Yet, the basic gesture by means of which a community is constituted is always an act of exclusion: the constitution of a 'we' presupposes the exclusion of Others. Inclusion and exclusion logically and intrinsically belong together. A paradigmatic example of the kind of gesture by means of which a community is constituted is the Holy Communion, a ritual of sharing and involvement. Yet, in the Christian liturgy (and most notably in its Roman Catholic version) the actual communion is preceded by another ritual, one of exclusion, in which the community members testify and re-establish their adherence to the Christian articles of faith. Those unwilling to take part in this ritual of adherence are denied access to the subsequent ritual of sharing.

The dialectics of inclusion and exclusion have displayed a series of decisive historical shifts. Whilst medieval society was a huge, heterogeneous collection of local, professional and religious communities, of complicated social forms of inclusion/exclusion (of which the professional communities called guilds provided a telling and paradigmatic example), in the modern era, it has been liberalism's historical effort and achievement to diminish the social importance of such communities in favour of a common market into which every individual is allowed to enter – in principle – and from which no one is to be excluded – again, in principle. A market is a form of social intercourse devoid of traditional biases in terms of social rank and privilege. It is a 'community' that includes all individuals, indeed, the entire population, and therefore it is no longer a community, but rather a huge collection of competing individuals. In the nineteenth century, however, when this idea of a free and common market came to be firmly established, it still conveyed a somewhat cynical vein. For although *de jure* every individual was granted the right to enter social intercourse, *de facto* many forms of exclusion still proved to be at work.

In contemporary Western society, liberalism's basic moral objective of constituting forms of social intercourse devoid of traditional ('natural') restrictions, still remains, but on a significantly expanded scale. Modern society's ultimate goal now seems to be that of realising complete *de facto* access to public social intercourse for all individuals – or at least for the greatest possible number and to the greatest possible extent. This basic moral objective of contemporary society is to be realised with the help of public policies aimed at extinguishing existing forms of social disadvantage. Notably, this objective applies to the three cardinal social practices by means of which social intercourse is constituted and maintained: education, labour and health care. In this chapter, I will focus on the practice of health care, most notably on the way the problem of scarcity of resources and health care facilities is to be solved. The moral principle guiding a liberal allocation policy for health care facilities could be formulated thus: every individual is entitled to a fair share of health care facilities in order to allow him to participate in social life (that is, in order to allow him to continue or even to improve his participation; see Zwart, 1993).

It must be stressed from the outset, however, that liberalism as I will use the term (that is, liberalism in a philosophical sense) is not to be identified with any particular political conviction, party or trend. Rather, I will use the term in order to address what I consider to be a basic moral view on social life; one, moreover, that happens to be dominant in contemporary society. But it could also be referred to as 'modernism' or even 'humanism'. I would not consider the famous Marxist claim, for example, that every individual is to contribute according to his abilities and to receive according to his needs, as being at odds with liberalism. Such basic convictions can no longer be considered as belonging exclusively to any particular political programme. Rather, they have become what – using a term borrowed from Rorty (1989) – could be referred to as the basic 'platitudes' of contemporary moral discourse, regardless of whether one personally happens to prefer its socialist, its Christian, or even its 'liberal' version (where 'liberalism' is used in a more restricted and particular sense).

The basic paradox of liberalism

The problem is that the liberal view of social life, convincing as it might seem at first glance, actually finds itself confronted with an ever-growing enigma. Despite its effort to establish a large-scale (and ultimately even global) community that would include all human beings and would allow us to satisfy all existing health care needs, we are actually faced with (at times alarming) forms of scarcity and exclusion, perhaps even on an ever-increasing scale. Many *de facto* forms of exclusion still seem to be at work. One might conclude from this that, whereas liberalism's ultimate moral objective remains basically convincing, we nevertheless find ourselves confronted with a series of 'application' problems still to be solved. One might equally conclude, however, that for some reason or other, liberalism's moral objectives are basically flawed. The latter point of view will be referred to here as communitarianism and entails the claim that, as a basic moral view of social life, liberalism is thoroughly misguided since it does not really consider the human individual in terms of what he and his fellow human beings have in *common*. Instead of providing the ultimate answer to problems of scarcity and exclusion, liberalism happens to be the very thing that produced and caused them.

Liberalism is faced with what has been called the 'paradox of scarcity' (see Achterhuis, 1988). Before the rise of modern labour, the great majority of individuals in Europe belonged to countless rural communities which were for the greater part self-sufficient and self-supporting. Although *we* tend to consider their form of life as rather primitive and backward, they themselves seemed to be fairly satisfied with it. The diseases from which these individuals suffered were as simple and primitive as were their daily lives. To the extent that their existence became increasingly complex over time, however, the complexity of their physical ailings (and the number of potential diseases) tended to increase as well (see Foucault, 1963, 15). Their natural state of health seemed to diminish as their socio-economic position came to be enhanced, and by implication their clinical pictures became more and more diversified. As compared to the simple and very few diseases a primitive, fifteenth-century peasant would expect to be troubled with in the course of his life, the eighteenth-century bourgeoisie already found itself exposed to an astonishing number of physical afflictions, and the number of diseases has continued to increase ever since. Moreover, the care of the ill came to be transferred from its natural locus (the family, the neighbourhood) to the hospital, where the health of the general population became an issue of national political importance. Instead of being able to meet the individual patient's health care needs more adequately, liberalism is faced with a population whose health care needs increasingly exceed the medical possibilities society is willing or able to afford. Thus, one of the basic enigmas of modern medicine came to be established – the growth of medical possibilities increasingly falls short of the health care needs it produces.

Liberalism versus communitarianism

Communitarians argue that the moral assessment of human existence must start from what *we* have in common. They claim, for example, that it is still possible to distinguish on a public level between (on the one hand) reasonable needs and necessary care, to be provided by society at all costs, and (on the other hand) eccentric needs, which the individual must be expected to satisfy at his own expense – if such needs are to be satisfied at all. In order for society to be able to satisfy all reasonable health care needs (or at least the greatest possible number of them), eccentric needs are to be denied access to public funding. Liberalism, however, entails the idea that, if it is at all possible to distinguish between reasonable and eccentric needs, it is the individual himself who has the right to make this distinction, rather than society at large. No one should be denied access to any particular health care facility merely because their needs are generally considered unreasonable, inappropriate or eccentric.

Whereas liberalism basically appeals to the individual's right to self-determination, the communitarian view implicitly or explicitly implies a moral appeal to human nature, notably to the idea of a natural life span in the course of which some basic common ('natural') human goals can be achieved. In other words, communitarianism involves the idea that there are certain basic moral goals in life, to be realised in the course of a natural life span, and whose realisation is to be supported by society at large. Perhaps one could say that, in terms of philosophical allegiance, every communitarian is something of a Thomist, regardless of whether he happens to be aware of it or not.

For in a famous passage,[1] Thomas Aquinas summarises a philosophical tradition of long standing by pointing out four basic natural goals, to be realised in the course of a human life: (1) self-preservation, (2) securing the future existence of the human race and caring for one's off-spring, (3) seeking the company of others (participating in social and professional life), and (4) improving one's cognitive faculties; that is, one's knowledge about the world (or, as Saint Thomas himself puts it, one's knowledge about God). Now it goes without saying that the goal of preserving one's own life will still count as an important and reasonable justification for medical intervention and medical progress. As far as the first common goal of life (the preservation of life itself) is concerned, liberalism and communitarianism seem to be of one mind. Yet, the communitarian view will immediately add that the preservation of life is to be balanced against, and even must be considered instrumental to, the three other basic goals mentioned. Our basic goal is not the maintenance or extension of life *as such* but to live a full life, a good life, a life that would count as a perfect exemplification of human flourishing. Life as such is merely a precondition for the other goals to be realised. The moral quality of our life is determined by the extent to which the other natural goals of life are realised.

Furthermore, if goals 2 and 3 have been achieved, or if we allowed the opportunities to achieve these goals to pass, the effort to preserve our life would lose much of its urgency – had it not been for our final goal, goal number 4. For even in old age, opportunities for intellectual progress still present themselves, and this still justifies life-extending treatment even if we have been able to realise goals 2 and 3.[2] It is because of this final goal that elderly human beings are to be treated fundamentally differently from worn out animals. Still, the communitarian view implies that, if the goal of preserving one's life is not balanced by other basic (or 'natural') goals – that is, by an awareness of what 'we' humans have in common *as humans* – we will run the risk of falling victim to what Callahan elsewhere (1973) referred to as the 'tyranny of survival'. Indeed, Callahan claims that modernism (or liberalism) significantly *aggravated* the problem of scarcity because it tends to consider the preservation of life as an end in itself, rather than as a *partial* end, and as a precondition for realising other, more 'human' natural goals.

A liberal, however, will no doubt recoil from such a line of thought. Liberalism is marked by a basic fear of 'gouverning-too-much' (Foucault, 1989), by the fear that society becomes involved too intimately in the lives and decisions of individuals. By implication, the imposition of natural goals to be pursued by all individuals in the course of a natural life span, even if they are formulated in the broadest of terms, is likely to be considered a case of 'gouverning-too-much'. The individuals themselves are to point out what kind of goals they allow to shape their lives. Social intercourse is to be regulated, not on the basis of natural goals, but on the basis of reasonable principles, to be accepted by all individuals, regardless of what they consider as basic human goals to be realised in the course of one's life. These principles are: (1) the right to self-determination (already mentioned), (2) the harm principle, and (3) the principle of distributive justice.

In order to clarify the difference between a liberal and a communitarian approach, let me briefly refer to a recent case. Should it count as a reasonable need if an elderly woman, who has passed the menopause at a 'normal' age, applies for IVF in order to fulfil her wish to bear a child?[3] It could be argued that such a need should count as eccentric, in view of the fact that infertility due to having passed the menopause cannot be considered as pathological. It cannot be considered as a disease for which medical intervention would be indicated, unless it happened prematurely ('praecox'). According to what was pointed out above, anyone who argues in this direction is a communitarian, whereas anyone who would argue that we should allow the individual herself the right to make her own decision is a liberal. Restrictions, for the liberal, are only to be imposed if (1) some harmful consequences, either for herself or for the child, would undeniably result from her decision (the harm principle), and (2) if other human beings, whose health care needs should be considered as more pressing and urgent, are denied access to necessary health care facilities and resources (the distributive justice principle). In other words, whereas communitarianism combines two basic ideas – namely (1) the idea that there are some natural goals in life, and (2) the idea that, to every goal, there is a season – liberalism proceeds from the three basic principles just mentioned: self-determination, prevention of harm, and justice. Let this suffice as a preparatory lining-up of basic positions. In the subsequent sections, the communitarian and the liberal perspectives are to be clarified more carefully.

Traditional communitarianism: a closer look

In the famous passage already mentioned above, Thomas points out that every agent acts in order to achieve some good (the good being that which all things seek).[4] In fact, this phrase is a concise translation of the famous first sentence of Aristotle's *Ethica*.[5] According to Thomas, the first commandment of natural law must be formulated thus: the good is to be sought and done, evil to be avoided; and on this first principle, all precepts of the natural law, apprehended by practical reason, are based. In other words, practical reason implies the basic apprehension that all objectives toward which man is *naturally* inclined, are good. Subsequently, Thomas mentions four natural human inclinations. The first is the one we have in common with all other entities, namely the inclination to preserve one's natural being. This *natural inclination* corresponds with the *moral obligation* to preserve human life. The second basic inclination is the one we share with all other animals, corresponding with the law which 'nature teaches all animals', namely that male and female seek intercourse with one another, as well as the subsequent inclination to educate their mutual offspring. Next, there is a basic inclination which is peculiar to man, namely the inclination to discern the truth of things (most notably the truth about God). Correspondingly, natural law commands us that we are to shun ignorance. Finally, man is by nature inclined to live *in societate* and therefore commanded by natural law not to offend those with whom he ought to live in civility. In short, there is a basic correspondence between 'is' and 'ought', between natural inclination and natural law.

Indeed, in formulating these basic human goals or inclinations, Thomas heavily relies on Aristotle. Three of the four natural inclinations mentioned by Thomas (procreation, participation in social intercourse and the pursuit of knowledge) are mentioned by Aristotle on the first pages of two of his major works. In the first book of his *Politics* he claims that man and wife, unable to exist without one another, are bound to seek each other's company, for the sake of the continuance of the species, out of a natural drive we humans share with other animals.[6] And subsequently, he claims that 'Man is by nature a political animal',[7] bound to participate in the social and political life of the city-state. Finally, in the first sentence of the first book of his *Metaphysics* it is claimed that 'all men naturally desire knowledge'.[8]

In the second book of the *Nicomachean Ethics*, moreover, he points out that man does not display his natural behavioural patterns (his 'moral virtues') *automatically*. Rather, a moral virtue is to be regarded as a habit – *ethos* in Greek – which means that it is to be acquired through training and education. For although nature gives us the *capacity* to receive these virtues, this capacity is brought to maturity by habit.[9] Furthermore, it goes without saying that moral education presupposes the existence of a moral community. Without a moral community of some kind, there is no chance for the individual to receive his necessary education. And for this reason, natural law theory implies communitarianism, as well as vice versa. They necessarily coincide and mutually involve one another. The community is prior to the individual, and if human behaviour were completely determined by innate instincts and biological equipment, moral philosophy (as well as moral education) would of course be pointless. In the case of animals, however, a certain amount of training is often required as well and therefore the difference between human behaviour (determined primarily by moral education) and animal behaviour (determined primarily by biological equipment) is a matter of degree rather than of principle. Yet, although a great number of animal species display some kind of social life, Aristotle claims that man is a political animal *in a greater measure* than other animals, for he alone possesses speech, which means that he alone can distinguish between right and wrong. Therefore, the fourth basic goal also can be considered as being peculiar to man. Nevertheless, his moral life remains basically natural.

In short, the Aristotelian-Thomistic view acknowledges a limited range of natural human pursuits, directed at achieving natural moral goods, with the implication that the basic conditions of life are similar for all of us. Human life displays a common moral pattern, and this is the basic truth of traditional communitarianism. There is a limited set of moral goals (or goods) the pursuit of which all human beings share with one another and for every act, practical reason must determine whether these common human objectives are likely to be furthered or obstructed by it. Under such moral circumstances, medical decisions are likely to become quite manageable. The first moral question simply is, whether the medical intervention or decision can be expected to preserve human life as a prerequisite for other, more human goals. Next, it has to be determined whether the life extension which it is likely to produce, will further or obstruct the patient's physical abilities to procreate and educate his offspring, that is, to take responsibility for those entrusted to his care. Finally, it has to be determined whether the intervention will allow him to participate in social intercourse, and to improve his cognitive faculties (with the ultimate intention of beholding God in heaven). In times of scarcity, we must carefully distinguish between natural needs and eccentric ones. In fact, if medicine would restrict itself to merely satisfying natural needs, and to supporting human flourishing rather than life-extension, meanwhile carefully observing the natural finitude of human life and human life goals, the problem of scarcity would no doubt lose much of its present acuteness.

Now what prevents us from simply remaining (or becoming) Thomists? For several reasons, traditional communitarianism has become problematic. Even communitarianism itself has changed, and contemporary versions can no longer be considered truly Aristotelian-Thomistic. This is inevitable, rather than deplorable, for, on a very basic level, the moral conditions of human life have changed – man has become a different kind of being. The common moral pattern of human life has been fundamentally transformed and the fundamental truth of modern morality is the *discordance*, rather than the correspondence, of natural inclination and natural law – and this basic shift has affected communitarianism as well. Indeed, communitarianism has become the effort to *counter* some of the basic inclinations which manifest themselves in contemporary human behaviour and in order to do so, a typically *modern* argument is added to the traditional rationale of communitarianism: the argument from scarcity. But before turning to contemporary communitarianism, allow me to elaborate the liberal perspective somewhat further.

Liberalism: a closer look

In order to further elaborate the liberal perspective, I would like to start from the case already mentioned concerning the elderly woman who applies for IVF. The first principle of liberalism implies that the fact that the woman herself happens to consider her need a genuine one must suffice as a primary justification of her application for IVF. The second principle, however, stipulates that, although we are granted the right to pursue our private goals, we are not to pursue them at all costs, and our claims become inadmissible as soon as they involve serious harm – either to others (most notably the child, who would have a relatively great chance of losing a 'significant other' at a relatively young age) or to the individual herself (will she, for example, be able to bear the physical burden of pregnancy and delivery?). The third principle implies that, in order to realise individual goals and to satisfy individual needs, the individual has a right to a fair share of natural resources and existing health facilities. That is, natural resources and health care facilities are to be distributed fairly among individuals in order to allow them to achieve their private goals and to satisfy their private needs. Somehow, the urgency of the woman's needs has to be balanced against the health care needs of others (most notably in the case of direct public funding of the medical intervention as such, but also with regard to the distribution of research grants, long-term facilities and investments, etc.). In a rapidly increasing number of cases, the principle of distributive justice is bound to become a decisive moral limit set by liberalism on the use of health care facilities for the satisfaction of private needs.

In short, a liberal will ask on what grounds society has the right to intervene in such a case and to deny an elderly woman the right to apply for IVF, if it is not for the harm she will inflict either upon herself or upon her child. Such considerations, to be subsumed under the harm principle, are to be dealt with by medical and psychological experts. They are not to be decided by means of some kind of public moral ordeal or by relying on a common substantial view of what should count as a good life. The same goes for the justice principle. The costs and benefits of the intervention involved have to be carefully assessed by experts and balanced against other needs, in view of considerations of scarcity and fairness. That is, in a liberal perspective, nature is a standing reserve, to be managed in a fair and well-informed manner, rather than a standard for moral decision-making. This is quite unlike the communitarian perspective which demands that one proceeds from what we humans have in common – for what we have in common is first of all our body, our body's natural life-cycle and history, from which our basic goals and needs evolve. According to traditional communitarianism, we are to manage our life and body according to the natural inclinations which display themselves even in our physique. Bodily life is the incarnation of basic human goals, and its natural patterns provide us with a basic sense of limit. According to liberalism, however, all limits are arbitrary. They have to be *determined* in a reasonable and well-informed manner. They are to be considered the temporary outcome of the interplay between expert information and individual preference.

In short, whereas communitarianism tries to maintain an awareness of community, of what we have in common (our human nature), liberalism aims at reducing all 'natural' and traditional restrictions. The social practice of health care is transformed in accordance with the market paradigm of human interaction, while considerations of harm-prevention and fairness function as the only reasonable restrictions on the basic entitlement to self-determination. This means, however, that liberalism entails a logic of restriction and exclusion of its own. In its effort to recognise as few restrictions as possible, it inevitably finds itself faced with something of a paradox. In the absence of any substantial criterion for determining what should count as necessary health care, furthering human flourishing, and in view of the rapidly increasing complexity of health care as a social practice, liberalism is forced to develop an ever-expanding system of regulations that are to prevent harm and to foster fairness, and this implies an ever-increasing level of interference in private decision-making. That is, liberalism ends up with the very thing it tried to prevent from the outset: 'gouverning-too-much'. Whenever substantial criteria are absent, all measures have to be 'determined', all limits have to be 'set'. We can no longer rely on the practical reason of the individual patient and physician involved in order to apprehend the extent to which the proposed medical intervention would further the substantial human goods described above.

Communitarianism, however, is faced with a similar paradox. It relies on two substantial criteria for determining whether a proposed intervention should count as necessary care: (1) the idea that there are basic goals in life, the pursuit of which is to be supported by society at large, and (2) the idea that to every goal, there is a season, determined by the cyclical history of our body, from which reasonable limits are to be adopted. Yet, when it comes to applying these ideas to concrete cases, it seems inevitable that communitarianism will likewise end up with the very thing it tried to prevent from the outset, namely arbitrariness. For example: at what age *precisely* would a menopause be considered premature (with the implication that, in terms of basic human goals, IVF should count as reasonable and justified)? Can we really expect the age limit provided by communitarianism to differ from what the liberal experts would come up with? That is, can we really expect communitarianism to solve the problem of scarcity more adequately? In order to answer these questions, let us turn to an outstanding example of contemporary communitarianism, provided by Daniel Callahan who, in a series of articles and books, but most notably in *Setting Limits* (1987), aimed at developing a communitarian approach to scarcity (entailing a fundamental critique of the liberal view on allocating health care facilities – referred to by Callahan as 'modernism').

Contemporary communitarianism and health care ethics: Daniel Callahan

From the very outset Callahan's effort reveals the extent to which contemporary communitarianism differs from the traditional version described above – that is, it reveals the fact that communitarianism itself has become fundamentally and inevitably *modernised*. For instead of relying on a basic correspondence, a *pre-established harmony* between 'is' and 'ought', between basic inclination and moral guidance, contemporary communitarianism recognises the fundamental discordance between the two. According to Callahan, modern technological medicine is driven by a basic inclination to extend life beyond all reasonable limits. This drive, moreover, is to be considered a natural one, for it is part of our 'natural endowment' that we want to live and not to die[10] and therefore, many elderly people will struggle against death until the very end, rather than displaying a prudent willingness to accept the basic finitude of human existence. Furthermore, our bodily nature can no longer be considered as fixed and normative in itself. Rather, it seems to have become malleable to human purposes and construction.[11] These intrinsic tendencies at work in medical technology towards life-extension, vigorously reinforced by patient self-determination, are to be *countered* by ethics. Callahan's basic objective is that of setting limits in a technological society by 'determining what are sensible and proper human ends'.[12] These ends, however, have to be *determined*, these limits have to be *set*, not in conformity with, but in opposition to the basic human and technological inclinations at work. Although the appeal to 'sensible and proper human ends' is basically communitarian, the fact that these ends have to be determined by others, rather than being apprehended by the individuals themselves, is apparently a modern adaptation.

This is not the only modern adaptation which Callahan's modernised version of communitarianism displays. Callahan's objective of reaffirming the communitarian idea of a natural life span is connected with a second, and rather modern one: the objective of handling the modern problem of a fair allocation of scarce resources. The communitarian awareness that, at a certain point in life, our common and reasonable human ends will have been fulfilled, is connected with a modern policy issue by presenting age as a legitimate criterion for exclusion from life-extending medical facilities. Callahan's position, that is, provides us with a blend of traditional and modern ingredients. In order for health care to remain affordable in the near future, he claims, we are to re-establish some social agreement as to what should count as a good life. The place of the elderly in a good society 'is an inherently communal, not individual, question'.[13] And therefore it ought to be discussed publicly, not only for the benefit of the elderly themselves, but also because Callahan believes that 'there will be better ways in the future to spend our money than on indefinitely extending the life of the elderly'.[14]

His communitarian view also entails a basic critique of liberalism (referred to by him as 'modernism'). According to Callahan, modernism's 'thin theory of the good' maintains that the centre of meaning is the private self rather than the community. Public policy is to rest upon the right of individuals to seek their private happiness, as long as they do not do harm to others. The search for the good of human life is not to be pursued by the community as a whole, but must be left to the individual.[15] It is Callahan's firm contention that such a theory will prove insufficient when it comes to facing the problem of increasing scarcity. In the absence of unlimited resources, we are *always* inevitably harming others. The only way to solve this problem, is by reaching a public consensus about ultimate human goals and goods. We have to acknowledge that the proper goal of medicine is not the extension of life as such, but the achievement of a full and natural life span.[16] And this idea of a natural life span provides us with a moral justification for limiting health care resources available to the elderly. Beyond a certain 'critical' age, life-extending treatment is to be denied to them. The art of living a good life implies the ability to accept its natural limits, and limitation on health care for the elderly is a defensible idea: each age group should receive what it really needs to live a life appropriate to it.[17] Old age is a stage of life in its own right, with its own proper and reasonable goals and ends. At the same time, however, Callahan stresses that a public view of the meaning of old age, should not lead to an 'official, and thus dogmatic, repressive view'.[18]

Medical need does not provide a reasonable standard for health care allocation because, rather than being a fixed concept, it is a function of technological possibility and social expectation. Medical need in principle knows no boundaries. It cannot serve as a standard to resist the 'escalating' power of technological change. Therefore, it is Callahan's objective to reorient medicine away from this technology-driven, borderless 'need' model of care. A natural life span is such that it enables every individual to accomplish the ordinary scope of possibilities that life affords.[19] It serves as a standard to offer serious resistance to an unlimited claim on resources in the name of 'medical need'. Beyond the natural life span the government should not provide the means for life-extending technology. The proper goal of medicine for those who have already lived out their natural life span ought to be the relief of suffering rather than the extension of life. Medical need in the context of constant technological innovation is open-ended. In the face of potentially unlimited technological innovation, reasonable limits are to be set.

According to the accepted principles of medical ethics, Callahan argues, the patient is to be the ultimate judge of the benefits and burdens of life-extending treatment. The right to make such judgements rests on the principle of patient self-determination. The idea of a natural life span, however, will provide a moral standard to determine the appropriate *use* of the freedom provided by this principle. Callahan stresses, however, that a policy based on this idea presupposes the establishment of a strong public consensus, otherwise it is likely to be experienced as coercive and unfair. Moreover, Callahan is of course aware of the 'technical' problem that the elderly constitute a remarkably heterogeneous group (in terms of physical condition and similar parameters), but still he thinks that some generalisations can and should be made. To overstress their heterogeneity would create 'bureaucratic and public confusion'.

In short, Callahan is at first reluctant to identify the natural life span with a particular calendar age. He clearly seems to be aware of the fact that to do so would mean introducing an element of arbitrariness, as well as a failure to recognise considerable differences that exist between patients of the same age. Therefore, in 1987 Callahan still is in favour of taking individual differences into account. But before long he comes to recognise that in this manner, the arbitrariness still remains. Who is to judge whether in the case of a particular elderly patient the life span has been completed? The patient himself, his physician, the Ethics Committee, the Court of Law? One way or another, the question of whether or not the life span of a particular patient has been completed has to be *determined* in an arbitrary manner – by an *arbiter*. Before long, Callahan recognises that this would result in arbitrary differences. Thus, in 1990 he already regrets his earlier position: 'I would now say that, to be consistent in the use of age as a standard, no exceptions should be made.'[20] Only categorical standards, applying to all, formal and impersonal, determined by society and not dependent on subjective and uncertain clinical evidence, can effectively be used. In 1977, this option was still rejected as being 'Orwellian'.

We may now draw the conclusion that Callahan's contemporary version of a communitarian approach to health care issues and allocation problems inevitably differs from traditional communitarianism in several respects. In the case of traditional communitarianism, the common human pattern was present from the very outset, due to the natural inclinations of human beings to pursue their natural life goals, and to do so in due time. In the case of contemporary communitarianism, however, life goals (or 'sensible human ends') have to be determined through public debate. Subsequently, they are to be elaborated into health care policies. All this is inevitable, due to the fundamental change in the moral condition of those who dwell in a technological world, as compared to those who lived in less accelerated epochs. Our living conditions are permanently and relentlessly transformed, and therefore the moral patterns of life have to be permanently revised as well.

Callahan's position, however, does not seem to succeed in overcoming the very things it attempted to avoid, or at least to diminish, namely arbitrariness and self-determination. To begin with, there is indeed something Orwellian and arbitrary in the idea that elderly patients are to be denied access to life-extending health care facilities merely because they have passed a certain calendar age, and regardless of their physical condition and their prospects for realising some still outstanding 'private' goals. One of the reasons for this may well be the fact that, in his summary of natural human ends – to accomplish one's life work and to care for those for whom one is responsible – at least one basic human goal is persistently overlooked. For besides participation in social life and caring for one's offspring, traditional communitarianism also recognises yet another basic human goal: the acquisition of knowledge, insight or wisdom. Moreover, traditional communitarianism will add that old age is a stage of life in which crucial opportunities for cognitive growth and awakening present themselves – and if medical technology allows them to extend their life in order to achieve such goals, why should elderly patients be denied this possibility? Whether or not the proposed medical intervention will further the pursuit of cognitive awakening as a basic human goal of life, must either be determined in an arbitrary manner – the 'Orwellian' option of contemporary communitarianism – or in a private manner – by the individual himself, the liberal option entailed by the principle of self-determination. Similarly to liberalism, therefore, contemporary communitarianism is faced with an enigma: somehow it is unable to overcome the very things it attempted to avoid. Rather than criticising Callahan for something which simply seems inevitable, the consistent and well-considered manner in which he tries to articulate a solution to this dilemma reveals the profoundness of the problem.

In my view, a tenable moral position should firmly recognise the principle of self-determination, but at the same time encourage the establishment of an ongoing public debate on the use of freedom and the determination of the basic human goals of contemporary life. Liberalism and communitarianism both entail a crucial, but partial truth. It is in the ongoing debate between the liberal and the communitarian perspective on contemporary moral life (to which Callahan has contributed significantly) that our moral condition is revealed and clarified. In the course of this debate we become aware of the fact that moral life itself has become paradoxical. In the absence of publicly discussed criteria for the adequate use for freedom, there can be no freedom. Likewise, in the absence of freedom, whenever an 'Orwellian' society tries to enforce the good, human flourishing is diminished. The idea *as such* that there are common basic goals in life, to be realised in due time, still preserves much of its validity. As to the application of this idea, however, we have to rely on the prudent individual's faculty of apprehension, rather than on implementing general policies of exclusion for demographic reasons.

NOTES

1 Aquinas, Thomas, *Summa Theologiae*, Vol 28, London: Blackfriars, 1a2ae 94, 2.
2 Callahan, D., 'On Defining a Natural Death', *Hastings Center Report*, 7 (6), pp. 32–36. Callahan is an outstanding spokesman of the communitarian perspective on medical ethics, most notably on the issue of scarcity, and formulated these goals as follows: to accomplish our life-work and to care for those for whom we are responsible.

3 In December 1993 the Italian gynaecologist Antoniori reported that he had successfully applied IVF to two menopausal women, one of whom was 59 years of age, the other 62. This event was covered by all the major newspapers, and in The Netherlands it provoked an ethical debate (Zwart, 1994).

4 'Omne agens agit propter finem', Aquinas, *Summa Theologiae*, 1a2ae. 94, 2; p. 81.

5 'Every art and every investigation, and likewise every practical pursuit or undertaking, seems to aim at some good: hence it has been well said that the good is that at which all things aim' (*Nicomachean Ethics* I 1; p. 3).

6 Aristotle, *Politics* I i 4; 1252a., London: Heinemann, 1933/1967, p. 5.

7 Ibid., *Politics* I i 9; 1253a., p. 9.

8 Ibid., 980 a 22, p. 3.

9 Aristotle, *The Nicomachean Ethics*, London: Heinemann, 1926/1967, II i 1–3.

10 Callahan, D., 'Setting Limits: Medical Goals in an Ageing Society', p. 75.

11 Ibid., p. 26.

12 Ibid., p. 13.

13 Ibid., p. 32.

14 Ibid., p. 53.

15 Ibid., p. 58.

16 Ibid., pp. 76–77.

17 Ibid., p. 114.

18 Ibid., p. 33.

19 Ibid., p. 135.

20 Callahan, D., 'Afterword: Daniel Callahan Responds to his Critics', p. 311.

3

RETURN TO COMMUNITY

The ethics of exclusion and inclusion

Chris Heginbotham

Introduction

'Community' is, rather like justice, an essentially contested concept, for which there are as many definitions as there are observers. It was once said in the 1930s that when 'five economists are gathered together there will be at least six opinions'. Community invokes the same impression. There are very many different definitions of 'community'; and the term is used variously in common parlance. We speak of 'communities of interest', 'community care', 'community policing', 'community centres' and simply of 'community'.

'Community' implies some sharing, participation and accountability – yet each of these concepts can be challenged, and may be neither necessary nor sufficient for an effective community to flourish. In this chapter I shall consider what we mean by community and its extension into versions of 'communitarianism'. What is the 'value of community' and to what extent is a consideration of relationships a prelude to a consideration of the inclusion or exclusion of individuals in or from this notion of community? Let us take just one example at this stage. If we do not value our relationships with people who have or have had mental illnesses, we will, to a greater or lesser extent, exclude those people from our community. By considering community in this way it will be possible to consider the ethics of such exclusion and inclusion and to a degree the way in which nationalism, discrimination and normative value setting arise.

Community also involves a notion of structure or corporateness, a notion of being and a set of common asssumptions. It is these common presumptions which lie at the heart of community. Rather than 'communitarianism' we might simply think of a commonwealth of individuals, or more simply the 'commons' – a very English concept though one often misunderstood. Alternately we might adapt the European notion of solidarity as a politically left of centre formulation of broadly the same concept.

Much of this is woolly and ill-defined and this goes to the heart of difficulties associated with basing any ethical or jurisprudential scheme on notions of community or communitarianism. Quite simply the crucial weakness of community is that it is an idea which can be made to appeal to all, to mean something to everyone. It can be both libertarian and socialist, individualist and collective. At best it can offer a synthesis of individual responsibility in an interdependent civil society, constraining the worst features of individual greed through collective action for the common good, whilst allowing opportunities for personal growth and creativity. Community – the collective – thus frees people to develop, by taking away fear of disability and deprivation. It is in this context that we will debate later the use and abuse of community care.

Community, communitarianism or commons

On first contact, communitarianism sounds like a softer version of socialism, something less threatening than communism, but more encompassing than labourism. Communitarianism's American antecedents are worth noting. Is communitarianism simply a handy cloak for a transatlantic attempt to recapture something of social welfare? Indeed there is a 'communitarianism' of both the centre left and centre right; the communitarian ideal attempts to balance individual worth with collective responsibility, to fuse liberal economic ideals with market socialism, and to recognise the interplay between the central and local state, on the one hand, and disparate groupings of local people – loosely called community – on the other. For some, communitarianism offers a vision of non-demeaning welfare coupled with empowerment, a democratic, authentic 'consumerism' and a social contractarian system in which local people can truly influence the circumstances of their lives. For others the communitarian ideal is not far distant from those twin pillars of continental philosophy – subsidiarity and solidarity.

Unfortunately communitarianism is highly unstable both as a concept and as a practical politics. At first blush it offers a romantic encapsulation of emotional containment, a fairy tale ideal of life, if not without distress, at least one with supportive social structures and processes. On closer examination however communitarianism cannot sustain this utopian promise. For 'community' can become both punitive and coercive, either by the imposition of community norms (communism), or by the imposition of the values of a (possibly elected) small clique which is empowered by the community to rule (national socialism). Furthermore, community judgements tend to drift 'down market' to the lowest common denominator of community acceptance rather than to that highest common factor of community satisfaction built on the creative tension of self-interest and altruism. Community goes beyond individual utilitarian ideals to a recognition of relationships and the value of interdependence.

That essence of community – the face-to-face close comfort of regular personal contact with valued others – is the underpinning of the common good. This, controversially, is at the core of community. Whilst we can talk of communities of interest, communities of people from different backgrounds, communities of need, and so on, for the purposes of this chapter community will be defined in a gently idealised form as a community of self-seeking others who find ways of achieving that face-to-face contact, even if they do not lead their lives in day-to-day geographical proximity.

Whilst community must be inclusive of all as people, the rules of community need not allow nor include all behaviours and attitudes. The criteria for including individuals' attitudes into normative rules will differ from the criteria which are used to exclude individuals from normal discourse. The inclusion of certain attitudes into the normative rules of society does not and should not imply the exclusion of any individual from the society which is governed by those norms. Unfortunately, in liberal societies this often happens. Once the norm is set anyone who departs from that norm is seen as at least deviant and sometimes as wholly aberrant and unacceptable.

At this point it may be valuable to borrow a phrase from Tom Campbell's discussion of justice[1] where he talks of individuals as having equal moral worth but unequal moral worthiness. An individual's contribution to society may be of equal worth he suggests (that is, from the person as having equal human worth with all others), but of unequal worthiness for inclusion in the normative rules by which that society is governed. This distinction of equal worth but unequal worthiness is helpful for two reasons. First, it identifies as essential the need to establish democratic processes and criteria for determining which rules will be included; and second because community members whose behaviours and attitudes lie outside those which have become normative under democratically constructed rules should not be criminalised or discriminated against simply because their behaviours do not accord with the normative rules of society. In other words we legitimately discriminate in constructing norms; but behaviours and attitudes which lie outside those norms are still in themselves legitimate.

The creation of social norms is inherently difficult and requires careful political and social management if it is not to scapegoat and exclude further the very people which an encompassing community must include. Cohesion amongst the dominant group is often bought at the expense of minorities. In wartime this may, exceptionally, be a 'real' enemy, although the creation of enmities to reinforce geopolitical advantage has occurred many times on spurious grounds. In civil society, the creation of a common 'enemy', the 'other', the scapegoated minority, provides a rallying point for a majority and deflects attention from other more important but less easily focused concerns. The Conservative government in the 1980s identified the trades unions as the 'enemy within'; and racial minorities have often been identified as the butt of societal anger, even when the minority in question provides much of the economic wealth. Throughout history minority groups have been subject to discrimination solely because they were identified as different – e.g. those with leprosy or seen as mad – even though they were already disadvantaged by their condition.

Unfortunately, communitarianism, which for some would reflect an inclusive approach to social discourse, has been used by others as a way of narrowing personal options. The communitarian critique focuses especially 'on the autonomous individual of liberal social theory who is supposed to exist prior to an independent of "social relations"'.[2] The Kantian emphasis on respect for individual autonomy plays down the interdependence of human existence. As such communitarianism challenges the principalism of much ethical discourse, a principalism which elevates autonomy to an overarching imperative. Making such principles 'untouchable', first rarefies and then stultifies debate. If every ethical issue can be reduced to a four-principle problem it is unsurprising that both discourse and humanity are the losers. We need clarity, yes; but we also need a broader conception of the common good.

This is not to say that principles are not valuable in themselves. Indeed, as Mike Parker has shown, whilst it is possible to generate a set of communitarian principles for the purposes of ethical analysis,[3] often we are left feeling dissatisfied with the result. We know that the world is more messy than simple principles can describe. We know that people respond with emotional impulses to tragedy and suffering. Let us take as an example the ethics of resuscitating a person found comatose following an apparent suicide attempt. If we know the person, and have reason to believe she had taken a deliberate decision to kill herself, do we have the 'right' to resuscitate, or should we respect the patient's apparent wish to end her life? The 'pure' legal principle demands respect for the patient's autonomy; but the health professional, at the moment of crisis, makes the untested assumption that either the suicide was unintended, or that she will be grateful for rescue. This counter-factual stance rooted in the 'thank you tomorrow' principle enables the professional to ignore the subtle aspects of the situation and to get on with providing care.

An acceptable form of communitarianism is a way of encom-passing those humanising impulses to do good.[4] It is concerned with solidarity and interdependence. No person can exercise their autonomy completely in an interdependent society. The maximisa-tion of one person's autonomy means placing some restrictions on the autonomy of others, and thus, on the autonomy of all. Of course, some restrictions are less onerous than others; some are trivial and some significant. In practice, however, we do not straightforwardly accept people's decisions to do what they want with or for themselves. Let us take the case of suicide again. We impulsively try to stop people committing suicide and resuscitate them when we can. Yet we also respect those who explicitly and thoughtfully decide to end their lives for what some will determine to be good reasons. There is within this a difficult paradox involved with the nature of community. By definition community is an interplay of individuals. Those individuals affect one another in complex ways. As Walzer has put it 'we are in fact persons and...we are bound together. The liberal ideology of separatism cannot take personhood and bondedness away from us. What it does is to take away the sense of personhood and bondedness.'[5]

It is liberal societies' principles, particularly those that focus on individualism, which in part take away that sense of personhood and bondedness. The fact of such personhood and bondedness has not gone. We know this by challenging ourselves and examining carefully what we ourselves want from 'community'. The sense of bondedness may sometimes be diminished but the fact often remains. From our own experience we know that what seems to distinguish for us as 'authentic community' (from the diaspora of autonomous individuals) is that sense of regular face-to-face interaction in which personal support is achieved from the very proximity of significant others. This is well summed up by an advertisement from the National Westminster Bank which was prominent during the 1980s. It showed a strongly growing tree with the caption – 'our roots are in our branches'. The idea of the transposition of roots and branches, of above ground and below ground, of what nourishes and sustains, and what flowers and is visible, offers an analogy for the structure of the *common good*.

Common good

Achieving that common good – and what might reasonably be described as a left of centre view of communitarianism – demands the recognition of some important barriers to its achievement. As MacIntyre put it, the problem 'is not to reform the dominant (existing) order but to find ways for local communities to survive by sustaining a life of the common good against disintegrating forces.'[6] Those disintegrating forces are the nation state, the market, transnational companies, the breakdown of traditional caring patterns, appeals to egotism and individualism, and the acceptance of cultural colonialism. The worst effects of each must be ameliorated through collective action which recognises individual worth in a community of others of similar value.

But who determines what is that common good? What is good? Being good is a form of egotism; doing good is a form of altruism. The transition from 'being' to 'doing' should not be a requirement of inclusion within community, but too great an insistence on 'being' at the expense of 'doing' places an emphasis on self-interest to the exclusion of others. Actions often speak louder than words. What we do is usually more important than what we say. We should also accept that being good is not necessarily a condition for doing good. The 'politically correct' demand, that people must always be seen to be good before they can be accepted as doing good is unhelpful in creating a sustaining community. By conflating the two spheres of 'being good' and 'doing good' the beneficial effects of an individual's actions can be negated by a perceived lessening of that person's ontological value.

Michael Walzer has warned against the conflation of antagonistic or mutually independent spheres of activity. These need not necessarily be spheres of justice as such, but may be spheres of community importance. For example, as a rule we should not expect people who are very disadvantaged as a result of mental illness to be at the forefront of fighting for better services. The sphere of improving care should be kept separate from the sphere of empowering service users. That does not deny the value of service users being at the forefront of such battles, but only if they want to be and only once they are empowered to take such action. Simply pushing them into the vanguard risks disadvantaging them further.

A key part of the communitarian discourse is an attempt to challenge enlightenment orthodoxy. Too much social policy, communitarians suggest, is predicated on the notion of the rational actor, with appeals to reason. Economic theory makes assumptions about 'rational utility maximisers' as if all consumers act rationally at all times and seek to maximise their own goods and happiness. Part of Etzioni's early project was to revise this idea of the rational with an appeal to emotional and personal values. Etzioni is an economist and although he is now seen as one of the main founders of communitarianism he has also been a significant critic of neo-classical economics.[7] In practice people are altruistic, they do work within a community of others. And this appeal to and an understanding of what may be seen as at best non-rational behaviour has parallels in the post-modern belief in relativism. Too strong an emphasis on relativism at the expense of universalism, or too powerful an appeal to inherent irrationality at the expense of reason are also fragmenting forces. We need a new balance, an interplay of the personal and the professional, an acceptance of the worth of each person's view, but an acceptance, too, of specific skill and ability harnessed in the sense of the community.

This point is well put by Jeffrey Alexander in *Fin-de-Siècle Social Theory*.[8] In discussing a rational approach to social development he describes the way in which the dream of reason may have turned into a nightmare, and posits three possible reactions. The first is to believe that universalism was never a real possibility. Everything is relative and local. Relativism and localism are the only standards that can inform a good society and the community must accept all ethnic and cultural differences, however barbaric or however much they abrogate the rights of others.

His second suggested response is to say that there are no goals worth striving for but only good processes. He suggests that this is a form of reductionism; reason – rationality – is reduced to a method rather than a substantive goal; reason is simply a strategy. He then suggests that there is a third and better response. This is to incorporate a degree of relativism and social construction without giving up on a universalising intent. Being reasonable, objective, tolerant, inclusive, are symbolic of tradition and do not necessarily reflect innate human capacity. But despite their construction (rather than their innateness) they are, none the less, products of groups of individuals, and can thus create an environment which induces a sense of responsibility and mutual respect.

Thus the normative rules of society must respect a degree of relativism, whilst accepting some rational limits to individual autonomy and behaviour, in a way that is wholly transparent and democratically accountable to the community at large. Ulrich Beck[9] has suggested that only by achieving slower changes in society, based on community ownership, accountability and democracy, will it be possible to achieve a society which is at one with itself. Perhaps the most important challenge is to slow down, to be reflective, to involve and participate, to provide time for hearing and sharing the views of others, and to work out those normative rules by which we all are expected to behave.[10]

We do not have to accept the worst excesses of the political left or right; on the left those who would constrain us in the name of community; on the right those who would – paradoxically – constrain us in the name of freedom. But if we allow social decisions to be speeded up constantly it will be impossible to achieve the balance which Jeffrey Alexander and Ulrich Beck describe in their own distinctive ways. Speeding up leads to centrifugal forces which throw those whose behaviours are seen as most distant from the norm further outwards towards the edge of society. These are the homeless, the unemployed, the disadvantaged and disabled, whose needs are not perceived as important by a society which values community for those who can use it but not for the rest. Each of these people has individual moral worth and in the *commons* they must be respected.

Practical implications

Let us now turn to some of the practical implications of these concerns. First, we will consider NHS mental health care from a communitarian perspective; second, we will look at active citizenship as a manifestation of the libertarian community; and third we will investigate in some detail the ethical implications of community care.

NHS mental health services

Mental health implies a concept of the integration of the person and an authentic interaction between the person and society.[11] For effective fulfilment, inclusion requires some minimum activity within a community of others and a series of interactions which situate the person in an acceptable supportive context recognising and respecting difference whilst seeking to achieve the greatest autonomy for each person commensurate with the maximum autonomy for others, subject to continuing disability. As we have seen this autonomy must be moderated by the recognition of the interdependence of every person in the social context or milieu in which he or she lives.

This is especially true of mental disorder and harm to others. Persons who suffer from mental illness do not lose their human worth; but neither do they gain the right because they are ill to cause harm to others. Their illness may be an exculpating reason if found guilty of such harm but is of itself not an acceptable reason why such harm should be caused in the first place. The fact of the harm however does not destroy the individual's human worth. At root communitarianism must provide a vehicle for respecting all human worth and difference, whilst providing a core set of values intelligible and acceptable to all.

This ethic has been dominant in health and social care, except at the margins. The 'best face' of the NHS is that it will always care regardless of sex, age, disability, sexual orientation, race, or any other feature of a person's condition whether within or beyond their control. And yet the NHS contains significant discrimination against those for whom it purports to provide care.

The delicate balance which had been struck in the NHS between collective action for the common good and the personal responsibility of clinicians has been eroded by the imposition of quasi-market mechanisms. The purchaser–provider split has led to another form of 'splitting' – the 'denial of the other'. Purchasers (health authorities) can now make tough, possibly discriminatory, resource allocation decisions whilst distanced more than ever before from the results of those decisions. By and large those who allocate budgets do not have to face the inevitable personal backlash from patients denied care. Such splitting is the contradiction at the heart of a market philosophy in health care. Although the contradiction affects all patients it is most evident in mental health care. Competitive markets, with winners and losers, identify those less able to fend for themselves and mark them as scapegoats for society's wider ills. Markets tend to widen disparities of income and wealth; and markets if left to themselves will lead to increasing levels of homelessness, family break-up, lack of personal resources to provide care to relatives, and the mentally distressing effects of job insecurity and unemployment. If markets create distress, how can a market system in health care offer a way to improved services.[12]

Markets provide mechanisms to exchange legal (or quasi-legal) claims to goods, services or property, not the physical goods or services themselves. 'These rights are dependent for their existence upon the duty of others to respect the right being upheld, with sanctions against those who do not exercise their duty being enforced.'[13] In other words the purchaser–provider split has led to two transaction levels – the 'managerial' level, exchanging quasi-legal rights in relation to services to be provided; and the clinical level, exchanging patient need for clinical care. In the main, clinicians do not see the first level of transactions as contributing anything meaningful to the clinical transaction, other than a negative effect of removing the power to allocate resources locally and immediately to clinical need. This distancing of the clinical from the managerial creates further alienation.

In all probability, the market will only create further alienation within health services of clinicians from managers, of providers from purchasers, and of the health care system generally from politicians, such that the service is less able to cope with the increasingly distressing effects of an unchecked market. This leads to further contradictions in the way services are organised. The market becomes the rationale for everyone's activity rather than the needs of patients. This schism at the heart of health services is presented to the mentally distressed patient as a therapeutic milieu. It is not surprising that the market in health care thus appears to many patients simply to mirror the distressing circumstances in which their lives are led, thus creating further alienation from statutory or mainstream mental health care and an incentive to turn more and more to under-funded alternatives.

Active citizenship

A second practical manifestation of communitarianism is the notion of the 'active citizen'. This idea is one that has grown and developed over the last two decades and has antecedents in both the political left and right. Margaret Thatcher once famously claimed that 'there is no society, there are only individuals'. This restatement of rampant individualism flies in the face of even the least structured societies and is wholly antithetical to social development for the common good.[14] Thatcher was reflecting the Conservative project of the 1980s which was, as she put it, to roll back the frontiers of the state. Ironically the key objective of this philosophy was essentially that of communist ideology – to free the worker from the shackles of the modern productive state in order to achieve maximum personal potential.

Deregulating social forces[15] has been an objective of centre-right governments for some time, but the effects of this deregulation have compounded a cultural structure already starting to fragment. Few people emerge as winners, but for many a denial of social place and personal fulfilment leads to alienation.[16] Local democratic structures become ever less effective leading to further deregulation. Across the political spectrum the reaction has been to promote the active citizen. For Thatcher, and the political right, this is the 'self-made' entrepreneur, who, having achieved financial security, can afford to take some public role. On the left the promotion of active citizenship is for very different reasons – to achieve a sense of empowerment through the discovery of self-worth.

Community care

A third example is provided by care in the community. What community? Does it care? The detractors of community care often draw attention to these problems. They say that asking the community to care is unacceptable when professional services are either patchy or non-existent. But a different reading of community care is that it is concerned with that humanising impulse to achieve solidarity and support, to offer disadvantaged people the right for their moral worth to be recognised. Perhaps the worthiness of some people's behaviour during illness or disability may be questioned but their worth as equal citizens should not. Community care provides valued settings in which people can rebuild and sustain valued lifestyles. Community care is none the less a paradox and challenges communitarian thinking and enlightenment principles. To what extent do we intervene in the lives of people who have become disadvantaged? To what extent do we allow individuals to be autonomous? Rational utility maximisers create large institutions with 'economies of scale'; irrational liberals let them roam the streets to neglect or harm themselves (and occasionally others). Communitarianism balances universal concerns with local personal responses; it does not assume that individuals 'become' their diagnoses, or that every person is as sick as the person with the most serious illness. Community is about valuing; community care is about rebuilding valued lives; communitarianism is about valuing each other's contribution to the greater good.

In essence this is the principle of normalisation,[17] within which resides a serious and enduring paradox concerning social norms and professional power. Helping disadvantaged people to achieve valued lifestyles means adopting norms which lie at the root of the discrimination which devalued them in the first place. The status quo must be challenged whilst aspiring to the status quo! As disadvantaged people and health service users become empowered they will rightly challenge professional power, especially but not only where it is seen to be used to reinforce both professional power and the cycle of deprivation – the continued devaluation of the service user.

We must recognise a dichotomy. Many service users need, or can make use of professional expertise, where appropriately directed; but professional power must be reduced or shared such that wherever possible service users can take control over their own lives. In other words, the accretion of power in whatever form to the professional helper disempowers the service user and reduces his or her capacity to achieve the maximum autonomy of which he or she is capable.

We noted earlier that a more subtle context must be used in which to debate the rights and wrongs of 'community care'. 'Community care' has been the dominant theme for thirty years in services for people with long-term continuing health and social care needs. Put simply, it is argued that people with mental illnesses, learning disabilities, physical and sensory disabilities or infirmity as a result of age, are entitled to care either in their own homes or in settings which approximate as much as possible to usual domestic environments. On this argument large Victorian hospitals isolated from the natural environment of the 'patient' can never be an appropriate setting in which to provide care.

Community care, as envisaged by pioneers in the 1950s and 1960s was a humanising impulse to revalue people whose human worth had not been respected by those purporting to provide care. The large institutions were the dark side of the industrial revolution, the utilitarian response to the breakdown of rural communities and the aggregation of people in towns and cities. Community care by contrast was (and still is) an idealistic attempt to re-establish the humanity of each person by providing care in settings likely to provide life-enriching opportunities.

To others community care has been a confidence trick pulled by successive governments with the active connivance of well-meaning professionals who fell into a trap of their own making. Titmuss described community care as 'a myth conjured up by cheese parers under the banner of progress'. Community care became care by the community not care in the community. Care by the community rapidly came to mean care by (so-called) 'informal' carers, overwhelmingly women. Insufficient resources, either numbers of places in residential and day care settings, or numbers of staff to support those places led in many cases to a lower quality of life for disabled people and their carers than provided in the large institutions. Community care was idealistic, under-resourced, under-evaluated and, for many, an act of faith.

Yet no protagonist of community care ever argued it was a cheap option – always the reverse; community care was intended to be care in the community rather than by the community, although providing adequate resources to enable families to care if they wish should be one option. Community care was, and is, intended to provide that communitarian context of collective action for personal freedom and growth. The ethic is one of respect for the individual in an interdependent society which values all equally. Collective action, recognition of individual worth, and a striving for an authentic community of equals are the essence of community care. These are the civic virtues which informed the creation of the NHS, underpin the best local authority provision, and are at the heart of local integrated voluntary sector activity. 'Private charity', as Bevan put it on the inception of the NHS in 1948, 'can never be a substitute for social justice'. Social justice requires both a recognition of the equal worth of each individual and a determination to allocate society's goods to enable each person to be able to benefit equally. Community care is not a cheap option but under-resourcing has given its detractors the opportunity to point to failure.

It can be argued that community care was 'set up to fail', or more plausibly that it has only recently developed beyond an early nascent stage. That it is perceived as failing, and that some commentators appear to want it to fail, suggests possible explanations for the attitude of the state to community provision. The first is a straightforward fiscal explanation with somewhat less straightforward overtones. Community care has been the victim of the least possible expenditure commensurate with the policy of institutional closure. But this is unsurprising. Most (though not all) of those recipients of community care are unlikely to be or become productive members of the workforce. Any investment in them will thus be the minimum necessary to obviate scandal or pressure from relatives.

A second explanation is that many people feel community care cannot or does not work because they do not perceive 'community' except in terms of their own family networks. In practice community care is more concerned with place than person; it is essentially deontological – the right to a home but with no prescription for personal support. The double 'Achilles heel' of community care is that it is either depersonalised by definition, or it implies care by rather than in the community. Many people naturally resist the implication (even if that implication was not intended and does not become real) that they individually will have to take over caring for a disabled or disadvantaged person.

A third explanation has become evident recently, highlighting that the recipients of community care are often examples of personal or family failure in a society which now places too great an emphasis on individual achievement to the detriment of collective action. It does not matter that many reasons for needing care are beyond an individual's control – mental illness, learning disability, being elderly – the idea of individual responsibility blames the victim for his condition. Focusing on individual failure legitimises a 'lesser entitlement' for those whom society can scapegoat, regardless of the 'double jeopardy' this reinforces. Such trends can be seen best in recent attitudes towards homelessness and homeless people demonstrating vividly how a deprived minority can become institutionalised as a 'necessary evil' – one which is constantly before us as a reminder of what can happen to us if we fail in our insecure jobs and insecure lifestyles. Or, as Paul Sturdy has put it: 'concern for the well-being of others is not a prominent characteristic of the street-level society in which most mentally ill people are forced by circumstances to live'.[18]

Conclusion

An acceptable community must offer solidarity within a framework of collective values and the democratic opportunity regularly to amend the values upon which society operates. The community must sustain a dialogue between the haves and have-nots, the included and excluded. As Henry Tam[19] put in *Philosophy Today* recently – social environments, like natural environments should not be taken for granted. We need community – not simplistically, or idealistically – but by rebuilding trust, toleration, inclusiveness, democracy, steadfastness and accountability.

1 Campbell, T., *Justice*, Basingstoke: Macmillan, 1990.
2 Sayers, S., 'The Value of Community', *Radical Philosophy*, 69, Jan./Feb. 1995.
3 Parker, M., 'Individualism', in *Ethical Issues in Community Health Care* eds Ruth Chadwick and Marie Levitt, London: Arnold, 1998.
4 Heginbotham, C., *Return to Community*, London: Bedford Square, 1990.
5 Walzer, M., *Spheres of Justice*, Oxford: Blackwell, 1983.
6 MacIntyre, A., 'The Spectre of Communitarianism', *Radical Philosophy* 70, March/April 1995, p. 35.
7 Etzioni, A., *The Moral Dimension: Towards a New Economics*, New York: MacMillan, 1988.
8 Alexander, J., *Fin de Siècle Social Theory*, London: Verso, 1995.
9 Beck, U., *Ecological Enlightenment*, New Jersey: Humanities Press, 1995.
10 See also Rustin, M., 'Incomplete Modernity: Ulrich Beck's Risk Society', *Radical Philosophy* 67, 1994, p. 5.
11 Barham, P., *Schizophrenia and Human Value*, London: FAB, 1993.
12 Soros, G., 'Capital Crimes', *The Guardian*, London, 18 January 1997.
13 Mulberg, J., *Social Limits to Economic Theory*, London: Routledge, 1995, p.170.
14 Taylor, C., *Multi-culturalism and the 'Politics of Recognition'*, Princeton: Princeton University Press, 1992.
15 De Vries, K., *Organisational Paradoxes*, London: Routledge, 1995.
16 Durkheim, E., *Suicide: A Study in Society*, London: Routledge, 1950.
17 Wolfensberger, W., *Normalisation*, Toronto: National Institute of Mental Retardation, 1972.
18 Sturdy, P., 'Communitarian Ethics and the Ethos of Community Care', University of Warwick: seminar notes, unpublished, 1996.
19 Tam, H., 'Towards a Communitarian Philosophy', *Philosophy Today*. 19 May 1995.

4

COMMUNITY DISINTEGRATION OR MORAL PANIC?

Young people and family care

Donna Dickenson

Introduction

The spread of liberal individualism to the family is often portrayed as deeply inimical to the welfare of children and young people. In this view, the family is the bastion of the private and the antithesis of the contractual, rights-oriented model which underpins public life.[1] When the values of personal choice and individual rights 'infiltrate' families, Michael Hammond argues in chapter 5 of this volume, care within families is threatened. Examples might include proposals for freely negotiated marriage contracts,[2] or provisions allowing children to determine where they will live – even to 'divorce' their parents.[3] Although all family members suffer, in this view, the greatest impact will presumably be on children. They are more vulnerable, more dependent on care, and less able to do anything about its erosion. Thus children and young people are a touchstone for the decline in community standards and family life, on this account.

Conversely, the apparent lawlessness of children and young people is cited to prove that the thesis about family erosion is correct. The breakdown of community values is seen as both the cause and the outcome of poor discipline and bad childrearing practice. In the Jamie Bulger case, for example, the apparent amorality of the two children who killed was presented in the media as traumatic evidence of a decline in community *mores*. The Labour leader Tony Blair responded to the Bulger case by warning that 'If we do not learn and then teach the value of what is right and what is wrong, then the result is simply moral chaos which engulfs us all.' Labour proposed a curfew on children, a model which has also been suggested in the USA. The effective lowering of the age of criminal responsibility from 14 to 10 which quickly succeeded the Bulger case in March 1994 (reversed in March 1995) represented another attempt to shore up 'traditional' standards again.

The exponential increase in expulsions from schools is likewise cited as proof that young people, corrupted by 1960s notions of freedom and rights, are beyond teachers' control and the community's powers of socialisation. The case of 13-year-old Richard Wilding, for example, attracted national attention in April 1996 when teachers at his school threatened to strike if the expulsion order against him was rescinded at his parents' request. Later that year a supposedly anarchic school in Halifax, The Ridings, was the object of similarly intensive media scrutiny, swiftly followed by a series of stories on litigation mounted by unsuccessful GCSE pupils against their schools. All were meant to show that children are now in charge, and yet simultaneously out of control.

There are several possible ways of attacking this commonly held position about community disintegration, as exemplified by family breakdown. First, one might argue that reports of the family's death are greatly exaggerated, or even that moral panic has been deliberately cultivated. Both political parties in the UK, it can be argued, have contributed to these jeremiads because blaming the *family* for a breakdown in law and order among the young removes any responsibility from *government*. If the state represents the family writ large,[4] then any decline in the family's authority is also bound to frighten politicians. The media are likewise culpable: the tearaway adolescents in the film *Kids*, for example, have been said to demonstrate that 'tarnished innocence is big bucks'.[5] To put things less conspiratorially, childrearing is newsworthy simply because most of us are or will be parents, and all of us have been children. One journalist explains her profession's obsession with children in these terms: 'Childhood is the site for a collision of the great themes of our modern narrative: for us, it is the place where too much fondness for the past meets too great a fear of the future.'[6]

Second, there might be cause to celebrate rather than mourn the death of the 'traditional' family. In Anglo-American law, most ferociously expressed in the doctrine of coverture, the entire civil existence of the wife was suspended during marriage.[7] Her property and earnings were entirely under her husband's control, and she had no independent power to enter into contracts or conduct a business. Coverture actually strengthened rather than diminished in revolutionary America – under a regime devoted to the 'rights of man'. In the UK vestiges of it persisted nearly up to the millennium; only in 1990, for example, did married women in the UK earn the duty and right to file their own tax returns, rather than being covered on their husbands' statements. In addition the father inherited substantial control over his children from Roman law. The subordination of women and children in the common-law model of the family[8] casts into doubt the mutual trust, reciprocity and selflessless which advocates of the traditional family eulogise. Perhaps women and children had no alternative but to trust husbands and fathers, who may or may not have been able to distinguish between their own interests and those of the family as a whole. Perhaps reciprocity was really one-sidedness, and women's selflessness enforced by the lack of economic alternatives. Feminist theorists have also argued that men's freedom to enter into the social contract, which guarantees rights in the public realm, depends in its turn on the pre-existing subordination of women in the private sphere.[9] The family is, or should be, a site of struggle; the alternative is the enforced unity, in the person of the husband, which coverture represented.

I do not disagree with either of these counter-blasts against the 'community disintegration' thesis, but in this chapter I shall instead pursue two less theoretical and more empirical strategies. First, I shall argue that in many respects young people in liberal, rights-oriented systems, particularly the UK, *actually* have *less and less* autonomy.[10] Although the logic of rights is often said to be unstoppable and insatiable, I will offer case examples which demonstrate that young people's right to refuse medical treatment, for example, is considerably weaker than it was ten years ago. This radically undermines one of the most basic rights of all, on which other freedoms crucially depend: the right of bodily integrity, the freedom from invasion of the physical person. Children and young people are not covered by 'the premise of thorough-going self-determination' about what shall be done with their own bodies, the principle with which Anglo-American law has been said to begin.[11] If they lack that right, then *a fortiori* they lack others.

Instead the notion of the young person's 'best interests' or welfare dominates in current English law. This assumes that someone – the 'community'? the doctor? the judge? – is more competent to determine young people's best interests and true wishes than they are. A disturbing increase in the numbers of children between 10 and 14 who are admitted to psychiatric wards has also been interpreted as the medicalisation of 'conduct disorders': use of a psychiatric diagnosis to control unacceptable adolescent behaviour.[12] These two phenomena are linked: the cases which established that young people have no right to refuse medical treatment involved both psychiatric diagnoses and disagreement among practitioners about whether a psychiatric diagnosis was appropriate to control these young people's behaviour.

So rather than arguing that reports of the death of the family and of community values about childrearing are greatly exaggerated, I shall be claiming that young people's rights are grossly overstated. (In passing, I think that this also applies to reports of the unstoppable growth of women's rights within the family, but I will not be making those arguments here.)[13] I conclude that young people in liberal, rights-oriented systems, particularly the UK, actually have too little autonomy, rather than too much. If there really is a decline in family or community cohesion, it does not stem from the supposed triumph of rights language and personal choice, because that 'victory' is largely illusory where children and young people are concerned.

Second, I will look at other legal systems, particularly those which privilege community standards above individual rights. Such deontological codes are found in southern Europe, where they may well apply to all patients, not only children. In Greek medical law, for example, the mere condition of being a patient *ipso facto* precludes full autonomy: 'a patient is a person whose mental and bodily capacities have been diminished due to some serious malfunction in her bodily organs'.[14] In relation to adults, at least, the right of consent and refusal is now enshrined in legislation based on northern European models.[15] But the emphasis on doctors' duties rather than patients' rights persists, for example in article 441 of the Greek penal code, which punishes doctors who unjustifiably withhold their services and their duty of care.[16]

Likewise, the language of children's rights is less prevalent in these more paternalistic systems than the rhetoric of parental duties, and it is the notion of a moral community which underpins those duties. Whereas the Bill of Rights and the Constitution can be seen to symbolise Americans' communal commitment to the language of rights, the deontological codes and constitutions of southern Europe give voice to a different community consensus.

The Spanish Civil Code, for example, promises parents the help of the state in fulfilling their duties of care towards their children. This is a discourse of *patria potestas*, not of rights. Article 39.3 of the Spanish Constitution declares that 'Parents must give assistance of every kind to their children, both matrimonial and extra-matrimonial, during their minority and in other cases in which it is legally foreseen.'[17] Parental responsibilities under such deontological systems are considerable, and courts are willing to enforce them. In December 1996, an Italian court actually required a mother to continue supporting and housing her 24-year-old son for as long as he wanted to live with her. Advocates of communitarianism are sometimes accused of appealing to hypothetical or ahistorical notions of community, which provide no grip on how we should approach the breakdown of our communities that they castigate. I think that this criticism is justified, and that an examination of actual legal and moral systems with very different attitudes towards rights and duties can be productive. Are things somehow better in countries where the language of children's rights does not dominate the discourse of the family?

The rights of children?

Children and young people are the focus of fears about the breakdown of community *mores*, whether they are perceived as the victims or instigators of moral decline. But are those fears justified? Do children and young people suffer from an excess of freedom and a surfeit of rights?

The community disintegration thesis *is* probably correct in identifying a growing societal – or even world-wide[18] – consensus in favour of extending more decision-making powers to children, and of relying less on 'because I say so' as an adequate rationale for parental authority. Over some twenty years statute and case law, reflecting wider social and political trends, has indeed sought to give greater weight to children's expressions of their own feelings.[19] This trend was made explicit in the Children Act 1989, which emphasised the importance of a child's own choices.[20] Passed with all-party approval and after wide-ranging consultations by the Law Commission, the Act also built on the 1986 *Gillick* case,[21] which established that the child's full consent to examination, treatment or assessment is required if she or he 'is of sufficient understanding to make an informed decision'. Even before *Gillick*, section 8 of the Family Law Reform Act 1969 had specified that the consent of a young person aged 16 or 17 to medical treatment 'shall be as effective as if he were of full age'.

Recent case law in England, however, has run counter to this trend. Contradicting the spirit (if not the letter)[22] of the Children Act, a succession of judgements has sought to restrict young people's choices, especially those about medical or psychiatric treatment. The 'best interests' of the child have generally been interpreted in a paternalistic manner, ignoring the young person's ascertainable wishes and allowing even 'Gillick-competent' children no right to refuse treatment to which someone with parental responsibility for them has given consent. Essentially, children and young people under 18 now have no right to *refuse* treatment in circumstances under which English law would none the less allow them to *consent* to whatever is proposed. But it seems clear that the right to *give* consent must also entail the right to *refuse* consent; otherwise, the right to consent merely translates into a right to agree with the doctor.[23]

This is exactly what happened in *Re W* (1992).[24] The 16-year-old anorexic in this case was co-operating with non-invasive treatment that kept her weight low but stable. She was none the less transferred against her will to a clinic where she might possibly be force-fed, despite disagreement between the two presiding physicians over which course of treatment was in her best interests. The court determined that she had no right of informed *dissent* to feeding by nasogastric tube, even though she would have been permitted to give her *consent*.

The issue in *W* was *not* the young woman's mental condition, the diagnosis of anorexia nervosa. It was held in this instance that even a *competent* minor could not veto treatment so long as there was consent from someone with parental responsibility – in this case, the local authority. A 1991 case, *Re R*,[25] involving a 15-year-old girl who was given antipsychotic drugs against her will, had already found that a young person of *intermittent* competence was barred from refusing treatment to which someone with parental responsibility had consented. (Again there was conflict among the care teams called on to give consent, but the court chose to listen only to the more paternalistic evaluation of the psychiatrists; R's social worker, on the other hand, believed she *was* lucid and competent to refuse consent.) The effect of *W*, then, was to deny the right to refuse invasion of bodily integrity even to a competent young person. This in turn means that 'a child or young person whose competence is in doubt will be found competent if he or she accepts the proposal to treat but may be found incompetent if he or she disagrees'.[26]

A third decision, *South Glamorgan County Council v. W and B* (1993),[27] took this tendency even further. R and W had at least been formally diagnosed as suffering from mental disorders, borderline though those diagnoses may have been. But the 15-year-old girl in the South Glamorgan case – although she was extremely reclusive and had a poor record of school attendance – had not been diagnosed as suffering from any psychiatric or personality disorder at all. None the less she was compelled by the High Court to receive in-patient psychiatric assessment and treatment against her will, although (contra *Gillick*) the judge had found that she *was* of sufficient understanding to make an informed decision.

I do not wish to argue that these cases necessarily reflect a general backlash of communitarianism; both *R* and *W* came under the courts' inherent jurisdiction, a fairly narrow and specific area.[28] What these cases *do* demonstrate, however, is that children's 'rights' are not all they are cracked up to be, in the 'community disintegration' thesis. In the significant area of consent to medical treatment – which epitomises the crucial, foundational rights of bodily integrity and property in the person – they underline the rights of parents and physicians instead.

> It is important to remember that these problematic cases determined that doctors could, with the parents' approval, impose invasive treatment on an unwilling young person under the age of eighteen, whatever his or her mental competence, without having to seek approval from a court. In other words, the decisions were about medical power.[29]

Thus it would be possible 'as a matter of law', according to Lord Donaldson, the judge who delivered the decisions in *R* and *W*, for parents and/or physicians to force an abortion on an unwilling 17-year-old. One is hardly mollified by his observation that doctors would never do this, especially as Donaldson added 'unless the abortion was truly in the child's interests'.[30] Even more disturbing are the possible implications of a recent wardship case – admittedly involving a much younger child – which appear to subsume the child's identity and interests entirely to those of the parent. On this view, a child might well have no independent rights whatsoever, including the right of continued existence.

The Appeal Court case of *In re T* (1996)[31] held that a child of two with a serious liver defect, in need of life-sustaining surgery, had no right to the procedure when his mother refused consent. This is the logical obverse of the doctrine validated in *R* and *W:* that children and young people have no right to refuse consent to a procedure if someone with parental responsibility does consent. What was even more extraordinary about this recent decision is that Lord Justice Butler-Sloss stated that the mother and child were one for the purposes of the decision, because the welfare of the child depended on the mother. In a startling twist of the argument based on the child's welfare, Lord Justice Butler-Sloss then deduced that the mother's right to refuse the procedure – which will almost certainly result in the child's earlier death – is also in the child's welfare. Now one could perfectly well argue the rationality of refusing a difficult procedure with only a partial chance of success; but that does not require the extraordinary dictum stating that the child has no objective criterion of welfare apart from whatever the mother thinks it to be. (Butler-Sloss chaired the Cleveland enquiry panel into what were deemed to be over-zealous investigations of child abuse, and could perhaps be expected to be particularly sensitive to parents' wishes.) Whatever the judge's reasoning or motivations, this latest case underlines the consistent trend in English law over the past few years *away* from independence, rights and autonomy for children and young people.

The duties of parents?

I argued in the previous section that advocates of the 'community disintegration' thesis have mistaken the rhetoric about children's rights for reality. Recent UK case law has radically undermined the rights of children and young people, in particular the fundamental right of bodily integrity. In this section I will present an apparent mirror image: legal systems in which the liberal rhetoric of children's rights is absent, even fiercely resisted, in favour of the deontological language of parental responsibilities. These systems are prevalent in southern Europe, although they are evolving towards more child-centred attitudes under pressure from international and European conventions (whereas, in passing, the UK system might be said to be slipping backwards). On the face of it, these systems should appeal to advocates of the 'community disintegration' thesis. They seem to reflect a societal consensus, embodied in constitutions, codes and statutes, in support of the 'strong family' and against the dissolving, individualistic discourse of rights. For example, article 147 of the Italian Civil Code actually requires parents to impose their considered judgement over any disagreement from the child, although the code does call for reasoned discussion.[32]

The origins of this doctrine may make communitarians slightly more uncomfortable. The Italian Civil Code dates back to 1942, the Fascist period. Although its emphasis on parental authority was subsequently undercut by the Constitution of 1974, even adults do not enjoy unlimited self-determination. Article 32 of the Constitution upholds the principle that patients should not be treated against their consent, but with the rather surprising exception of compulsory treatment under Act of Parliament. However, informed consent is rarely sought in any other context than surgery: not, for example, in relation to invasive drug treatment or blood transfusions.[33] There is considerable reliance on implicit consent and reluctance to use the language of rights, which is perceived as extraneously Anglo-Saxon.[34]

The *child's* right to be informed of the likely risks and consequences of proposed treatments is legally vested in the *parent* by article 28.3 of the Constitution. The same article gives the *doctor* ultimate responsibility for the child's welfare, further overriding the young person's rights. However, recently at least one Italian jurist has argued that the spirit of the Constitution is consistent with greater autonomy for children and young people, at least as a limit on the exercise of the parents' power. It appears possible for courts to uphold a minor's refusal of treatment against the wishes of his or her parents, upon request by the Public Prosecutor or a third party.[35] If this interpretation is correct, the Italian duty-based system may sometimes award more effective powers of informed refusal to children and young people than our own 'rights-based' one. Similarly, the 1995 Deontological Code for Italian doctors enjoins an absolute duty of confidentiality for information received on trust from the child, which may not even be disclosed to parents.[36]

The direction of causation from duties to rights or rights to duties is a vexed question in philosophy. A contractarian approach, of the sort which underpins political liberalism, sees rights as prior, as existing in the state of nature and as secured by the rules of the social contract by which we choose to bind ourselves in order precisely to protect those rights. Deontologists, on the other hand, present rights as a second-order concept: your rights are contingent upon my duties.[37] Similarly, in a principle-based approach to medical ethics, rights are created by rules or principles.[38] But in actual legal practice, it seems plausible, at least, that the rights of minors in relation to bodily integrity and consent are more real in Italy than in England.

The distinction between societies emphasising parental duties and those stressing children's rights is further clouded when we look at *wider communities* than those of the nation-state. The movement towards international legal recognition of universal human rights is expressed in the UN Convention of 1989 on the rights of the child.[39] If these rights are absolute, they do not depend on capacity or competence; neither are they granted to children by adults or governments, but as a consequence of membership in humanity. As a consequence, countries are not called upon to *attribute* such rights to children, but to '*respect*' such rights because they already exist in themselves. The country must 'guarantee that they be enjoyed in practice (article 2)'.[40] The implications of this convention, for deontological systems such as Italy's, mean 'going beyond the fairly widespread view within the community at large according to which children are perceived as an appendix of an adult (parents, teachers, guardians, etc.) who, even when catering to the needs of the child, do so by exercising their own rights'.[41] Although the convention does contain a limiting clause concerning the child's 'sufficient discernment', this is not so far off 'sufficient understanding to make an informed judgement', the criterion for *Gillick* competence. But we have already seen that the effect of the *W* case is that even a Gillick-competent young person has no right to refuse treatment in English law.

An even more overt change to the language of rights can be found in the Council of Europe Convention on the exercise of children's rights, submitted to member states for ratification on 25 January 1996. The Convention is concerned with promoting children's substantive and procedural rights, particularly in relation to participation in, and sufficient information about, judicial procedures concerning them. Eschewing the language of child *protection*, the Convention freely uses the language of rights *promotion*. Member countries are urged to devise means by which children can participate directly in court proceedings, provide specialised assistance enabling them to express their opinions, and afford independent representation, particularly in family proceedings. The European Human Rights Convention likewise allows children and young people to submit claims against their national governments in their own name before the European Court. If the Italian system is serious about incorporating the Council of Europe and the UN conventions (the latter ratified by Italy in 1991 and incorporated into statute)[42] we may have the ironic situation in which 'paternalistic' Italy affords young people more autonomy than 'liberal' England.

Conclusion

It should be clear by now that I regard the notions of family and community disintegration, under the pernicious influence of children's rights, as an instance of moral panic. If anything, the rights of young people in the UK are less secure than they were in the past decade. Meanwhile, the Italian system has moved on somewhat from its earlier emphasis on parents' duties rather than children's rights – an approach which communitarians might well find sympathetic. Yet there seems little fear among Italian jurists of any breakdown in 'community'; rather, a sense that the demands of the wider European community, and the universality of member-ship in the *human* community, demand some recognition of children's rights. Perhaps, too, the rhetoric of all-encompassing parental duties has its own costs for the community. It is probably no coincidence that Italy has the world's lowest birth-rate:[43] the commitment required of parents – a lifelong duty of provision and support to their children, enforceable by courts – is ironically higher in that system than in one nominally oriented to children's rights.

Why are we in the UK subject to this kind of moral panic? In possible explanation, I want to end on what is admittedly a speculative note about the social construction of childhood. Perhaps it is no more speculative, after all, than other notions about ethical consensus and community, and appropriate to a chapter in a book on that subject.

The notion is this: that 'childhood is not a fact; it is a theory, namely a social theory...One is a child when, and only till the moment when, the society decides that he or she is a child, namely that he/she has different rights and obligations from an adult.'[44] It would be much easier if childhood *were* a fact, but it is not. Past societies, as Philippe Ariès argued in his influential *Centuries of Childhood*, frequently lacked any notion of children as anything other than miniature adults. Until the Victorian period, European children were dressed in the ruffs, furbelows and bodices proper to adults, and the passage from infancy to adulthood was mediated, at most, by a period of apprenticeship to adult life. Childhood was not idolised in the modern, post-Romantic manner, influenced by Wordsworth's and Rousseau's intimations of moral purity in children. This view may be somewhat simplistic, but it reminds us that childhood is what we make of it.

In this sense the community decides what the boundaries of childhood are. Perhaps we have a genuine and troubling sense that we are getting it wrong; or perhaps we rather envy our young people for what we perceive as their cosseted childhoods and prolonged adolescences. The German sociologists Ulrich Beck and Elisabeth Beck-Gernsheim offer a more charitable interpretation in *The Normal Chaos of Love*. Along with other attributions by formerly fixed status – 'status fates' – childhood, like the family, is an arena of contest and conflict.

> The bourgeois nuclear family has been sanctified or cursed; people have either focused only on the crises or preferred a vision of the perfect family arising from the ashes of disappointing alternatives. All these views are based on a false premise. Anyone labelling the family all-good or all-evil ignores the fact that it is neither more nor less than the place where long-standing differences between men and women come to the surface.[45]

When gender conflicts of interest *are* acknowledged in the family, 'everything one vainly hoped to find in the relationship with one's partner is sought in or directed at the child....Here an atavistic social experience can be celebrated and cultivated which in a society of individuals is increasingly rare, although everyone craves it.'[46] Childrearing unites too many of our most central fears and preoccupations: our veneration of love as a 'secular religion', our uncertainty about how to replace 'feudal' family relationships with modern democratic ones, and, most importantly, the endless possibilities for guilt that we have done too little.

> The very act of bringing up a child is emotionally highly charged. Loving it, the frail little creature, means protecting it, parents are consistently told. This injunction hits them at their weakest spot, the hopes and longings they invest in their progeny....What if something did happen? Could we ever forgive ourselves?[47]

DONNA DICKENSON

This is the converse of the greater emotional satisfaction which can be obtained from modern parenthood. Without constant childbearing, women have more emotional and physical energy to devote to their fewer children. Men, deprived of patriarchal powers over the children, none the less gain too; witness, for example, the popular belief that the praiseworthy 'New Man' plays an equally devoted part in childrearing to his wife. But whereas children simply shared their parents' lives in pre-modern agricultural Europe, the duties of parents have now evolved into a separate and very demanding set of tasks. 'A child used to be a gift from God or occasionally an unwanted burden, but now it is above all "somebody difficult to care for".'[48] The child is a screen upon which our deepest fears are played, and as 'a dependent creature always in need of an adult to define, care for and administer its physical, emotional, current and future needs'.[49]

But whatever our motivations, we ought to recognise that the moral panic over children and the family is actually an odd and misguided attempt at reforming a community consensus. In an ironic manner, it disproves its own thesis. The decline of community cannot be all that serious when the community is so apparently united in moral panic over its children.

NOTES

1 The version of this argument which has most influenced contemporary politics, through its adoption as Thatcherite ideology, is that made by Ferdinand Mount in *The Subversive Family: An Alternative History of Love and Marriage*, New York: Free Press, 1982.

2 See, for example, Margaret Sokolov, 'Marriage Contracts for Support and Services: Constitutionality Begins at Home', *New York University Law Review*, vol. 49, pp. 1,195 ff. (December 1974), and Lenore Weitzman, *The Marriage Contract*, New York: Free Press, 1981.

3 The Children Act 1989 has been incorrectly interpreted as giving children such unequivocal rights. In fact the 'ascertainable wishes and feelings of the child' constitute only one of several factors in the 'welfare checklist' (s 1[3]) which courts are directed to consider in relation to such matters as residence and contact orders. These include 'his physical, emotional and educational needs', 'the likely effect on him of any change in his circumstances' and 'any harm which he has suffered or is at risk of suffering (s 1[b], [c] and [e])'.

4 This position is usually associated with Sir Robert Filmer's 1680 treatise, *Patriarcha*, Oxford: Blackwell, 1949, ed. P. Laslett, attacked by Locke in his *Two Treatises on Government*, 1688. Although liberalism has rejected the parallel between the father and the sovereign, the association between the state and the family persists in the twentieth

century, bolstered, for example, by Margaret Thatcher's parallels between domestic budgeting and good public housekeeping.

5 Francine Stock, 'Commentary: Time to Revisit the Child in All of Us', *The Guardian*, 24 April 1996.

6 Rachel Cusk, 'How We Turn Children into our Battlefield', *The Guardian*, 3 December 1996.

7 Donna Dickenson, *Property, Women and Politics: Subjects or Objects?*, Cambridge: Polity Press, 1997, chapter 3, 'Contract, Marriage and Property in the Person'; Marylynn Salmon, *Women and the Law of Property in Early America*, Chapel Hill and London: University of North Carolina Press, 1986; Sir William Blackstone, *Commentaries on the Laws of England in Four Books*, ed. Thomas Colley, two volumes, Chicago: 1899, fourth edition; Tapping Reeve, *The Law of Baron and Feme, of Parent and Child, of Guardian and Ward, of Master and Servant, and of the Powers of Courts of Chancery*, New Haven, 1816.

8 This inequality was probably worse in the Anglo-Saxon countries than in Continental civil law jurisdictions, where community of property regimes gave the wife some independent property interests. There is some implication under community of property that marriage is an equal partnership. Each spouse retains all property acquired before marriage, and any property inherited during marriage – all of which would belong to the husband under coverture; but the earnings of each spouse, plus all other non-inherited property acquired during marriage, become the couple's 'community' or joint property under the husband's administration. A small minority of US states also operate community of property systems.

9 Carole Pateman, *The Sexual Contract*, Cambridge: Polity Press, 1988. Other feminist critics of Lockean liberalism, in addition to Pateman, include Jean Bethke Elshtain, *Public Man, Private Woman: Women in Social and Political Thought*, Oxford: Martin Robertson, 1984, pp. 108–146; Gatens, *Feminism and Philosophy*; Zillah Eisenstein, *The Radical Future of Liberal Feminism*, New York: Longman, 1981; S. M. Okin, *Women in Western Political Thought*, Princeton: Princeton Univerity Press, pp. 200–201; Nancy J. Hirschmann, *Rethinking Obligation: A Feminist Method for Political Theory*, Ithaca and London: Cornell, 1992, pp. 55 ff.; and Joan Cocks, *The Oppositional Imagination: Feminism, Critique and Political Theory*, London: Routledge, 1989, pp. 128–135. A more favourable reading of Locke is given by Melissa A. Butler in 'Early Liberal Roots of Feminism: John Locke and the Attack on Patriarchy', in M. C. Shanley and C. Pateman (eds), *Feminist Interpretations and Political Theory*, Cambridge: Polity Press, pp. 74–94. For a sympathetic but critical exploration of Pateman, see D. Dickenson, *Property, Women and Politics*.

10 For the purposes of this argument I am running rights and autonomy together, since that is usually what happens in the view about young people's excessive freedom as a cause and symptom of community disintegration.

11 *Natanson v. Kline*, Kansas 1960.

12 Department of Health statistics for the period 1985–1990 indicated an increase of 65 per cent in numbers of children aged 10–14 who were admitted to adult psychiatric wards, together with an increase of 42 per

75

cent for under 10s and 21 per cent for 15–19-year-olds. At the same time the number of adult admissions fell by 9 per cent. Although many of these admissions were informal, by parental agreement, this procedure deprives young users of mental health services of the rights of challenge provided under the 1983 Mental Health Act for patients admitted under compulsory order (s 3).

13 Those wishing to pursue this line might find some of the following helpful: Christine Delphy, *Close to Home: A Materialist Analysis of Women's Oppression*, translated and edited by Diana Leonard, London: Hutchinson, in association with the Explorations in Feminism Collective, 1984; Caroline Glendinning and Jane Millar (eds), *Women and Poverty in Britain: The 1990s*, Hemel Hempstead: Harvester Wheatsheaf, 1992; Sylvia Ann Hewlett, *A Lesser Life: The Myth of Women's Liberation*, London: Michael Joseph, 1987; Ruth Lister, *Women's Economic Dependency and Social Security*, Manchester: Equal Opportunities Commission, 1992; Mavis MacLean, *Surviving Divorce: Women's Resources After Separation*, London: Macmillan, 1991; Jan Pahl, *Money and Marriage*, London and Basingstoke: Macmillan, 1989; Carol M. Rose, 'Women and Property: Gaining and Losing Ground', in *Property and Persuasion: Essays on the History, Theory and Rhetoric of Ownership*, Boulder, Colorado: Westview Press, 1994, pp. 233–263; and Ann Whitehead, 'I'm Hungry, Mum: The Politics of Domestic Budgeting', in Kate Young, Carol Wolkowitz and Roslyn McCullagh (eds), *Of Marriage and the Market*, London: CSE Books, 1981, pp. 49–68.

14 I. Manoledakes, 'Scientific and Legal Problems Concerning the Phenomenon of AIDS', *Bulletin* (Quarterly Edition of the Hellenic Centre for the Control of AIDS and STDs), 2 (1996), p. 7.

15 Greek Law 2071/1992 on the Modernisation and Organisation of the Health Care System, Article 47, section 3: 'The patient has the right of consent or refusal to any diagnostic or therapeutic procedure intended to be performed upon him. In the case of a patient wholly or partially mentally incompetent, the exercise of this right falls upon the person who legally asks on his behalf' (translation by Filimon Peonidis). Peonidis points out that this article is modelled on a relevant Belgian act of 1979 ('A Moral Assessment of Patients' Rights Practices in Greece: A Preliminary Outline', paper presented at the sixth European Biomedical Ethics Practitioner Education Project meeting in Naantali, Finland, 6 September 1996). He believes that 'the language of patient's rights is in the process of supplementing [rather than replacing] the traditional duty-based framework of medical ethics' (p. 7).

16 Peonidis, 'Moral Assessment', p. 4.

17 Article 154, summarised in Joaquin Bayo-Delgado, 'A Drug-Addict Minor and an Incompetent Family: How to Act to Assure Therapeutic Support to the Minor? The Spanish Situation', paper presented at the first meeting of the European Biomedical Ethics Practitioner Education Project, Rome, 25 May 1996.

18 John Eekelaar cites the UN Convention on the Rights of the Child as evidence of 'a world-wide context of increasing sensitivity to children's rights' ('Commentary on "True Wishes" ', *Philosophy, Psychiatry and Psychology*, vol. 2, no. 4 (December 1995), pp. 304–306.

19 Donna Dickenson and David Jones, 'True Wishes: The Philosophy and Developmental Psychology of Children's Informed Consent', *Philosophy, Psychiatry and Psychology*, vol. 2, no. 4 (December 1995), pp. 287–303, at p. 287.

20 See (3) above. The Children Act, which came into force on 14 October 1991, also gave the child the right to refuse a medical or psychiatric examination when an emergency protection order is being contemplated, 'if he is of sufficient understanding to make an informed decision). (s 44(7)). This is the wording established in the *Gillick* decision (see below).

21 Gillick *v* West Norfolk and Wisbech Area Health Authority, 1986; 1 Appeal Cases: 112–207.

22 The Act is by no means a children's charter: the paramount principle is the welfare of the child, arguably a paternalistic criterion. See n. 3 above. The dominant concept of the Act is probably parental responsibility, and the decisions in *R* and *W* – contrary to the spirit of the Act though they first appear – can be interpreted as reinforcing the supremacy of parental responsibility over children's rights.

23 Commentary, *Medical Law Review*, vol. 1, no. 2 (1993), pp. 271–273; J. A. Devereux, D. P. H. Jones, and D. L. Dickenson, 'Can Children Refuse Consent to Treatment?', *British Medical Journal*, vol. 306 (29 May 1993), pp. 459–461. For a contrary view that there should be a higher tariff for refusal than for consent in minors, see Allen E. Buchanan and Dan W. Brock, *Deciding for Others: The Ethics of Surrogate Decision Making*, Cambridge: Cambridge University Press, 1989.

24 *Weekly Law Reports* 3: 758–782.

25 Ibid., 3: 592–608.

26 Devereux, Jones and Dickenson, 'Can Children Refuse?', p. 461.

27 *Family Law Reports* 1: 576–597.

28 This important distinction is made by Eekelaar (see above).

29 Eekelaar, 'Commentary on "True Wishes" ', p. 305.

30 Ibid., p. 306. The courts have also forced treatment on young people against their wishes even when parents do *not* consent, notably Jehovah's Witnesses (*Re E* [1992], *Family Court Reports*, 2:2 19; *Re S* [1994], *Family Law Reports*, 2: 1,065). In the *E* case the young man, whose refusal of a transfusion at the age of 16 was overruled, exercised his right of choice as soon as he reached 18, and died.

31 *In re T (a Minor) (Wardship: Medical Treatment)*, reported in *The Times*, 28 October 1996.

32 Paola Daddino, 'Conflict Between Minor and Parents in Cases of Therapeutic Treatment: The Italian Law', paper delivered at the first meeting of the European Biomedical Ethics Practitioner Education Project, Rome, 25 May 1996.

33 Carlo Calzone, 'Consent or Compliance? From Informed Consent to Informed Guidance', paper given at the sixth meeting of the EBEPE project, Naantali, 6 September 1996. Articles 28, 29 and 31 of the 1995 Code of Professional Ethics in Medicine do require informed consent, 'but in practice [the Code] subordinates it to the principle of beneficence' (Calzone, 'Consent or Compliance?', p. 4). The Code specifies that 'doctors ought to commit themselves to protect children, elderly and handicapped persons....In particular, doctors ought to do what is

in their power so that children receive what is needed for a harmonic psychic and physical development and so that children, elderly and handicapped persons are guaranteed quality and dignity of life' (Article 28, 'Assistance: duties of doctors towards children, elderly and handicapped persons', translated by C. Calzone). Whilst article 29 requires doctors to inform patients about diagnosis, prognosis and consequences of proposed therapy, it also warns them to 'keep in mind the patient's limited medical knowledge, his cultural level, emotions and ability to understand....Information on the diagnostic and therapeutic programme can be limited to the elements that the patient's culture and psychological condition make possible to accept and understand, and superfluous details on scientific aspects should be omitted.' The overall aim is 'to promote compliance with diagnostic and therapeutic procedures'.

34 Daddino, 'Conflict Between Minor and Parents'; Carlo Calzone and Maria Stella d'Andrea, 'New Offspring in a Family with a Handicapped Child', paper presented at the first EBEPE meeting.

35 Daddino, 'Conflict Between Minor and Parents', referring to articles 330–333 of the constitution.

36 Arts. 9. 10, 11 and 17 of the code, as summarised by Glauco Mastrangelo and M. Serena Mastrangelo in 'Divorce and Legal Separation: The Conflicts Among Parents and the Role of the Practitioner', paper presented at the first EBEPE meeting.

37 See, for example, Charles Fried, *Right and Wrong*, Cambridge, Massachusetts: Harvard University Press, 1978, pp. 9 ff.

38 Robin Downie and Kenneth Calman, *Healthy Respect: Ethics in Health Care*, London: Faber and Faber, 1987, p. 61.

39 Similarly, the Platform for Action of the UN Fourth World Women's Conference (Beijing, September 1995) presents women's rights as universal human rights which rightfully override particular societies' traditions.

40 G. Magno, 'The Rights of Minors in International Conventions', paper presented at the first EBEPE meeting.

41 Ibid.

42 Act number 176, 27 May 1991.

43 UN data put the Italian birth-rate at 9.6 per 1,000 inhabitants. The Greek and Spanish rates are likewise quite low, at 10.6 and 11.2 respectively. Compare the rate for Great Britain of 13.6, and the American statistic of 15.5. (Table reproduced in Ulrich Beck and Elisabeth Beck-Gernsheim, *The Normal Chaos of Love*, translated by Mark Ritter and Jane Wiebel, Cambridge: Polity Press, 1995.)

44 Emilio Mordini, 'Confidentiality in Child Psychiatry', paper presented at the first EBEPE conference.

45 Beck and Beck-Gernsheim, *Normal Chaos of Love*, p. 33.

46 Ibid., p. 37.

47 Ibid., p. 119.

48 Ibid., p. 132, citing H. Hentig, foreword to the German translation of Ariès, *Centuries of Childhood*, Munich, p. 34.

49 Beck and Beck-Gernsheim, *Normal Chaos of Love*, p. 137.

5

CONTRACTING CARE IN THE COMMUNITY

Michael Hammond

The colonisation of care in the community by the market

Four principles underlay 'care in the community' as it was conceived in the 1990 NHS and Community Care Act. These were: first, that the care people received was to be decided solely by their needs; second, that people were to be involved and consulted about these needs; third, that life incarcerated in institutions was inferior to life at home in the community and fourth, that statutory solutions to welfare problems were questionable. This final principle was linked to the first two in the sense that individuals were seen as best able to discern their own needs and preferences; and statutory institutions were seen as not well placed to decide for others what is in their best interests.

There was broad, all-party support for the Community Care Act. Most of this was based upon acceptance of the first three principles and I don't want to question these here. The fourth principle however has proved problematic. For, the way this has been responded to, and the way community care has developed has cast doubt on the possibility of the realisation of the aims of the other three principles. In short, 'care in the community' is being undermined first by the development of a market of providers and purchasers of care and second by the introduction of cost-led management into its provision. What I want to show is that the application of market concepts to 'care in the community' insidiously undermines both care and the possibility of care in the community.

Let me start by considering the fourth principle. There might be said to be political agreement on at least some aspects of this principle especially where there is a concern for autonomy (which lies behind both the first two principles). For what many people find objectionable about statutory solutions to welfare problems is their paternalism. At the time of the Act, the officers of the state – DSS officials, social workers – were seen by some to be deciding for clients what was in their best interest. This perception however ran counter to the perception of social workers themselves who believed that in their adherence to client self-determination they were not imposing solutions on clients. They were, they believed, valuing and respecting individuals, recognising their uniqueness, being concerned with opportunities for growth, increasing access to opportunities previously denied and providing resources which would enable and empower individuals rather than keep them entrapped. Nevertheless, what happened was that the concept of the 'nanny state' became built into the dominant perception of statutory welfare provision with the implication that people should be encouraged not to rely on the state; and this led to a policy of reducing state provision partly to encourage individual responsibility. Alongside this anti-paternalism, for which there was broad agreement, there were two linked crucial perceptions: (1) that statutory provision is inefficient i.e. it costs too much for the amount of need satisfied; and (2) that the most efficient mechanism for efficiency, maximum care for minimum cost, is the market.

The solution was seen to be the increasing privatisation of care. This has turned out to be privatisation in two senses. The first sense is entirely negative: 'private' means 'not public'. Care is increasingly not provided by statutory agencies: local authority homes for the elderly are diminishing in number; large institutions run by the health service for patients with various degrees of psychiatric disorder (including those with no disorder at all – like women incarcerated in mental institutions for moral incontinence (unmarried mothers)) are being closed down and their former patients are being cared for 'in the community' (In this context the sceptical thought arises that the only meaning that can be attached to 'in the community' is 'not in an institution'; the prevalence of the attitude of 'not in my backyard' with respect to these former patients indicates the degree to which there is no community for them at all.)

The second sense of privatisation concerns the *funding* of care. The providing agencies, increasingly former voluntary agencies, compete for funds from the purchasing agency, the statutory social services. The work of social service social workers becomes more weighted in favour of the purchase of provision from other agencies than in the provision of these services. This second sense of the privatisation of care clearly involves the market. But crucially it is not the market in its pure form whereby the purchaser and the person to whom the provision is given are one and the same person. For, in most cases the purchaser is the social service agency (perhaps supplemented by some financial input from the person requiring care – as when elderly people are means-tested for contributions for their care in residential homes or for domiciliary care).

What the first sense of privatisation alone could produce is a state of affairs in which the voluntary agencies might increasingly be seen as an additional *alternative* to the state provision. These voluntary agencies could both in their style of provision and in their critical perspective on state provision (e.g. MIND on mental health provision, SHELTER on housing policies, NCH on provision of care for children) constitute a challenge to the paternalistic tendency within statutory provision and a challenge to received wisdom on welfare provision. The addition of the second sense of privatisation however has made a significant difference. For it has meant that statutory agencies increasingly treat the voluntary sector as an agent of provision and the form that the relationship between the statutory authorities and voluntary agencies takes becomes one of *contract*. The agency contracts to provide specifically identifiable services for specific amounts of money which the statutory authorities pay. To obtain these funds the voluntary agencies have to fulfil contractual conditions laid down by the statutory agencies.

The effect of this contractual arrangement is that the state can exercise control over the provision of care. And this means that it is possible to stifle criticism. For it can be a condition of the contract that there be no political activity critical of statutory policy (e.g. the prevention of members of hospital trusts from making public comments on the internal running of the system), or the providing agency can fear that if it does publicly criticise it will not have its contract renewed. Given that the larger voluntary agencies earn up to 80 per cent of their income from directly contracted services one can appreciate the power of the fear of loss of income.

Two examples help bring out the kind of control possible here. The first concerns care of the elderly. It is becoming clear that in many cases the paramount consideration in the allocation of care is often cost rather than client need or preference. There are cases where despite a person having expressed a need or preference for remaining in their own home albeit with support from home help, domiciliary nursing etc. and despite the expression of an aversion to living in a residential home they have been pressured into accepting a 'package of care' that involves residential care because it is cheaper. One instance is of a 79-year-old woman in Gloucestershire referred for reassessment for a care at home package which was costed at between £780 and £900 per week (1994). After this costing, going home was no longer an option due to its cost. The making of decisions under tight budgeting constraints has had three implications. First, there are clearly unmet needs; and second the private sector is affected: the UK Home Care Association and its 900 members report not getting work or having rates cut down to uneconomic levels because councils are opting for residential care because it is cheaper (Dobson, 1995a, 18–19). Third, care managers feel limited in the kind of services they could provide or arrange[1] and it is clear that a central factor in statutory authority control here is cost.

The second example is of self-help for people with HIV/AIDS. A recent study by the National Network of Body Positive reveals that various voluntary support and self-help groups were in danger of collapse because they were being refused funding by local health authorities (Williams, J., 1995). The crucial factor in this refusal involved the nature of the contract these self-help groups had to make with these authorities. Some groups were refused funding because they had not developed the presentation of their 'provision' in accordance with contractual requirements. Six of the groups had been forced to change their agenda(s) after demands from the funding agencies. The nature of some of these changes is revealing. In one case there was a demand for the release of the names of people who were either HIV positive or had AIDS. (Ostensibly this was to ensure that the number of people being helped was accurate and to develop monitoring and surveillance of HIV infection.) There was another case where money was made available to fund work with women when the greater need was for a gay men's worker and in order to obtain the funds the Body Positive Group had to employ a female worker (Ibid., 20).

What has proved particularly problematic has been the emphasis upon self-help which is characteristic of these groups (the 'buddy' system):

> If the current and potential benefits of self-help – particularly its balancing component within community care – are not realised by statutory funders, the self-help movement

will continue to be squeezed by the contracting system into becoming service providers, due to the extreme difficulty in quantifying self-help.

(Ibid., 39)

This highlights an important point which is that some forms of care are, by their very nature, resistant to being quantified; and what can't be measured can't be paid for. The model of care as determined by what can be paid for sees care as something like legal services where a client pays a solicitor, say, for a particular service (e.g. a conveyance which takes X number of hours at £Y per hour, plus the cost of telephones, letters, etc.). But care cannot always be expressed as a 'service' and if the kind of self-help offered in the HIV/AIDS case is 'professionalised' into a service in order to meet the conditions of the contract then one is also in danger of losing the important sustaining sense of community that HIV/AIDS sufferers (and their friends) have developed.

These two examples enable a number of relevant points about 'care in the community' to be made. First, the control exercised via the power of funding and the withholding of funding has clear paternalistic overtones; hence the practice of 'care in the community' is inconsistent with its own rhetoric of giving power to non-statutory agencies and to individuals. Second, the care provided has to be perceived in a particular way. It is a service to be bought, a service which is a means for satisfying an individual's needs, independently identified. Third, the nature of social work changes. Instead of being providers of care, social workers become 'managers of care' (in social work literature they are often referred to as 'care managers'). This leads to a reported reduction in job satisfaction. For social workers are forced to change from being carers to being purchasers of care, and the latter is not so psychologically sustaining.

The philosophical language of 'care in the community' is predominantly individualistic. Or at least it is framed by a dichotomy between public good and private interest. Previously, statutory welfare provision was seen as public good, rather like clean air or unpolluted water; now, the range of public goods is so much smaller – mainly concerned with protecting our security, life, etc. And if the meeting of need is not a public good it must be a private good. Add to that the belief that the best way to satisfy private interests and needs is by allowing the agent to purchase what he or she needs and one has the basis for the kind of market we find in 'care in the community'. The agent, in this situation, is not always able to purchase care; so someone does so on his or her behalf. Care on this model is a quantifiable means of satisfying an individual need. What I want to show in the rest of this chapter is that this is an odd kind of care; and that if it becomes the dominant mode of care then it will have systematically undermined the possibility of the many kinds of care that do exist – but which cannot easily be captured by this public good/private interest dualism.

One such source of care in this other sense lies in the 'communities' on which 'care in the community' so clearly depends. If one puts aside the sceptical thought that 'community' as it occurs in 'care in the community' has only a minimal, negative meaning then one sees that there is in fact a community (in a sense) of unpaid carers. There clearly is a great amount of care in the community which is neither statutory nor provided by voluntary agencies. This is the care provided by family, friends, fellow sufferers or neighbours; and this care has the virtue (from the point of view of cost-conscious governments) that it is freely (at least in terms of money) given. But this point of view overlooks both the variety of care possible and the variety of communities in which this care takes place (Jewish communities which run day-care centres or provide social work services for those who prefer a Jewish social worker; Asian groups operating day centres; the buddy system supporting people with AIDS). The individualist framework of 'care in the community' is blind to these different kinds of care, despite the programme relying on this care. This blindness is the subject of the next section.

Care

Caring takes many forms; there is a variety of things one can care about; and there is a variety of motivations to care. Here are some instances of each:

i Forms of care

1   worry; concern; anxiety: as in the parental 'I care whether or not you come home safely' or in 'cares of life'.
2   nurturing, nourishing, as in parental care: looking after the physical and emotional development of those in our charge.

3   protecting, as in Care Orders – e.g. when a child might be withdrawn from an abusing family for its own protection. The child is placed in the care of some trusted third party (e.g. foster parent).

4   affection, as in 'I care for you' (even better when it is non-verbalised). This can involve all the ingredients 1–3. Its special feature is that it need not have the paternalistic overtones of 1–3.

5   interest, as in 'I care about Liverpool's success in the League.' Here care is an expression of one's interest in the well-being of the recipient of care; but this care need have no causal power on that well-being (though this isn't the belief of supporters at the ground!).

ii   Objects of care

1   people (individuals): children, siblings, parents, friends, lovers, partners, neighbours, colleagues, oneself, etc.

2   people (groups): family, religion, ethnic group, gender, underprivileged, etc.

3   sufferers: the ill, criminals, mentally disturbed, injured, bereaved, dying, threatened, etc. (This can take individual or group as object.)

4   'things': cars, bicycles, homes, tools, etc.

5   living things: gardens, landscape, nature conservation, flowers, plants, etc.

6   abstractions: truth, honesty, life, health, duty, art, music.

iii   Motives of care

1   'moral': loyalty, duty, obligation, fairness.

2   self-interest.

3   role obligations: teacher, nurse, social worker, care assistants, home helps, etc.

4   vocational: certain norms, ideals, virtues that go beyond 3.

5   disinterestedness: care given for the benefit of the recipient (not as in 2 merely for the benefit of the carer).

6   friendship.

All these differentiations – of *type*, *object* and *motive* – of care are problematic. Particularly problematic are the relations within each group and across each group. The permutations of care are obvious enough (at least 100 possible combinations of the above!) and this alone should make us wary of conceiving 'care in the community' as only one kind of care. To simplify matters I am going to concentrate in the remainder of this chapter on: (i) 2 and 3: the nurturing, nourishing, protection forms of care; (ii) 1: care of individuals, and (iii), 1 to 6: all the motives. This means that the main focus of the rest of the discussion will concern motives. Why do people care for others in this way? Approached from this perspective several questions emerge:

1   Is it the case that all care is really in the interest of the carer? (An affirmative answer implies that care for the welfare of others should be seen as nothing but the pursuit of one's self-interest.)
2   Is it the case that all care is disinterested?
3   Does it matter what the motive of care is?
4   Is care in any of these categories more typically displayed by women than by men?

The last question has obvious implications for care in the community, for unpaid carers are typically women. And if the result of other (employment) policies (if they can be called that) is a growing proportion of women working (albeit on short-time temporary contracts) then there is likely to be a fall in the number of those available to care. Whether unemployed males can step into the breach remains to be seen; but if there is a different psychological history of males and females, where males are encouraged to become autonomous rational individuals and females are encouraged to become caring, communal, connected emotionally, sensitive family members, then the prospect is none too happy (Gilligan, 1982).

For present purposes, the importance of this fourth issue is that of its relevance to current moves to strengthen the moral sense of duty between members of families. The attempt to re-enforce the sense of familial obligation most typically felt by women is an attempt at a corrective to the increase in breakdowns in care which demand (costly) state intervention (in the form of provision of services). There is a growing awareness that a society of preference-satisfying individuals is a society which loses any sense of obligations to others. But this strategy isn't the only possible response; though it might seem to be such by those who think in terms of a *dichotomy* between public good – ascertained by reference to impartial, objective standards of duty, obligation, etc. – and private interest. It seems to me to be a result of poverty of thought (and practice) that this is seen to be the only alternative.

Before trying to explain why, I want to link this dichotomous thinking to the third question concerning the relevance of motivation to care. In the special case of 'care in the community' under consideration motivation is systematically ignored. From the point of view of a care manager it does not matter what the motivation for care is as long as the care is given. From this point of view, which is concerned to maximise preference satisfaction at least possible cost, the only relevant motivation is self-interest. The discounting of other kinds of motivation in this way is an instance of the dichotomous thinking referred to above. This is likely to prove important for there is the danger that it will lead to a tendency towards the lack of recognition (and therefore a lack of encouragement) of more complex kinds of motivation.

In order to consider some of the complexities of the motivation of care I want to concentrate on the first two of the questions I listed above. It is worth noticing that there might be a hidden presupposition here: that care is either self-interested or it is disinterested. It is this presupposition that I want to question.

I want to suggest that on one reading of question 2 above (i.e. on one reading of 'disinterested') the answer to both questions 1 and 2 is: 'No'. To question 1, the answer is 'No' because there are cases of care which are morally motivated, to question 2 it is 'No' because there are cases of care which are selfishly motivated. This reading of 'disinterested' is one which stresses impartiality: one should care for those who deserve or need it regardless of their special relation to oneself. The danger in this reading is that it seems to presuppose the kind of dichotomous reasoning I detected lying behind 'care in the community'. In this case care is seen as either impartially justified (the impersonal demand of morality) or as self-interested (Blum, 1994, Ch. 4).

The account of 'disinterested' that I gave before – when listing types of motivation – is, I think, the crucial one. For this high-lighted the *direction* of motivation, suggesting that care was for the benefit of the recipient; there is no essential reference to benefit to the carer. It is possible that the carer gains satisfaction from caring; but it only counts as not being disinterested caring if the caring is *merely* for the benefit of the carer – despite any benefit the recipient of that care receives. So if a 'dutiful' daughter looks after her mother rather than put her in a nursing home in order to ensure her inheritance this care is not disinterested, even though the mother may benefit from this care.

So some care is carer-centred; and some care is an attempt to satisfy the demands of impartial morality (duty, etc.). Some would argue that both kinds of care are self-centred (guilt, etc.) – but resisting that move is not my concern here. What I want to highlight here is that much important care is not clearly either of these; and this is why *role-obligations*, *vocation* and *friendship* figure in my list of motivations. (Blum, 1994, Ch. 4.)

What seems to be involved in vocation is: (1) a sense of personal identification with the relevant activity: one sees nursing, teaching, etc. as an important aspect of oneself because the activities involve values and ideals to which one also subscribes. It is not usually that there is a role and one makes an independent existential choice to identify oneself with it; rather it is, given the type of person one is (the type of values typically displayed in one's behaviour), one will feel drawn to particular vocations (or not – as in the case when one works for solely other reasons, such as, security, means for private satisfaction, to maintain family, etc.). Vocational demands will not be felt as external/impersonal demands. They will be felt as personal demands: I would be lacking if I did not respond to a particular call on my sense of vocation. And (2) there is a response to some particular person which involves going beyond the mere call of duty. For this to be a vocational response (as opposed to, say, a friendly one) this has to be a response to a person in particular need of one's vocational capabilities. So a nurse acting out of a sense of vocation would on occasion not merely be conscientious in giving medicine, keeping the patient comfortable, being available for consultation, etc. but could respond to a patient with special needs for example, as someone who requires additional or special nursing. In this the nurse is responding to a particular call as a nurse. So it is not a response due to anyone, but a response to a particular need only seen as such because of the nurse's perception of the values and ideals of nursing i.e. the need is seen as a medical need (breathing difficulty, inability to urinate, lack of confidence in the prescribed drug, etc.).

The particularity of this response and the fact that the vocational norms are the carer's personal norms mean that the care provided is not independent of personal characteristics (either of all or of a restricted group). What might still be true however, is that the care is impartial in that it would be given to *anyone* who had this particular degree of difficulty. The temptation (in such cases) might be to see acting out of a sense of vocation as acting for one's personal good, for one might feel badly about oneself if one did not provide the extra attention to someone in a particular plight. It is true that the sense of value here is one's own – hence the vocation – but it would seem misleading to portray this vocation as a pursuit of one's own self-realisation, or of one's own happiness, or even of one's own perfection. For this is not the *aim* of the motivation. The aim is the relief of a particular kind of suffering which is perceived in a particular other. (The motivations here can, of course, be more complex – one shouldn't assume there is only one motive. Often what we do is overdetermined so some vocational action might also be due to wanting to impress, to help friends, for love, etc.)

In this account of vocation I have concentrated on actions which go beyond the call of role duty – as in the special additional help given to an anxious patient – but there is a sense of vocation which could be manifest in all the activities of a practitioner who has a sense of vocation. An example would be a nurse who in fulfilling his nursing duties – thereby satisfying the demands of the role as nurse – does so in a way sensitive to the needs of those in his care. He might spend extra time with a frightened patient; be lightly humorous with another; take care to explain procedures to another. And these sensitivities contribute to the care provided. Some will be expressions of the caring qualities of the nurse himself not solely as a nurse: he might display the same sensitivity in other aspects of his life. Others will be expressions of him as a nurse in that he might feel it important to perform his nursing duties in a particular way but feel no such pull in his personal life. The strain of his vocation might be such that he could not sustain this level of sensitivity.

What is important here is that the sense of vocation is manifested in a variety of ways: specific acts of kindness, compassion, nurturing, specific sensitivities displayed in a variety of acts, e.g. being sensitive to issues of confidentiality as a social worker; having a sensitivity to the needs of adoptive parents when one's central focus of care is the adoptive child; being sensitive to colleagues (in so far as their stresses and strains might affect the overall care provided) and so on. There is a response to needs. The motivation for all these kinds of care, embodied in the various virtues, kindness, compassion, sensibility, etc., might be complicated: it might include a strong sense of public duty – which determines why one chooses to be a nurse or social worker in the first place; it might be that one feels 'naturally' drawn to a certain caring profession because of the kind of person one is; it might be that one has a deep underlying sense of guilt at one's fortune which one wants to expatiate through care for others; it might be that one is moved by a compassionate desire to relieve suffering. But whatever the answer – and what I want to resist is first that there is only one kind of answer viz. self-interest or public duty and second that motivations are simple (single) – it is clear that certain kinds of care (vocational) are provided because there exists a relationship between the carer and his or her particular dispositions, values and ideals and the particular needs of those in his or her charge.

If one tries to provide an independent specification of these needs – as in an assessment of need – which is able to form part of a contract between the local authority purchaser and some provider then the care bought (the service) is no longer vocationally given; whatever care is given has been specified in advance (and for which a specified payment has been made) so the care is not for a particular other – but for another whose need satisfies certain objective criteria.

The undermining of care in the community

The nature of the care offered has changed: for now care is a 'service' provided to an individual consumer, where there need be no special relationship between carer and charge; and in practice the tight conditions for the provision of care – certain number of patients to be seen; limitations on budget; reduction of waiting time for first appointments; increasing efficiency (lower costs per client) – mean that there are fewer opportunities for the kind of vocational care which has been a feature of the caring professions. When one adds the fact that the institutions which used to embody an idea of public service have been systematically replaced by quangos whose whole ethos is managerial efficiency then one sees the conditions for the continuing deterioration of a certain kind of care. Of course it is possible that individuals working for a 'private agency' like a nursing home can still have a sense of vocation and respond to those in their care in the way I have been emphasising. But the climate for this is not one in which this is encouraged (*Cardiac Arrest* on television is a caricature of this tendency within the NHS).

What I am suggesting then is that there is (or was) a kind of care typically offered by carers in public agencies which cannot form part of a contract between purchaser and provider. The provider cannot contract to offer this kind of care because to do so is to transform it into a contractual duty so it operates more like role duty rather than as something which transcends such duty. And the purchaser (or the person on whose behalf the care is being purchased) cannot demand this kind of care.

One might not worry too much about this state of affairs for two reasons: First, this kind of care, as I have suggested, is slightly capricious; one cannot rely on it. So isn't it better to offer care clearly specified and paid for so that one can know that it will be provided? To which the answer might be: not if the quality of care suffers due to the resentment of carers operating under alien conditions. And second, there are plenty of other kinds of care offered which can be relied upon: from family, friends, neighbours and communities.

The clearly specified care referred to first will be paid for, whereas the care referred to second will be unpaid. And if the latter can be expanded or the former be cost-conscious then the aim of reducing the tax burden can be achieved. Are there any problems with the strategy of expanding unpaid care? I will mention one and discuss another. The one I want to mention is important: indeed it is part of the problem for it concerns the very need for 'care in the community' – at least in some cases. What seems to be happening is that care for family members seems to be breaking down. We see increasing violence within families – child abuse, battered wives, elderly abuse. We see breakdown within relationships bringing problems for the care of children. We see the decline in care by families of children with special needs or of the elderly. Part of the cause of this decline is connected with the pursuit of individual autonomy by those who used to be saddled with caring. In a climate of giving priority to the individual as the best judge of what is best for him or her this is not surprising. For those who are the unwitting victims of this process decisions have to be made about the appropriate forms of care. Where the victim has a clearly acknowledged 'right' to care, e.g. abused children, then statutory provision is arranged – though even here there is a tendency not to use publicly owned children's homes but to use publicly 'purchased' foster homes – which are cheaper.[2] In other cases, 'packages of care' are arranged subject to the usual budgetary constraints. So what happens is that care is either seen as right – or as yet another consumer good to be paid for. So the 'mentioned' problem is that unpaid for care is diminishing.

The other problem related to this is that the process of the enactment of community care contributes to the drying up of unpaid care. This can occur as the causal consequence of contracting procedures (as in the Body Positive self-help groups). But I am more interested in something deeper. The message of 'care in the community' is that care is *either* a public matter (when there is a clear moral duty to provide it) *or* it is a private matter, in which case the care should be given or paid for (either by the needy, or by someone on behalf of that person).

The trouble is that much of the care that is given is not given because the donor feels morally obliged (in the impartial/impersonal sense) but because of some special relation to the person in need. The donor could be a fellow family member, friend, colleague, a member of some religious group, ethnic group, etc. Seeing the range of motivations for care in all these groups as subsumable under either being morally obliged (the resurgence of duty calls) or as called for by private interest is to misrepresent the complexity of motivation here. A temptation, as in the vocation cases, to resist is the thought that if the care I give to a friend, fellow-believer, fellow-sufferer, is only given because that individual has a special relationship to me then this care is given for reasons of self-interest (as it is seen as clearly not morally demanded). But the possible motivations are more varied than this.

1   One can provide care for an individual because one is moved by their plight. One so acts not because they fall into the relevant category but because their plight touches you.

2   One can provide care for an individual because he/she is a friend or because he is a member of the same community. Here the guiding motivation is the felt obligation of friendship, the felt demands of the community: one would feel one owed this to anyone who was a friend etc. Acting to protect a group might be one kind of example.

3   One can provide care for an individual because of the specific relationship (and its history). It is only because of particular trust/expectations and particular awareness of needs that certain forms of care are offered. Why they are offered is something to do with the care being the expression of that relationship.

In none of these cases need the demand be felt as an impersonal moral demand; nor need it be the pursuit of private interest – though there is a strong personal element here. But the central message (as I hope was seen in the case of vocation) is that these types of cases are difficult to extricate from the relationship: to focus on the carer's motivations tempts one, because this is an expression of his or her needs, desires, attitudes, dispositions, virtues, ideals, to see this as only self-interest. To focus on the help given tempts one to underestimate the element of care given that is because the person is a friend (or because of a special relationship). Take the example of Body Positive self-help groups. Most of the members of these groups are people with AIDS, and this fact contributes to the kind of care received. Those helped are less likely to feel patronised; they feel there is more possibility of being understood. If one tries to provide an objective account (i.e. independent of the specific relationship between fellow sufferers) of the care such self-help groups give one is reduced to items like advice, counselling, support, campaigning against discrimination. One might then be tempted to think that anyone can offer these – which to a degree might be true (i.e. if one accepts certain restrictions on the 'anyone'). But if the care offered by original self-help groups is not in the equation then an important dimension of that care will be lacking.

One response to the second temptation could be to identify the need of the individual as one which involves support from fellow sufferers. Then one can, if it is lacking, or in danger of collapsing because of lack of funds, fund such self-help groups. In this case this seems possible: indeed it seems to be what the National Network of Body Positive wants (i.e. recognition of the special element of 'self-help'). But this certainly does not seem to be possible in all cases e.g. friendship caring (one cannot purchase friendship – though, one might be able to provide financial support to friends to enable them to care for their friends, though I suspect that any such funding would not take any notice of the friendship element here). All that would be of concern would be how much help the individual needs and what is the cheapest way to fund it.

The first temptation (i.e. the temptation to think of care as self-interested) is the one which concerns me more, since it is so dominant. For in so far as such cases are seen to be pursuing their self-interest – as seems to be the case in the official thinking behind 'care in the community' – then the special nature of that care is not recognised, for it *is* more than this. Even if I am wrong to think that a philosophical case can be made for differentiating these various motivations for care such that they are not reducible to self-interest it is clear, I hope, that people act as if they think there are such distinctions. Someone who helps a friend without considering what he or she has to gain from giving the help would be upset if the friend thought otherwise. Similarly for the other kinds of motivations. But if the message received is that all such motivation is at bottom self-centred then the culture encouraging such motivation declines; and hence one might expect the requisite psychology for the kind of community care on which 'care in the community' relies to begin to be less in evidence.

Another factor contributing to the same process is that people who previously would have cared for family, friends, etc. because of their special relationship to those in need might feel in the contractual climate of 'care in the community' that they are being taken for a ride, exploited. This could breed a resentment which could have deleterious effects on the care provided; or even result in a withdrawal of the care. But they are caught in another way: if financial support is given there is always the danger that the care given will be seen (by the cared for) as only given for that financial support and this can have dire consequences on the care provided/received.

One final line of thought. I have argued that in relation to the caring professions and to caring voluntary agencies contractual/market funding can undermine the possibility of some important kinds of care. This is I think the more reliable argument. I have also argued that the unpaid-for care is in danger of diminishing even faster thus putting more pressure on statutory services (and so exacerbating the first problem) and that this is in part due to the sparse view of the motivation of care on offer – that it is motivated either by moral duty or by private interest. It could be, however, that I have imposed this dichotomous view on the proponents of 'care in the community'. It might in fact be the case that it is only the public provision of such care that is vulnerable to the charges of inefficiency and paternalism. It may well be legitimate to claim that friendship care, family care, community care are neither. They are not inefficient for they do not cost the tax payer any money; they are not paternalistic (or at least not in the same league as public welfare) because this kind of care pays special attention to the voices of the recipients of care. This leaves open the possibility that we have minimal public provision plus either alternative voluntary agency provision, voluntary agencies being the agent of state provision, plus the network of unpaid-for care, with its variety of motivations, which need not be seen as only self-interested. The tax-saving task of government would be to re-encourage all those kinds of motivations for care that have been my concern.

I say this is a possibility, but in order for it to be realised one might have to re-examine the case against public provision; for it is in that case that we first saw the power of the stress on individual self-interest. The central message is: don't rely on the state – look after your own interest. It is in the resonances of this clarion call that 'care in the community' is transforming both care and community.

NOTES

1   Dobson. R., 'Social Nightmare', *Community Care*, Supplement, 27 April–3 May 1995, contains a report of a survey of care managers which has 71 per cent of these reporting clients with unmet needs because of budgetary constraints.
2   It is arguable that these are not 'purchased': because the rates for foster carers are so low they barely cover costs. This is a clear exploitation of the goodwill of foster carers.

6

VIRTUAL GENETIC COUNSELLING

A European perspective on the role of information technology in genetic counselling

Ruth Chadwick and Kim Petrie

Introduction

In the fast-paced world of clinical genetics, the role of the genetic counsellor is constantly being redefined. There is a consensus that genetic counselling should precede testing to ensure an informed choice is made. However, debate persists whether it should be a mandatory precursor to testing or should simply be made available. Also, the traditional guiding principles, client autonomy and non-directiveness, are currently being challenged on the basis of their interpretation, attainability and effectiveness in modern clinical genetics. Genetic counsellors must also grapple with the sensitive and revealing nature of genetic information and hence with its communitarian implications on two fronts: maintaining client confidentiality from third parties such as insurance companies; and dealing with the unresolved issue of familial rights to genetic information that may disclose vital health information. A clear definition of the role and purpose of genetic counselling is made further elusive by rapid advances in genetic mapping and screening technology, as each new genetic screening procedure made clinically available raises new medical, legal and ethical considerations.

Even genetic counselling itself is not immune to the technological advances. An interactive CD-ROM has recently been developed to ostensibly supplement or replace genetic counselling in testing for BRCA1 and BRCA2 mutations, which are potential indicators of a genetic predisposition to breast cancer.[1] This computerised counselling technology forces a thorough consideration of the requirements and challenges of genetic counselling into the foreground. This chapter will discuss the current position on genetic counselling in Europe. Then, against the accepted criteria, we analyse whether an interactive CD-ROM can be considered a form of genetic counselling at all, and if so, whether it can effectively deal with the pressing dilemmas facing the modern genetic counsellor. For whilst the use of CD-ROM counselling might be seen, on the one hand, as a genuinely communitarian development shifting power away from practitioners and other experts and towards the community, it could equally be interpreted as an abdication of communitarian responsibility by practitioners (because it is now patients who have to decide what ought to happen with the information).

Genetic counselling as an integral part of genetic services

Genetic counselling is a central component of the provision of genetic services from both the private and public sector.[2] Advances in genetics have made it possible to reveal carrier status and susceptibility to serious genetic disorders. However, due to the complexity and unfamiliarity of contemporary genetics, the possibility of misunderstanding the testing results, by both medical professionals and the public, is substantial. Also, genetic testing brings serious social and psychological risks which may affect both the individual and their family and may not be realised. For example, genetic testing may reveal future health information and if released to a third party may result in genetic discrimination or health insurance being denied. Consequently, it is generally agreed that genetic counselling is a necessary precursor to genetic testing.

It is however controversial whether pre-test genetic counselling should be mandatory or simply made available and participation left up to individual discretion. Although it is accepted that counselling may be crucial to understand the nature and many implications of genetic testing, mandatory counselling can be criticised as paternalistic. As will later be discussed in more detail, the biomedical principle of autonomy necessitates that people have all the information required to make a fully informed, autonomous decision. However, autonomy can also support the right to choose whether or not counselling is desired. Another view is that some degree of paternalism may be necessary, as people may not realise the implications of what they are refusing until it is too late. This debate is ongoing, but for the purposes of this chapter there is consensus that genetic counselling must at least be an option made available to anyone considering genetic testing.

There is a view that new genetic testing technologies are creating a greater demand for genetic counsellors than limited health care resources can supply, and a CD-ROM would be a more realistic way to meet the current demand.[3] It is agreed that limited resources is a serious problem facing genetic services.[4] However, before we embrace computerised counselling, it must first be questioned whether it can be considered a form of counselling at all.

The fundamental principles of genetic counselling

The primary purpose of genetic counselling is to assist an individual in deciding whether or not to undergo genetic testing. However, the term 'genetic testing' is deceptively simple as there are various types of clinical genetic services available. For example, people may seek personal genetic information before making reproductive decisions; they may elect foetal testing for certain disorders; and finally, people may consider being tested for either carrier status or genetic predisposition to certain disorders. Each of these scenarios raises different issues that the genetic counsellor must address and therefore a general definition of what genetic counselling should entail is impracticable. However two universal principles have traditionally guided the genetic counsellor: client autonomy and non-directiveness.

The principle of autonomy is strongly endorsed by biomedical ethics and health law alike. An autonomous moral agent has the right to self-determination and, in the biomedical context, to make her own health care choices. To truly exercise this right to autonomous choice, an individual must be able to deliberate on all available information and options pertaining to the choice being made, including any implications or consequences that may result. From a legal perspective, fully informed consent must be obtained prior to medical intervention or else the supplier of the service may face liability.

There is general agreement in Europe and North America that certain information is indispensable to understand the implications of a decision to undergo genetic testing. The genetic counsellor must make a client aware of the nature and inheritance patterns of the disorder in question, as well as inform about the purpose, limitations and proven accuracy of the desired test. The counsellor must also gather detailed personal information and family history to provide an assessment of the client's personal risk of developing a disorder. The individual must be informed of the potential psychological and social implications of either a negative or a positive result on themselves and their family. Finally, the counsellor must discuss available prevention and treatment options and their limitations. It is generally agreed that this is the minimal information needed to make an informed decision on genetic testing.[5]

Can a CD-ROM meet these informational requirements? Presumably, a sophisticated program could allow an individual to key in personal and family history information and give a statistical analysis of the person's risk of developing the disorder. With respect to the other minimal requirements it is possible a CD-ROM could be specified to provide this information; however, much detail would be required and all risks and potential social and emotional implications must be addressed. For example, the client should be made aware of possible adverse emotional responses to different results which they may not anticipate. False positives may create unfounded anxiety, while false negatives may give unfounded reassurance. True positive results may cause great anxiety even though this does not indicate when or if the disease will develop. Finally, a true negative may result in unexpected depression and feelings of guilt.[6] If all details are included, it is arguable from a purely informational perspective that provision of information from a CD-ROM may be adequate.

However, there are problems with such a proposal. First, it would be difficult to ensure that all the information was provided. The person could skim over important information or could quit the program before important information was given. Second, new information is published daily that may change or invalidate the information contained on the program. Vast quantities of a CD-ROM could be created one day and then invalidated the next. Will a market-driven economy allow for these to be destroyed and new ones created? This is dubious as all subsequent productions will face the same risk of being rapidly outdated. There is also a problem that old CD-ROMs will remain in existence after the information they contain has been proven inaccurate. It would be difficult to prevent a previous user from lending it to a friend or family member who may not be aware it is outdated. Also, it can be strongly argued that young children should not be counselled on their susceptibility to adult onset disorders.[7] Again, this would be difficult to regulate with a CD-ROM. A third concern is that simply providing information does not ensure that the information is understood. However, this issue will be given a more in-depth analysis under the discussion of effectiveness of genetic counselling. The second general principle of genetic counselling will first be discussed.

Along with being fully informed, an autonomous decision must be made voluntarily and any indication of coercion will raise concerns of paternalism and the legality of the consent. To safeguard against potential coercion, the principle of non-directiveness has become a cornerstone of genetic counselling. Essentially, non-directiveness means that the genetic counsellor must not guide or direct their client and must respect all decisions. Recently, however, the notion of non-directiveness has been critically examined. Clarke argues that non-directiveness is impossible as even acknowledging the opportunity to undergo a specific genetic test indicates that this test may be an appropriate choice.[8] However, although total non-directiveness may be impossible, there are degrees of non-directiveness and it can be argued that genetic counsellors can strive to be as non-directive as possible.[9]

It is arguable that there is less risk of coercion or directiveness from a CD-ROM than a human counsellor. This position may be countered by the view that a computer program misleadingly gives the appearance of objectivity, although it was originally pro-grammed by a person and values may be systematically imposed. However, in general, if the presentation of information and options are strictly balanced, there is arguably less risk of values being imposed by a computer program.

However, this increased non-directiveness may not be considered a benefit considering recent analysis. There is the view that striving for the highest degree of non-directiveness may reduce risk of coercion but may be ineffective counselling. The UK Nuffield Council on Bioethics states that, to some, a neutral approach seems cold and unhelpful.[10] Another view is if non-directiveness is interpreted as limiting counselling to questions and issues raised by the client, the minimal informational requirements may not be provided. Also, it is recognised that preconceptions may affect the quality of an individual's understanding.[11] There is a position that overcoming these barriers to decision-making may require the counsellor to identify preconceptions and raise important unsolicited information.[12] A recent report from the Royal College of

Physicians of London acknowledged that different degrees of directiveness may be preferable in different situations.[13]

Current interpretations of autonomy are now focusing on maximising the quality of the decision-making process, rather than an interpretation stressing self-determination.[14] The emphasis on maximum non-directiveness is being reduced, although new approaches must be monitored very carefully to ensure that the values, opinions and decisions of the individual are respected. None the less, there is developing consensus in Europe that empowerment and enablement are the new guiding principles of genetic counselling.[15]

Effective genetic counselling: enablement and empowerment

To discuss what empowerment and enablement in genetic counselling may entail, we will examine the special challenges of genetic counselling for susceptibility to breast cancer. Studies have linked BRCA1/2 mutations to a predisposition to breast cancer and testing programs are available. This form of counselling was selected for two reasons. First, a CD-ROM is most likely to be marketed for adults seeking information about their health status and genetic susceptibility to adult onset, multifactorial disorders. Second, a CD-ROM recently proposed purports to replace or supplement this form of counselling and therefore general discussion is timely. It must finally be noted that some of the concerns and considerations are unique to breast cancer susceptibility testing, while others are common to other forms of testing.

It is unlikely that the goals of empowerment, and enablement in genetic counselling and decision-making can be achieved by provision of information alone. Genetic information, in particular the concept of genetic risk, is complex and may be difficult to convey to an individual. Evans *et al.* found that individuals do not always understand the notion of risk when described as 'gambling odds', although this is a common strategy for explaining this concept.[16] The way information is presented is important, as the assimilation and comprehension of information can be specific to each individual. Therefore, a counsellor must assess understanding and reformat information as necessary.

In addition, assimilating information may be an emotional process and this must be taken into consideration. Significant psychological stress may accompany the fear of genetic susceptibility to serious disease. This contention is supported by a study showing there is little difference in mood disturbance between women with BRCA1/2 carrier status and those actually diagnosed with breast cancer.[17] Many women fearing inherited breast cancer disposition have lost a close family member and may feel intense anxiety, despair, guilt and resentment towards other family members and even their bodies.[18] Studies have shown that these emotional responses may seriously affect judgement.[19] In addition, Williams argues that the client must believe the information given to them and 'relate it to themselves in a meaningful way'.[20] It is possible that someone may be in a state of denial or wilful blindness to the personal implications of the information. Emotional and psychological responses may also act as barriers to making a free decision. Due to the familial nature of BRCA1/2 testing, there is increased fear that guilt or responsibility may make a person believe that testing is her only ethical option. To ensure that an empowered autonomous decision is made, the counsellor must provide support during a difficult time and give reassurance that the decision is theirs to make and alternatives may be available.

Another obstacle a genetic counsellor must overcome is individual variation in risk perception. For example, a positive result still leaves open the uncertainty of when or if the disease will develop, although some may perceive it as a certainty. How people perceive genetic risk percentage varies greatly and is affected by many factors such as, *inter alia*, family dynamics, age, personality and coping styles.[21] Studies have also shown that the perception of risk of inheriting breast cancer is affected by prior beliefs and personal experiences with the disease. For example, studies have shown that a woman's perception of risk may increase with the number of mammograms she has received.[22] Risk perception has been found to have a significant affect on health decisions.[23] Therefore, dealing with inaccurate perception of risk is extremely important in maximising the quality of the decision-making process.

Can a CD-ROM address these barriers to empowered decision-making? To reach the objective of client empowerment, provision of full information is necessary. However, it must be accompanied by professional support to minimise preconceptions and other emotional barriers to true understanding and autonomous voluntary decision-making. It is argued that even the most sophisticated CD-ROM may not be able to provide the necessary individualistic support to maximise empowerment. Information provided on a computer screen would be subject to a serious risk of misinterpretation. Although checks can be programmed to test an individual's knowledge, it must also be ascertained whether the answers were not just regurgitated, but also understood and related effectively to themselves.

In addition, preconceptions and prior beliefs may pose an extra problem for computer counselling as they may negatively alter what information is focused on while navigating the program. Also, although our society is becoming more familiar with computers, we are not at the point of universal familiarity. Many people may not feel comfortable with this method of counselling, let alone empowered by it. Even the most user-friendly computer program can not replace empathy, compassion and support. A final criticism is that there is no way to ensure or ascertain that the counselling was effective.

As a final point, a serious problem facing genetic counselling is that often genetic testing procedures may be made available despite limitations of the accuracy of the testing procedure. There are significant limitations with current testing procedures for BRCA1/2 mutations[24]and the implications of the presence of these mutations are not fully understood.[25] There are also concerns regarding available methods of prevention and treatment for breast cancer. Self-examination of breasts and mammograms are often considered to be methods of prevention as early detection may be possible and methods of treatment pursued. Available 'treatment' includes prophylactic mastectomies, oophorectomy, and tamoxifen treatments. There are however strong criticisms of these methods of prevention and treatment. First, these options for both prevention and treatment bring their own medical and psychological risks to the individual.[26] Second, none of these options has been proven to lower incidence of breast cancer or significantly decrease morbidity.[27]

It can be argued that due to these serious limitations, clinical genetic testing for breast cancer susceptibility should not even be permitted. Although BRCA1/2 testing is still made available, an individual considering testing must be aware of this position. However, this is a catch-22 situation as the very act of counselling on this subject legitimises the testing procedures. Full empowerment requires that a client understands these crucial limitations and any inaccurate assumptions of the efficacy of the tests or treatments must be addressed. The innate endorsement of a CD-ROM offering such counselling may counteract statements pertaining to these serious limitations. Finally, some of these concerns may not be able to be handled by a genetic counsellor at all. There is agreement that professional support in genetic counselling may also require that referrals to psychologists or medical professionals be offered. For example, to understand fully the available treatment options, referral to a plastic surgeon to discuss options for reproductive surgery after mastectomy may be required.[28] It seems unlikely that a CD-ROM could provide this necessary support.

To analyse fully computerised genetic counselling, other advantages and disadvantages such as commercialisation, privacy and confidentiality must also be considered. These are not simply problems for those who develop such technology or for patients and practitioners. They are problems which concern the community as a whole. Most notable amongst these is the problem of what to do with genetic information.

Commercialisation of genetic services

Commercialisation of genetic counselling may exacerbate problems already addressed. There is a fear that commercialisation of genetic services will result in market and consumer demand driving the course of biotechnology. For example, there is a concern that a market-driven economy may alter or delay the course of research as an announcement of new information may render a product obsolete. Also, it can be argued a commercial interest is raised in keeping the CD-ROM on the market for as long as possible. It is problematic that an interest other than the welfare of the individual may be considered. Another concern is that some genetic services will be made available before adequate testing has been done on their reliability and effectiveness. This may be supported by the argument that individuals should have the option of choosing to undergo genetic services if the technology is available. However, this 'supply and demand' mentality may override quality control and careful accreditation of privately supplied medical services. A corollary to this is the concern that if genetic services supplied direct to the public are shaped by consumer demand, a certain definition of 'normalcy' may emerge.[29]

Other issues of quality control may arise. As was mentioned earlier, there is a problem of misuse of outdated CD-ROMs. Also there may be a move to provide such services over the Internet to increase accessibility. A criticism of CD-ROM counselling is that although numbers are increasing, at present, a significant number of people do not own a computer or have access to one.[30] Although the Internet may promote accessibility, it will be unregulated and quality control rendered virtually impossible. Finally, if computer counselling is used in conjunction with mail order genetic testing services, there are concerns that the human element may be eliminated from a complex and sensitive decision-making process. The UK Advisory Committee on Genetic Testing recognised the complexity of genetic testing of adult onset disorders and recommends that services supplied direct to the public and outside of a professional medical relationship be limited.[31]

Privacy and confidentiality

A key consideration in genetic counselling is confidentiality which, like autonomy, is recognised by both law and ethics. First, it must be noted that the terms privacy and confidentiality are not inter-changeable and are distinct concepts. Private information is information that an individual has not made known to another person and another person has no right to know. On the other hand, confidential information has been *confided* to someone. If information is confided to a counsellor, the duty to keep this information confidential then arises. Although confidentiality is not an absolute principle in biomedical ethics, it can be justified on the principles of autonomy, utility and beneficence.[32] One of the risks of medical genetic information is the possibility of predicting future health status and this information may result in denial of health insurance or employment discrimination. Therefore, the case for maintaining individual confidentiality from third parties is strong. However, a controversy exists between the individual's right to keep their genetic information confidential and the duty to provide shared genetic information to family members and broader communitarian duties and responsibilities.

Dickens *et al.* state that there is no legal duty to warn relatives. However, it is suggested that a court may override the right to confidentiality and may consider disclosure of test results as 'justifiable or excusable' under certain circumstances.[33] The Royal College of Physicians of London suggests that in very limited circumstances there may be reasons to reconsider disclosure of information to family members. It is stressed that this would be considered in extreme circumstances, but the possibility is raised. A reason for this suggestion is the notion of common genetic property or shared ownership of genes among members of a family. With third parties, such as insurance companies, disclosure of the information can only result in an alteration of behaviour towards the person tested. However, family members may have a personal interest in knowing the information and it can be used for their own health care planning.[34]

There is also a stronger position that medical geneticists and counsellors have a duty to inform a family member of important health information, and consequently breach the duty of confidentiality to the individual that was tested.[35] A study group to the European Commission concluded there is a strong presumption in favour of individual confidentiality. However, disclosure may be possible in exceptional circumstances. They stated that the need to disclose must outweigh interests in maintaining individual confidentiality and the interest in protecting the principle of professional confidentiality in general.[36] Although the presumption of individual confidentiality is supported, absolute assurances of confidentiality of test results may be unrealistic.

Arguably, a CD-ROM could offer counselling under conditions of optimal privacy. An individual could seek genetic counselling for a disorder and no one else would need to know. In this scenario, the threat of disclosure would be avoided and this may be considered a significant advantage as the risks of genetic discrimination would be avoided. The question then is whether this increased privacy can outweigh concerns of quality of counselling. It can be argued that a CD-ROM does not provide effective counselling as it does not supply the necessary professional and emotional support to empower an individual in autonomous decision-making. In addition, studies have shown that individuals seeking anonymous testing are often those that are the most vulnerable and in need of professional support.[37]

However, it is important to remember the debate whether genetic counselling is a mandatory precursor to genetic testing. It can be strongly argued that autonomy supports that individuals should be able to choose whether or not to seek genetic counselling and that a mandatory requirement is paternalistic. For some, concerns of confidentiality may be a barrier to seeking genetic counselling at all and a CD-ROM may be the only option they wish to pursue. Also, there are degrees of support that can be offered in a counselling interaction and someone may prefer one approach over another. At this point, focus returns to issues of quality control and what are the minimal standards of genetic counselling.

Conclusion

The purpose of this chapter was to assess whether computerised genetic counselling can be considered a form of genetic counselling, and if so whether it is effective genetic counselling. However, there is a view that this distinction should not be made as effectiveness in itself is a fundamental criterion. The new view of autonomy in genetic counselling moves away from simple provision of information to the quality of the autonomous decision-making process. There is general consensus in Europe that the genetic counselling relationship must strive to empower and enable an individual to make an autonomous decision. For example, barriers to understanding must be addressed and professional and emotional support provided. This chapter put forth many reasons why a CD-ROM is likely not to meet these requirements and therefore should not be recommended. However, it is recognised that this contention may be criticised as paternalistic. If we take the position that counselling should not be mandatory and should be left to individual discretion, it is arguable that people should also be able to choose the form of counselling they pursue. For example, some may value increased privacy and prefer a virtual genetic counsellor. However, such safeguards against paternalism can result in a consumer-focused mentality which raises many concerns of quality assurance.

Once a CD-ROM is advertised as a replacement to genetic counselling, it is argued that certain minimal standards must be met. People generally do not know what to anticipate from genetic counselling.[38] Therefore, a CD-ROM advertised as a replacement for genetic counselling may be accepted without question or examination. This weakens arguments that selecting a CD-ROM over a human genetic counsellor is necessarily the result of an autonomous choice. In addition, determining a generally acceptable minimum standard for a program will be difficult as achieving empowerment and maximal understanding is an individual process. Finally, it can be argued that some forms of genetic services should not even be sanctioned outside of a professional medical relationship. The UK Advisory Commission on Genetic Testing states that certain genetic services supplied directly to the public must be limited due to their complexity and the serious implications of the decision.[39]

As a final note, it is recognised there is a strong impetus towards computerisation of services in our society. Clinical genetics is not immune to this trend and computerised counselling will undeniably challenge our conception of modern genetic counselling. There have been reports of computer therapy that have been effective in helping suffers of depression. However, in these instances, the CD-ROM was used for self-help purposes and not to make important medical decision carrying serious and potentially unanticipated implications.[40] Also, it is agreed that a CD-ROM may be a useful educational tool, but only under the surveillance of professional medical care. The trend towards computerisation must not overwhelm the need for high quality generic services as the social, emotional and medical implications of clinical genetic testing on individuals and their families are significant. It is contended that the many concerns discussed in this chapter are limiting factors to the endorsement of CD-ROM genetic counselling in Europe.

NOTES

1 Green, M. J. and Fost, N. (1997) 'An Interactive Computer Program for Educating and Counselling Patients for Genetic Susceptibility to Breast Cancer', *Journal of Cancer Education*, vol. 12, no. 4, pp. 204–207.

2 Council of Europe: Official Statement on Genetic Testing (1994) *Bulletin of Medical Ethics*, February, p. 10. EUROSCREEN (1997) *Genetic Screening: Ethical and Philosophical Perspectives, Final Report*, February, Contract no. BMH1–CT93–1348, p. 6. Advisory Committee on Genetic Testing (ACGT) (1997) *Code of Practice and Guidance on Human Genetic Testing Services Supplied Direct to the Public*, September, London: Health Departments of the United Kingdom, p. 3.

3 Green and Fost, 'An Interactive Computer Program', pp. 204–207.

4 A Report of the Clinical Genetics Committee of the Royal College of Physicians of London, *Clinical Genetic Services in 1990 and Beyond*, London, UK, 1991, p. 11.

5 ACGT, *Code of Practice*, pp. 5 and 13. Chadwick, R. (1993) 'Human Genome Analysis: Implications for Genetic Screening' *Proceedings of the International Seminar on Bioethics*, 22–26 Knox College, Dunedin, New Zealand, November 1993, p. 8. Statement of the American Society of Clinical Oncology: Genetic Testing for Cancer Susceptibility (1996) *Journal of Clinical Oncology*, vol. 14, p. 1,730–1,736.

6 Shickle, D. and Chadwick, R. (1994) 'The Ethics of Screening: Is "Screeningitis" an incurable disease?' *Journal of Medical Ethics*, vol. 20, pp. 12–13. Huggins, M. *et al.* (1992) 'Predictive Testing for Huntington's Disease in Canada: Adverse Effects and Unexpected Results in Those Receiving a Decreased Risk', *American Journal of Medical Genetics*, vol. 42 , no. 2, p. 508.

7 Biesecker, B. *et al.* (1993) 'Genetic Counselling for Families with Inherited Susceptibility to Breast and Ovarian Cancer', *Journal of the American Medical Association (JAMA)*, vol. 269, no. 15, p. 1,973.

8 Clarke, A. (1991) 'Is Non-Directive Genetic Counselling Possible?' *Lancet* 338, pp. 998–1,001.

9 Chadwick, 'Human Genome Analysis', p. 11.

10 Nuffield Council on Bioethics (1993) *Genetic Screening Ethical Issues*, London, December, p. 37.
11 Vernon, S. *et al.* (1993) 'Factors Associated With Perceived Risk of Breast Cancer Among Women Attending a Screening Program', *Breast Cancer Research and Treatment*, vol. 28, pp. 141–143.
12 White, Mary T. (1998) 'Decision-Making Through Dialogue: Reconfiguring Autonomy in Genetic Counselling', *Theoretical Medicine and Bioethics*, vol. 19, no. 1, pp. 5–8.
13 A Report from the Clinical Genetics Committee of the Royal College of Physicians of London (1998) *Clinical Genetic Services: Activity, Outcome, Effectiveness and Quality*, January, London, UK, p. 2. The report recommends that different degrees of directiveness are desirable for different types of genetic counselling. They suggest maximal non-directiveness is necessary in counselling on reproductive decisions; however, in counselling on adult onset disorder, the counsellor should advise on recommended methods of prevention.
14 Ibid., p. 9 states that the ultimate aim of genetic counselling must be a healthy adjustment to the possibility or diagnosis of a genetic disease, although they acknowledge that this concept is difficult to measure.
15 Clarke, 'Is Non-Directive Genetic Counselling Possible?', pp. 998–1,101. Chadwick, 'Human Genome Analysis', pp. 11–12. Royal College of Physicians of London, *Clinical Genetic Services*, p. 9.
16 Evans *et al.* (1994) 'The Impact of Genetic Counselling on Risk Perception in Women with a Family History of Breast Cancer', *British Journal of Cancer*, vol. 70, p. 936.
17 Vogel, V. (1993) 'Breast Cancer Risk', *Breast Cancer Research and Treatment*, vol. 28, p. 92.
18 Biesecker *et al.*, 'Genetic Counselling for Families', p. 1,973.
19 Lerman, C. and Schwartz, M. (1993) 'Adherence and Psychological Adjustment Among Women at High Risk for Breast Cancer', *Breast Cancer Research and Treatment*, vol. 28, pp. 147–152.
20 Williams, Ann (1994) 'Genetic Counselling: A Nurse's Perspective', in Clarke, A. ed. (1994) *Genetic Counselling: Practice and Principles*, Routledge, p. 47.
21 Vernon, 'Factors Associated With Perceived Risk', p. 137.
22 Vogel, 'Breast Cancer Risk', p. 92.
23 Lerman and Schwartz, 'Adherence and Psychological Adjustment', p. 149.
24 Parmigiani, G. *et al.* (1998) 'Determining Carrier Probabilities for Breast Cancer – Susceptibility Genes BRCA1 and BRCA2', *American Journal of Human Genetics*, vol. 62: pp. 154–155. For example, available models cannot take into consideration spontaneous mutations, environmental factors or the potential effect of yet undiscovered genes that may play a role in conjunction with or distinct from BRCA1/2.
25 King, Mary Claire *et al.* (1993) 'Inherited Breast and Ovarian Cancer: What are the Risks? What are the Choices?' *Journal of the American Medical Association (JAMA)* vol. 269, no. 15, p. 1,978. For example, a lifetime risk percentage of 85 per cent has been given to people with BRCA1/2 mutations. However, this percentage has arisen from studies

with families with very high incidence of breast cancer and it is possible that some BRCA1/2 mutations are not as severe as others.

26 Lerman and Schwartz, 'Adherence and Psychological Adjustment', p. 145. It is unclear what effect accumulated radiation from mammograms may have. Also, studies have shown that women at risk of familial breast cancer often undergo frequent surveillance and testing and may exhibit a disabling fear of the disease. Lerman found that this constant fear can even act as a barrier to following recommended surveillance or treatment.

27 Chadwick, R. and Bundred, N. (1998) 'It is Unethical to Offer Gene Testing for Cancer when the NHS Cannot Afford to Deal with the Consequences', forthcoming paper. King et al., 'Inherited Breast and Ovarian Cancer', p. 1,979. Schrag, D., Kuntz, K., Garber, J., Weeks, J. (1997) 'Decision Analysis: Effects of Prophylactic Mastectomy and Oophorectomy on Life Expectancy Among Women with BRCA1/2 Gene Mutations', New England Journal of Medicine, vol. 336, pp. 1,465–1,470.

28 ACGT, Code of Practice, p. 13. Biesecker et al., 'Genetic Counselling for Families', p. 1,973.

29 Caulfield, T. (1997) 'Regulating the Commercialisation of Human Genetics: Can We Address the Big Concerns?', Paper presented at the International Conference Genetic Information: Acquisition, Access and Control, December 5–7, Preston, England.

30 USA data http://www.usadata.com/usadata/category/mmk95com.htm and http://www.survey.net/ There is unofficial evidence that access is not universal and is related to individual circumstances such as level of education, age, type of employment and levels of income.

31 ACGT, Code of Practice, pp. 4 and 10. The ACGT Code of Practice states that testing for inherited dominant and X-linked disorders, for adult onset genetic disorders regardless of inheritance, or for the genetic components of multifactorial or acquired diseases that are supplied directly to the public must be limited due to the complexity and serious implications this sort of testing involves.

32 Chadwick, 'Human Genome Analysis', p. 12.

33 Dickens, B., Pei, N. and Taylor, K. (1996) 'Legal and Ethical Issues in Genetic Testing and Counselling for Susceptibility to Breast, Ovarian and Colon Cancer' (1996) Canadian Medical Association Journal, vol. 154, no. 6, p. 815.

34 A report of a working group of the Royal College of Physicians Committees on Ethical Issues in Medicine and Clinical Genetics (1991) Ethical Issues in Clinical Genetics, October, London, UK, pp. 4–8.

35 Ngwena, C. and Chadwick, R. (1993) 'Genetic Diagnostic Information and the Duty of Confidentiality: Ethics and Law', Medical Law International, vol. 1, p. 87.

36 Chadwick, 'Human Genome Analysis', p. 12.

37 Burgess, M. et al. (1997) 'Dilemmas of Anonymous Predictive Testing for Huntington's Disease: Privacy vs. Optimal Care', American Journal of Medical Genetics, vol. 71, pp. 199–201.

38 Hallowell, N. et al. (1997) 'Women's Need for Information Before Attending Genetic Counselling for Familial Breast or Ovarian Cancer:

A Questionnaire, Interview and Observational Study', *British Medical Journal*, vol. 314, no. 7,076, pp. 281–283.

39 ACGT, *Code of Practice*, pp. 4 and 10.
40 Pope, Nicki (1998) 'Computer Therapy, How CD-ROMs are Helping Sufferers of Depression', *Telegraph Magazine*, Saturday, 28 February 1998.

7

CULTURAL DIVERSITY AND THE LIMITS OF TOLERANCE

Sirkku Hellsten

Introduction

Some of the most difficult social problems facing modern multicultural societies arise out of the demand of tolerance. This problem becomes apparent when we discuss liberal values such as individual autonomy and equality in relation to the question of the degree to which modern liberal society should support cultural diversity and to what degree it should require cultural integration. For, whilst on the one hand the requirement for pluralism and tolerance demands that a liberal society allows and even encourages cultural diversity and different ways of living, on the other clear moral conflicts arise when cultural beliefs and traditions themselves turn out to be the enemies of autonomy and equality.

This chapter addresses the problematic nature of multiculturalism, equality and tolerance in pluralist modern Western democracies. It discusses why individual citizens, and particularly those working in the field of health care, face problems when it comes to the promotion of tolerance and respect for autonomy in a modern multicultural society. It also shows how easily the requirement for tolerance and pluralism can erode our reasoning towards ethical relativism and moral nihilism. To demonstrate these problems, the justification of female 'circumcision' is considered. The tradition of female 'circumcision' provides a relevant example in this context for two reasons: first, it is time to leave this cruel and discriminatory tradition finally in the past; and, second, the paradox that the victims of this practice are also its strongest proponents demonstrates well the problems that occur when we are dealing with the requirements of tolerance and respect for autonomy in real life situations.

These problems of tolerance are discussed within a contemporary liberal-communitarian framework: in pluralistic Western societies' expansive international economic and political integration, accompanied by increasing immigration, have created deep conflicts between the universalist liberal principles of constitutional democracies and the particularist claims of ethnic communities to preserve the integrity of their values and ways of living. I shall argue that in a pluralistic, multicultural society there need not be a conflict between the liberal and communitarian approaches to justice. Instead these approaches should be seen as complementing each other: the intellectual justification of liberal politics can be seen to both presume and to enforce the existence of communitarian ethics within modern societies. When the core values of the liberal and communitarian line of reasoning are explicated, it becomes evident that both views promote the realisation of individuals' autonomous moral agency. From this point of view I shall propose an alternative approach to ethical pluralism which I shall call 'moral individualism'. Moral individualism, as I shall define it, attempts to combine the liberal and communitarian approaches in order to promote the individual's capacity to engage in autonomous and critical self-reflective questioning. That is, the individual's ability to distinguish his or her own views and moral judgements from those he or she has adopted from the social environment. This view also suggests that the moral identity of an individual is not in itself directly connected to any particular culture, but rises above particular cultural values, traditions and social ties, even those of the Western competitive and subjectivist market culture, reflecting the individual's capacity as an intellectual, moral and political agent. Moral individualism presumes then that when we discuss moral autonomy we shall see it as providing an account of well-being, that is the final goal or the human *telos*, that modern multicultural welfare democracies are built to promote.

Western democracies, female 'circumcision' and the problems of subjectivism

One of the central theoretical and practical problems of our age is to reconcile the aspiration of political equality with the fact of social and cultural difference within modern multicultural states. This reconciliation appears to be a challenge particularly to a contemporary liberal view that sees justice as blindness to difference. Such blindness or neutrality means that civil and political rights, primary social goods such as education, employment and health care ought not to be distributed on the basis of morally arbitrary characteristics such as sex, race, age, social position, cultural background or individual choice of values. A state must be governed by principles of justice that do not presuppose any particular conception of well-being or 'the good life', whether this well-being is described in cultural, religious, ideological or other such terms. Since no individual's conception of the good life is nobler or superior to another's, the modern liberal state is required to advocate value pluralism and tolerance as far as possible when it comes to different value and belief systems, ethical views and ways of living. This means that if any individual with a particular communal or cultural background voluntarily persists in maintaining certain cultural or communal traditions and values, he or she should have the right to do so without interference from the institutions of the state.[1]

In principle this requirement for the neutrality of the state means that the functioning of public state institutions, such as education and health care ought not to be based on any particular view of well-being either. Instead they are required to be run according to the ideals of equal concern and respect for autonomy. Particularly in the field of health care however, this demand for neutrality can be confusing. After all, the very concept of health is closely related to the concept of human well-being; a central part of human flourishing is to enjoy good health. If there is no generally accepted definition of well-being, there can simultaneously exist various interpretations of what is meant by the concept of health, as the debates on euthanasia, abortion, mental illness, sexuality, and self-inflicted harm (substance abuse, dangerous lifestyles, etc.) have shown us. Even if we could quite unanimously agree that health meant the lack of serious illness, disability and abnormality, opinions on what might be considered as threats to health would vary considerably according to time, place, scientific knowledge and medical technology available. Moreover, there are great differences in opinion when it comes to the health care measures to be taken to promote individual well-being. The question also arises as to whether we should in health care emphasise the prevention of or the remedy and rehabilitation from illnesses.

The modern, liberal view asserts that individuals should be free to choose their own values, religion, culture, language, traditions and even their own concept of well-being. Its response to the multiplicity of religious, cultural and moral traditions in modern society has then been to advocate the tolerance of different ways of living as far as possible. It is this requirement of tolerance combined with the promotion of autonomy that makes the questions of cultural integration and multiculturalism one of the most controversial questions in liberal pluralism. First, a liberal state cannot promote social and cultural integration as long as it does not explicate any account of the well-being such integration is to embody. Instead modern liberal multicultural society remains fragmented with isolated cultural minorities, each of which have their own sets of values and beliefs which seldom in practice truly respect liberal ideals. Second, citizens of the multicultural liberal welfare democracies face a curious dilemma when it comes to the promotion of the requirement of tolerance: as people from different cultural backgrounds try to adapt to the Western ways of living and Western values without losing their own cultural identity and traditions, we are asked to be tolerant and respect their choices. We feel the danger of paternalism in interfering with the lifestyles and values of individuals from different cultures. Nevertheless, cultural traditions and practices may sometimes directly oppress individual equality, autonomy and rights and thus violate the very principles we were taught to respect to begin with. We are then asked to be tolerant while simultaneously being expected to seek out the limits of this tolerance. The problem again is that when we have no common account of 'the good life' or well-being to be promoted, we have no ethical guidelines in our search for the limits of tolerance. These problems are particularly pressing for many of those who work in the field of health care or social services and who have to deal with the question of whether people from different cultural backgrounds should be allowed to maintain traditions that may cause serious risk or damage to their physical or mental health.[2]

One such controversial traditional practice which has lately attracted much attention is that of female 'circumcision'. This is a custom which is widespread in Africa, north of the equator, as well as in many African communities within Western societies.[3] For anyone working in the field of health care and social services it is apparent that such a tradition is most harmful to one's physical health and should not be practised.[4] After all, even in a liberal society individuals cannot do whatever they want. They cannot for instance harm others or suppress their autonomy[5] This means that intervention is justifiable in such cases in which we can prove that without intervention the recipients would inflict grave harm on themselves or others and secondly that the recipients of the interventions are not at the time capable of reasonable voluntary decision-making, but are suppressed or coerced.

In the case of female 'circumcision' violation of the harm principle is evident. There are no medical reasons for such mutilations of the female genitalia. The physical consequences of this practice are extremely harmful, causing pain and illnesses for the rest of the victim's life. In the worst scenario the operation can lead to death.[6] However, even if the harmful implications for one's health are evident the fear of paternalism remains. Many may still doubt whether it is justifiable to try to convince people from different cultural backgrounds that they would be happier if they adapted to our ways of life and left the past behind. Our fear of causing psychological harm by acting paternalistically easily makes us ignore the fact that within pluralistic liberal society there may exist cultural minorities or ideological communities that themselves restrict the moral autonomy of their individual members.

The problem is that the theoretical formulation of the liberal view which sees a just society as one existing within a reciprocal social contract between equal and fully rational autonomous decision-makers takes for granted what it sets out to prove. Thus, it derives 'ought' from 'is' and with this naturalistic fallacy nullifies its own moral foundation. It presumes individual rationality and autonomy in the derivation of principles of justice that are to promote this very same autonomy. The abstract image of the liberal subject causes us to see autonomy at the same time as a descriptive and as a prescriptive attribute of the good human life and thus confounds values and facts. Its starting position is also its ending position. Instead of demanding that we respect an individual's potential capacity for autonomy, the liberal view asks us to respect the presumed autonomy of a real person. What is believed to be and what should be are seen as the same thing.[7] In both of these uses, descriptive and prescriptive, the abstract idea of moral agency and human equality notoriously fail to recognise prevalent real life injustices on two accounts. First, the assumption of natural moral and political autonomy of human beings makes us *overestimate* the real autonomy of people. It assumes that the relations between dependence and interdependence do not exist when in fact these relations are central to most human lives in reality. Second, the assumption of autonomy and equality also makes us easily *underestimate* the potential autonomy and the real moral and political decision-making capacity of those who in real life have not had the opportunity to achieve autonomy in a social context. It seldom asks itself whether these people were able to obtain autonomy in the first place. Furthermore, if autonomy is seen to be the presumption of our moral worth, those who do not seem to have it are then considered less human and thus less worthy. Thus, by defining justice through a process of reasoning which is blind to difference and which totally abstracts from social particularity, liberal reasoning has an inbuilt bias in its method of deriving the principles of justice themselves. What appears just from within a theoretical and hypothetical decision-making situation in practice often functions in ways that reinforce and reproduce the subordination and marginalisation of certain individuals or social groups. There is then a real danger that liberal justification of pluralist democracy can be used also to legitimate the subordination of individual will in an established order.

The liberal conception of freedom and autonomy may protect people against the suppression of the liberal state itself but it consistently disregards the values and ties of communities that people are born with. Modern liberal reasoning has then misdirected its emphasis on the supposed atomistic, rational and autonomous individuals and may thereby have become an uncritical booster of a fragmented civil society which is prone to a naive collectivism which works against the ideals of liberal pluralism and tolerance. For some of those social collectives within modern state that are protected and promoted by the liberal requirements of tolerance, equality and autonomy can themselves be enemies of these very same values.

The liberal requirement for tolerance then works well only in societies, if there ever were such, which already truly respect equality and promote the realisation of moral autonomy. When we talk about individuals who are members of communities in which the boundary of the self is strictly limited to existing norms and traditions which do not respect the presumed autonomy of an individual, problems are inevitable. If an individual's moral autonomy is bounded by its existing capacity rather than as a potential capacity, our hands are tied when it comes to the prevention of this suppression. Such liberal ideals as autonomy, equality and freedom can be interpreted either as values or as facts, depending on other (political) aims. Only if the core value of liberal democracy, the actualisation of moral autonomy, were considered from the teleological point of view and seen as the human potential that is to be realised within the liberal order, could we justifiably interfere in such cultural traditions and practices that prevent the development of moral autonomy; the very same quality that is needed in choosing or revising one's values and one's conception of the good life. Should we see moral autonomy as the human *telos* in liberal justification, our task would be then to build societies that secure such circumstances in which this autonomy can be achieved in the first place.

From this point of view, in the case of female 'circumcision' we can easily prove that there is actual violation of autonomy when we show that the individuals involved are forced to participate in these traditions and cannot be seen as making voluntary decisions for themselves.[8] When it comes to the tradition of female 'circumcision' we can then point out that despite the apparent willingness of the victims involved, empirical study of the circumstances proves that this practice is not originally *chosen* by autonomous agents but is mostly maintained by social coercion and mental suppression.

First, if we talk about migrants from traditional cultures this tradition is usually associated with poverty, illiteracy and the low status of women. In patriarchal communities uncircumcised women are stigmatised and not sought in marriage, which helps to explain the paradox that the victims of this practice are also its strongest proponents. They can scarcely afford not to be. In these circumstances, women are reluctant to question the tradition or take an independent line lest they lose social approval. In poverty-stricken patriarchal communities struggling to survive, social acceptance and support may mean the difference between life and death. Thus, women in these communities have no alternative but to go along with the practice. Their chances to leave their community are also only hypothetical. When 'circumcision' is required to guarantee a girl's chastity and fitness for marriage, and when marriage may provide the only means of survival, the decision to follow the ritual is rational. If the only way to guarantee the future for your daughter is to circumcise her, the mother's decision too is rational, even loving, given the circumstances.

Second, in multicultural Western societies where there are more opportunities for an independent life and much greater access to information, these traditions are maintained both by patriarchal oppression and by appealing to the importance of communal integrity and cultural identity. Thus, these women still often tend to defend the practice by appealing to the perilous and menacing practical consequences that would follow from abandoning the tradition. These decisions are not, however, independent or autonomous in the way a liberal view requires. If *de jure* autonomy, i.e., the inalienable right to self-determination, is interpreted as an option to check the validity of one's authorities and traditions whenever one feels it is necessary and rational, it can be seen that these women lack this option. They still live in social circumstances which are coercive and oppressive and which prevent the development of one's autonomous moral judgement and moral identity which is separated from one's cultural identity. Since the development of moral identity and personal autonomy cannot occur in oppressive or coercive circumstances and since autonomy is, according to the liberal view, what makes individuals valuable both to themselves and to their fellow creatures, oppression which thwarts the development of independent moral judgement must be condemned.[9]

Finally, in the case of female 'circumcision' the most urgent point is the fact that this operation is generally carried out on small children, the age range being anywhere from one week to 14 years. Children of this age do not yet have an understanding of what is being done to them and why.[10] They are not autonomous agents and such an operation physically harms them and prevents them later on from being integrated into their new societies. This ritual victimises little children with unnecessary violence and physical harm that will limit their opportunities to choose the best possible life for themselves in the future. Neither do the children have any means of avoiding this physically and mentally violent and painful ritual. When all this empirical evidence is considered, it is clear that this particular tradition is based on constraint, coercion and suppression of individual will. After all, women and children involved with this tradition can hardly be considered to be autonomous decision-makers consistent with the liberal view. For, their decisions are based on ignorance, false beliefs and social pressure. Many women and children have no real option but to go along with the custom. Interference is therefore justified and this tradition and others like it have to be rejected by the liberal view.[11]

Communitarianism and the problems of cultural relativism

I have argued that despite its subjectivist tendencies, in the end, the liberal view has to reject harmful and oppressive cultural traditions. However, some ethnic groups and cultural minorities within multicultural Western societies will feel that the liberal demand for moral autonomy is another example of Western cultural imperialism and may attempt to defend their old traditions by appealing to the communitarian justification. Thus, the question remains whether the communitarian line of reasoning and the appeal to the importance of common values; communal ties and cultural traditions could offer any grounds for rebuttal that could be used to justify such traditions as female 'circumcision'.

Such communitarian critics of liberal justification as Alasdair MacIntyre, Michael Sandel, Charles Taylor and Michael Walzer all note that modern liberal society ignores the fact that principles of justice are always rooted in history, discourse and traditions of actual communities and that nobody is ever totally free to choose his or her values and ways of living. Any conception of an individual presupposes always some view of society and community, since all individuals are social beings. All the values and norms we have chosen, we have chosen as members of a particular community, ethnic group or social collective. More often than not these social attachments are involuntarily acquired during the course of our upbringing and socialisation, independent rational choice having played no role whatsoever in this. We do not choose the society we are born in, and thus we have not voluntarily chosen our culture and traditions either. Social influence communitarians argue is not merely a contingent fact of our actual social and moral identities, but the original social context of a human life which shapes it to be the kind of life it is. Our will is thus always more or less formed by our social environment. The tendency to conceive of a human being as an abstract and rational moral agent entering into a scheme of political association, independently of knowing what its particular, socially constituted nature is, gives liberal reasoning its incoherent nature. Social co-operation cannot build on the image of social agents that are constituted independently of societies – as pre-social individuals. Instead, by virtue of its basic structure, liberal society has to be communitarian, since the promotion of value pluralism assumes that there are different sets of values among which we can choose.[12] The individualist premises of liberal justification are unacceptable because any conception of an individual always presupposes some view of society and community since all individuals are social beings. Even the values and norms we have *chosen* we have chosen as members of a particular community. Communities with their value systems and their social relations, cultural practices, norms and traditions actually give our lives their moral meaning rather than the apparently neutral political order.[13]

Communitarians hit home by pointing out the problems that liberals have with the abstract concept of fully rational and autonomous self and the idea of natural equality. If we stopped here, followed the communitarian advice and paid more attention to the social influence that affect all our choices, we should be more apt to recognise the suppression of individual autonomy in reality. A communitarian viewpoint, however, goes further and states that since our morality is always tied to a certain society, there is no reason to believe that we can derive in any abstract and universal sense absolute principles of social justice. Since the values that people hold in general, and the concept of justice in particular, are derived from their communal relations, there is no way for this concept to be universal or absolute. Communitarians suggest then that we should instead recognise that there are different – though often overlapping – spheres of justice. The claim that those communal relations to which people are tied should be taken into account if we are to discuss the questions of social justice together at all, is one to which traditionalists like to appeal. The traditionalists often interpret the communitarian conception of an individual embedded in particular community or culture to be in strict contrast to the atomistic liberal individualism. The communitarian emphasis on common values and traditions is then taken as support for traditional ties and community rules.

Thus, whereas the problems of the liberal view start with the abstract, liberal conception of subject, the problems of the communitarian view start with an abstract conception of community. The same sort of circularity we found in liberal reasoning is evident in communitarian reasoning. If the communitarian concept of community refrains from separating moral and political community from cultural (or some other close historical) community, it does not make any distinction between moral reasoning and cultural beliefs. The tendency to see communal norms as moral norms leads towards cultural relativism. Cultural relativism, for its part, easily legitimises the suppression of individuals in the name of custom and traditional social norms. If the values and practices of a certain culture or community justify themselves by their mere existence, there can be no room for moral autonomy or for the correction of prevailing injustices. In practice this easily results in the enforcement of nationalism, political conservatism, the tyranny of the majority, oppression or totalitarianism. The common values and common good of a certain society may easily harm and suppress some of its individual members.

Relativism considers then that our cultural or communal norms are also our moral norms and that our cultural identity determines also our moral identity. According to relativism there are no *general* moral standards that we can use in order to evaluate the practices or norms of different cultures and different communities. If the communitarian line of reasoning presented a merely relativist ethical stance there would be no criteria against which the values of different communities or cultures could be evaluated. This would lead the communitarian view to the same Nietzschean nihilism of which it accuses liberalism.[14] In the name of the common good or tradition societies can endorse traditions that oppress the weak, whose weakness is constituted by their subordination in the established order.[15] There would be no right or wrong, no good or bad and no reason for individuals to use or try to develop their moral identity and judgement. Without standards of justification there would be no reason to reject even such harmful traditions as female 'circumcision', slavery, cannibalism, etc. The question of values and the discussion of moral judgements would become irrelevant and meaningless. Therefore it should always be kept in mind that our cultural identity should not be equated with our moral identity.

Cultural relativism is an inconsistent ethical stand involving serious conceptual problems and can therefore provide no grounds for the defence of cultural or communal rights or autonomy as such.[16] One of the conceptual problems is in its account of 'culture' or 'community'. No social collective is ever a permanent, independent entity. Change and development are characteristic of any social collective. This development, for its part, is always taking place through the work, interaction and ideas of the individual members of these collectives, in their striving for a better and more perfect society. All social collectives are composed of individuals, and their acts are only the collective result of the actions of these individual components. Thus, whatever is said about any culture or community must, at some stage, be related and in some way reduced to discourse about the doings, beliefs, attitudes and dispositions of its components. We have to ask who actually did and thought what, and what led an individual to act and to think the way he or she did and not some other way. The idea that there are such things as social collectives gives false premises to the requirement for cultural autonomy or minority rights. The only rights that could be respected in order to maintain cultural pluralism are the rights of an individual as a member of a particular community with a particular cultural background. What really matters then, in the end, are individuals and their choices within a community or culture. Thus, what really have to be protected are the rights of these individuals whatever their cultural backgrounds are.[17]

The weakness of the communitarian approach is in its refusal to identify the limits that a community can place on its members. The communitarian ethical model fails to show where one would get the motivation and will to criticise the *status quo* in one's community if what is just is defined in terms of communal values, cultural identity and traditions. While communitarians succeed in pointing out that history and social ties matter in the actualisation of individual morality, they do not provide us with any normative guidelines that would tell us how much they should matter or that would define the limits of the influence a community can have on its individual members. The danger in the communitarian account of justice is then that the individual becomes too easily identical with the values, goals and beliefs of community and that respect for autonomy and free will is buried into the tradition and forgotten. Under such circumstances the potential autonomy of an individual can easily be *underestimated*. On the other hand, if the communitarians presume that these embedded individuals could also have the will and power to criticise the prevailing values or traditions of their communities, their actual autonomy can be as easily *overestimated*.

The teleological value of autonomy as moral agency

The main dilemma liberals and communitarians share, though it is emphasised differently in both accounts, is the balance between the influence of culture and the autonomy of an individual will. Communitarians see aptly that the abstract liberal concept of the self that is designed to protect the self from the contingencies of its environment calls 'into question the dignity and autonomy that liberalism seeks above all to secure'.[18] However, the communitarian image of the self that is as easily restricted to the existing values, norms and traditions of one's community and culture has a great risk of drowning the individual in a sea of social ties, experience and circumstances instead of providing a political and cultural atmosphere in which the more abstract and instrumental liberal values could fulfil their task as the means to achieve moral autonomy and to develop one's moral identity independently of one's cultural background. The problem then is that despite their opposing attempts neither liberal nor communitarian lines of reasoning leave room for the development of one's moral identity. However, if we were to promote the social actualisation of moral autonomy, one's cultural background should not decrease one's capacity for independent reflection, critical scrutiny and the correction of one's beliefs and the beliefs of one's society.

In order to overcome these natural tendencies to reason egocentrically and sociocentrically, we have to move from the relativist pattern of thinking towards a more adequate ethical pluralism which promotes an individual's capacity to engage in self-reflective questioning. This questioning shows that our belief and value systems are, by definition, irrational, if we are incapable of abandoning a mere belief in reliance on rational reasoning. Critical thought and moral identity must be predicated on the ability to discover the insights of opposing views as well as the weaknesses of our own beliefs, and particularly the weaknesses of those beliefs and traditions that we have been indoctrinated with within our culture.

Despite their methodological differences, both liberals and communitarians base their emphasis on the importance of culture and community on the assumption that culture and community provide the common good and value standards for its members. For the communitarians, membership of a community is seen to have its own intrinsic value for an individual as a social being. Being a part of a community is an essential part of human life and human flourishing. The community, as a body with some common values, norms and goals, in which each member regards the common goals as his or her own, is intrinsically good, because it is a precondition of the moral autonomy of an individual. This same view of the value of cultural influence is also found in the texts of such liberal theorists as J. S. Mill and Will Kymlicka as well as in Rawls (particularly in his later writings). Mill, Kymlicka and Rawls all see that people can become aware of the options available to them and intelligently examine their value only when they have a rich and secure social and cultural structure. Thus, social ties and cultural membership can be seen as having intrinsic value, not as having some moral status of their own, but as providing the context of choices that people make in their lives.[19]

Thus, in addition to the usual individual rights of personal liberty and associative freedom, there are further justifications for the existence of different cultural or ideological groups with different value systems. One most important reason for the existence of different value systems is that each of us has our own view of the good life. It is a necessary component of this interest in our will to choose our own way of life that we need the capacity to frame, pursue and revise our conceptions of the good life. Testing and choosing for ourselves among the options give life much of its value. However, because no one can really choose the whole context of one's choice, the cultural backgrounds in which we find ourselves are for the most part not of our own choosing. It should then be taken into consideration that it is not our own fault (and sometimes it is no one's fault at all) that the culture in which we begin life provides an insecure foundation for the development of our autonomy.[20]

Communitarian reasoning does not, any more than liberal reasoning, mean that any one community with common beliefs and values is as good as any other. Good communities are those that not only leave space and aim to secure the individual's autonomous moral judgement but also promote the development of this judgement. Communitarians think in terms of 'reflection', 'critical scrutiny' and 'corrections' of beliefs and values in communities which are engaged in the democratic process of public debate and self-criticism. The self that is the reflection of its traditions is not meant to drown the self in its traditions, but the complexity of traditions is rather seen to foster immanent critiques.[21] This normative aspect that promotes the development of the individual's autonomous moral agency and moral identity is, however, often misinterpreted or overlooked in the communitarian approach by traditionalists as well as by liberals. The reason for this misinterpretation is quite simple: communitarians refrain from defining any particular community, culture or political system as the best, much in the same way as liberals refrain from defining any particular way of life as the normative model of the good life.

Communitarianism as well as liberalism sees the reasoned critical rejection of old values and practices on the basis of new facts or new knowledge or new understanding and new interpretations of old facts as an important part of the good of an individual. The promotion of individual moral autonomy and moral identity is central to both liberal reasoning and communitarian reasoning. In both approaches the capacity to form independent moral convictions is seen as an important part of a good human life or human flourishing. A just society is a society that gives room to different value systems but also protects the autonomy of the individual members of the different communities.[22]

From relativism to ethical pluralism

I have tried to show that despite their methodologically incompatible premises liberal and communitarian lines of reasoning both promote the same common value of human flourishing as the realisation of moral autonomy within a rich and open cultural context. They both also share the reluctance to explicate this normative point that has a somewhat teleological structure. This reluctance, for its part, results in a situation in which both the liberal and communitarian views coexist in modern multicultural society, but instead of complementing each other they tend to clash, leading towards ethical relativism.

In order to avoid these logically and socially unfortunate tendencies, we should explicate the core value common to both lines of reasoning, that is, the actualisation of individuals' moral identity and moral autonomy. In order to promote this value modern multicultural societies are to avoid ethical relativism and instead promote *value pluralism*. Unlike relativism, value-pluralism demands respect for the right to hold divergent beliefs, but implies neither acceptance of actions based on those beliefs nor respect for the content of these beliefs by their mere existence, as relativism does. If any cultural practice or belief can be proven to be incoherent, controversial, harmful or oppressive it should be rejected. Thus, value pluralism could be defined as the proper and critical tolerance for diversity of ideas and value systems.

This means that when we ponder the distinction between cultural identity and moral identity we should focus on the development of moral identity, moral autonomy and reasoned moral viewpoints. Ethical pluralism requires us to recognise the existence of other views, but it does not assume their blind acceptance as such. Instead, ethical pluralism demands not only emphatic but also critical assessments of differing perspectives. Ethical pluralism requires that different belief and value systems can be critically evaluated and assessed and that the basis and validity of their norms can be questioned. If we can show certain cultural practices to be incoherent, contradictory and even harmful, we have grounds for rejecting them. Many cultural practices such as female 'circumcision' can be shown to be the result of attempts to maintain the prevailing unequal power relations between sexes, and they are themselves based on prejudice, false beliefs and ignorance and thus bear no moral justification.

If we are ready to accept that it is ethical value-pluralism rather than ethical relativism that both liberals and communitarians are after, we can agree that cultural traditions and irrational value judgements can and should be evaluated on at least the three following accounts, in order to promote a successful and fruitful cultural integration through which we can develop our moral identities by learning from each other. First, when such harmful practices as female 'circumcision' are defended by reference to cultural differences, one can always question the *factual validity* of this defence. One can ask if it is really true that there are societies in which genital mutilation is considered desirable? By whom is it considered valuable and on what grounds? Is female 'circumcision' actually consented to by those subjected to the practices, and if so, is their consent free, considered and uncoerced? What are the real goals achieved by this practice? Are these traditions really the best means of reaching the given goal? Can we find any other equally good or even better means to attain the same goals? Are these goals themselves justifiable or are they concealing some other political purposes?[23]

Second, without giving up on tolerance, it is also possible to challenge the *consistency* of the practices, norms and prohibitions prevailing in a culture as a whole. There may be communities in which female 'circumcisions' are condoned although cruelty towards women and children is otherwise rejected. There might be a society that, in principle, promotes tolerance, but ignores intolerance within its minority groups. For instance when refugees are seeking equal political rights and liberties, they should be ready to give up those traditions of their culture that violate these very principles. In these cases one can point out that since the moral code of society is self-contradictory, the requirement of consistency prevents rational and morally autonomous individuals from accepting the dictates of the system.

Third, if these internally oriented critiques prove to be ineffective, the moral system under consideration can be *conceptually extended*. While it is true that many of our moral judgements are relative to ethical theories or shared opinions, it is by no means the case that only existing sociocultural entities should be defined as the source of valid moral judgements. Even if we accept that our social environment affects our values, there is no reason why cultural traditions should be equated with moral standards and why our moral identity should be fully determined by our cultural background.[24]

It should also be noted that the term 'cultural difference' is often used by the traditionalists as an excuse for or as rationalisation of old power relations which otherwise have no moral justification. In the same way, the concept of 'individual autonomy' can be used as an easy defence for retaining prevailing social structures. By appealing to cultural differences or individual autonomy, we can find an easy way to ignore value conflicts and reject open dialogues that could question the old values and power relations. Thus, by accepting everything, including intolerance, we do not have to re-evaluate our own value and belief system. By not questioning our own views, we never have to be afraid that they are not as consistent and as correct as we believed them to be. With an attitude that says anything goes, we never have to bother thinking about the differences between good and bad or right and wrong. This uncritical acceptance of everything is, however, moral laziness or even moral incapability. Both of these relativist lines of reasoning – cultural relativism and subjectivism – work against proper tolerance and pluralism and, in the end, they also work against the actualisation of individual moral autonomy. This leaves an individual's moral identity undeveloped and can thus result in moral indifference towards other people.

However, should we learn to integrate the liberal and the communitarian viewpoints we could promote ethical pluralism in the form of *moral individualism*. Moral individualism encourages the development of a person's moral judgement. Its objective is to promote the realisation of a person's true moral identity as an autonomous moral agent without requiring him or her to abandon his or her cultural heritage. In order to develop a moral identity distinguishable from one's cultural identity, we need to learn to clarify our values and beliefs and ponder which of them we have chosen as morally autonomous agents and which of them we have either blindly adopted from our social environment or had forced upon us. The only way to do this is to openly investigate different sides of every issue. We have to respect the existence of divergent beliefs. Instead of accepting or rejecting them offhand, we should focus on assessing the validity of opposing views and different belief and value systems. This process of ethical inquiry is central to individual moral development and through this it is also central to communal and cultural development. In fact this process also provides an implicit definition of 'the good life' and human flourishing in modern multicultural societies. If seen from a teleological viewpoint, the presupposition of and the requirement for autonomy demand that the liberal state promote a political and cultural framework which in turn promotes the actualisation of this autonomy.

A richly varied and secure cultural structure can then have intrinsic value, not merely some moral status of its own, and can provide the context for our choices. Moral autonomy, that is, the ability of an individual to make choices for the good life requires not only freedom from coercion, but also cultural diversity. In multicultural societies, the diversity of choice can provide concrete, living alternatives, life experiments that will facilitate our intellectual growth and moral development. And when it comes to our children, this pluralistic, and multicultural atmosphere provides them with a multiplicity of choices and opportunities in the global village. At its best, the influence of cultural background can make people aware of the options available to them. It can help us to examine intelligently not only others' values, but also our own. At its worst it can stifle individual will and prevent one's moral autonomy from developing at all.

Conclusion

In modern multicultural democracies liberal and communitarian views complement each other. The liberal view provides the political frame and the communitarian view explicates the source of diverse values systems within modern Western societies. Despite their methodological problems and tendency towards relativism, both of these accounts are based on value pluralism, which is related to the development of reasoned moral viewpoints and to the willingness to recognise the existence of other views, rather than their acceptance or rejection as such. Should we understand the interdependence of the liberal and communitarian approaches within a modern, multicultural society, we would learn that the demand for tolerance in a pluralistic state does not mean acceptance of all divergent views and practices by virtue of their mere existence. Neither does it mean voluntary indifference to these views. Instead it means emphatic but also critical assessment of differing perspectives. Maintenance of tolerance and value pluralism requires the promotion of moral individualism. Moral individualism demands that different moral judgements and divergent value systems can be and should be critically evaluated and assessed. This means reflective and critical subjective and intersubjective questioning of the basis and validity of different norms, beliefs and values systems.

Particularly in medical and health care ethics it is important to realise that within both liberal and communitarian lines of reasoning there is the core value of human flourishing or well-being, defined in terms of the realisation of an individual's moral identity as moral agent. This agency is the goal for which our political system and its institutions should strive. *Moral individualism* combines the liberal and communitarian lines of reasoning and sees as its goal the realisation of the individual's moral agency in a social context. Moral autonomy as the realisation of one's moral agency is then the human *telos* to be striven for within modern pluralistic and multicultural society. Thus, to summarise, we can say that within modern multicultural society there is then always room for more than one conception of the good – as long as there is some conception of the good. There is, and should be, always room for tolerance as long as we remember that there are also limits to this tolerance.

NOTES

1 See for instance Danley, 1993, 172; Kukathas, 1992, 108, 118–119; Kymlicka, 1989, 11–13, 164–166; M. S. Williams, 1995, 68 and also Rawls, 1971, 1993.

2 This is naturally according to a Western concept of normality and health. In modern Western democracies the questions of what is natural or normal are in general linked to the development and findings of modern science and the latest medical technology whereas in more traditional or primitive cultures the same questions are rather linked with the harmony of the nature or harmony of the society.

3 However, history reveals that female 'circumcision' of some kind has been practised at one time or another on every continent. In Britain and in the USA during the last century clitoridectomy was thought by some to be a remedy for all manner of 'ills', from epilepsy and hysteria to nymphomania and masturbation.

4 In its most radical form, called infibulation, the operation involves amputation of the clitoris and the whole of the labia minora, and at least the anterior two-thirds and often the whole of the medial part of the labia majora. The two sides of the vulva are then stitched together and an opening is left for menstrual blood and urine. The stitches are often done with silk catgut or thorns, and a tiny sliver of wood or a reed is inserted to preserve an opening for urine and menstrual blood. In this context it should be noted that there are two other milder types of female 'circumcision'. These are (1) Circumcision proper, known in Muslim countries as sunna (which also means 'traditional'), is the

mildest but also the rarest form. It involves the removal only of the clitoral prepuce and; (2) Excision which involves the amputation of the whole of the clitoris and all or part of the labia minora. In these milder forms the practice of female 'circumcision' is reported in some countries in Asia, too. WHO Chronicle, 40 (I): 32 (1986).

5 Dworkin, 1977, 267; Rawls, 1971, 244; Feinberg, 1973, 25–31. This tradition is naturally not the only harmful tradition. In more traditional communities there exist particularly many such traditions that tend to harm and suppress women. However, even in our own apparently equal society, for instance, the idealisation of youth, beauty and slenderness can become a threat to the health of many women. Some of the harmful consequences of this idealisation are eating disorders, mental problems, plastic surgery and unnecessary implants and their medical implications.

6 There are several adverse effects of infibulation on physical health. The immediate dangers of the operation are haemorrhage and shock from acute pain, infection of the wounds, urine retention and damage to urethra or anus. Gynaecological and genitourinary effects are haematocolpos, keloid formation, implantation dermoid cysts, chronic pelvis infection, calculus formation, dyspareimia, infertility, urinary tract infection and difficulty of micturition. Obstetric effects are perineal lacerations, consequences of anterior episiotomy e.g. blood loss, injury to bladder, urethra or rectum, late urine prolapse, puerperal sepsis, delay in labour and its consequences, e.g.: vesicovaginal and rectovaginal fistulae, fetal loss, fetal brain damage. WHO Chronicle 40(I)(1986):32–33.

7 Rawls's, as well as Kant's, political concept of justice sees citizens as free and equal persons, as they according to the liberal justification of self-government of people ought to be. This leads to a vicious circle in which autonomy is required in order to guarantee the actualisation of autonomy. Autonomous subjects in political decision-making were then those who already had the opportunity to make autonomous choices in their life. Those who lack the real opportunity were seen to also lack the status of autonomous subjects. Thus, they can be considered as less human and their oppression can be justified by the very same principles of liberalism. Autonomous decision-making is then the privilege of those whose capacity is not limited by social and economic conditions of the given society. Rawls's own theory of justice is apparently tied to the values and possibilities already available within liberal democracies, whereas Kant's theory was limited to those values and possibilities accepted in his time and in his society. By this I mainly refer to Kant's political equality, which left women, servants and other people who were 'not their own masters' outside legislative decision-making.

> Anyone who has the right to vote on this legislation is a citizen. The only qualification required of a citizen (apart, of course, from being an adult male) is that he must be his own master (sui iuris), and must have some property (which can include any skill, trade, fine art or science) to support himself. In cases where he must earn his living from others, he must earn it only by selling that which is his, and not by allowing others to make use of him.

The domestic servant, the shop assistant, the labourer, or even the barber, are merely labourers, not masters of an art or members of the state, and thus unqualified to be citizens. A citizen must in the true sense of the word serve no-one but the commonwealth.

(Kant, 1990, 131)

8 Coercion typically involves explicit or implicit threats and being conditionally structured: if you do not agree to do something unpleasant the coercer will see to it (or at least claims that he or she will see to it) that something even more unpleasant will happen to you or perhaps to somebody else (family, friends). A successful instance of coercion has occurred when the coercer (whether state or an individual) has managed to get you to do what he or she wants as a result of a threat to interfere with your person, or your interests, either by positively attacking you (and your interests) or by withholding benefits from you. Airaksinen 1988a and 1988b, 214.

9 Feinberg, 1973, 21–22; Rawls, 1971, 261. On the conception of autonomy and limits of paternalism in medical ethics see Häyry, H., 1991, 46–63, 74–80.

10 WHO Chronicle, 40(I):32(1986). The operation is usually performed by the traditional midwife, who does the mutilation while a number of women including the child's female relatives hold the victim down to prevent her from fighting. It is also rare that local anaesthetics even are used to ease the pain.

11 Liberals then would not only have right but a duty to interfere not only when this tradition consenting physical damage is practised within liberal society but also when it is practised in non-Western cultures which do not respect the equal moral status of all human beings. This interference itself should not be coercive, but it can be done by invalidating the reasons that maintain the practice by giving adequate information on the physical and sexual aspects involved and educating women in general. Helping women to achieve better living standards and improving their position gives them better chances to make independent and well-grounded judgements about their own culture and its practices. After all, probably the best way to change unreasonable and inhuman traditions is the reasoned internal critique from within the culture itself.

12 Bell, 1993, 4; Haldane, 1993, 204; MacIntyre, 1984; Sandel, 1982.

13 Deontological liberalism requires that the various participants in social life agree to be bound by principles of a strictly impartial sort in which no reference is made to the identity that constitutes facts of particular individuals and communities. Liberal justice, as we have defined it, is blind. The communitarian objection to the abstract liberal account of justice is that liberal reasoning requires us to think of ourselves as characterless, atom-like agents constituted as subjects of one or another political community without reference to the distinctive circumstances and histories which have influenced us. This totally ignores the dependency of self-consciousness upon social environment. MacIntyre, 1984; Sandel, 1982; Taylor, 1979, 1989; Walzer, 1990, 1987, 1983.

14 See Taylor's criticism on the concept of freedom in deontological liberalism. Taylor, 1979, 159.

15 Avineri and de-Shalit, 1992, 4–7; MacIntyre, 1984, 1988, 346–352; Walzer, 1987, 65–87.

16 Bell, 1993, 11; O'Neill, 1993, 1–3. For the problems of cultural relativism as an ethical stand see Howard, 1993, 318–319 and Williams, B., 1972, 34–35. The heresy of cultural relativism has been cleverly pointed out by Bernard Williams in his *Morality* (1972). Williams claims that relativism consists of three propositions: that right can be coherently understood as meaning 'right for the given society'; that 'right for a given society' is to be understood in a functionalist sense; and that therefore it is wrong for people in one society to condemn and/or interfere with the values of another society. This view is clearly inconsistent, since it makes a claim in its third proposition about what is right and wrong in one's dealings with other societies which uses a non-relative sense of right not allowed for in the first proposition. The problem is that if an individual or a community is regarded as a unit of morality, and as such identified in part through its values, then any talk about morality becomes a tautology: it is tediously a necessary condition of the survival of a group with certain values that the group should retain those values. At the other extreme, the survival of a society could be understood as the survival of certain persons and their having descendants, in which case many communitarian propositions about the necessity of communal or cultural survival would be false and would lead back to individualism. Williams, 1972, 35.

17 Flew, 1991, 61.

18 Alford, 1991, 9; Sandel, 1982, 95.

19 Green, 1995, 260; Kymlicka, 1989, 164–166, 1995; Mill, 1986 (1859), 65–67; Rawls, 1971, 560–564, 1993, 29–43.

20 Green, 1995, 260.

21 Alford, 1991, 16–17.

22 Kymlicka, 1989, 164–165; Kukathas, 1992, 108–118; also Rawls 1971, 1993.

23 The reasons for the practice are said to be as follows: even if the origins of this tradition have been impossible to trace, a variety of other reasons are advanced by its adherents for continuing to support the practice today. Some say it is just a means of suppressing female sexuality and attempting to ensure chaste or monogamous behaviour; others believe that it was started long ago among herders as a protection against rape for the young girls who took animals out to pasture. It is also said to be the trademark in the Egyptian slave market. Circumcised female slaves were sold for a higher price, because they were less likely to be sexually active and get pregnant. Some Muslim people believe that it is religiously ordained, even if the Koran does not support this assumption. Other adherents believe that intact female genitalia are 'unclean', that an uncircumcised woman is likely to be promiscuous and even that the operation improves the life chances of a woman's offspring. Others say it is a ritual initiation into womanhood.

None of these given reasons bears close scrutiny. They are in fact rationalisations for a practice that has woven itself into the fabric of some societies so completely that 'reasons' are no longer particularly relevant, since even invalidating them does not stop the practice. These reasons as such give no moral justification for the tradition. This tradition – as well as many other ones – is based on prejudice, false beliefs and ignorance, not on critical judgement of its justification. As Mill notes, the problem is that customs are not often questioned by individuals who are involved in them because 'people are accustomed to believe and have been encouraged to in the belief that their feelings are better than reason and render reasons useless.' Mill, 1986, 12. See also Häyry, M., 1992, 55.

24 See also Häyry, M., 1992, 55.

8

ETHICS, COMMUNITY AND THE ELDERLY

Health care decision-making for incompetent elderly patients

Mark R. Wicclair

It would be ageist to assume that all elderly people are unhealthy and 'senile'. Even the 'oldest-old' (i.e., people older than 85) can enjoy good physical and mental health (Neugarten, 1990). Nevertheless, as people grow older, there is an increased likelihood that they will require acute and/or chronic care and will experience more or less substantial mental impairment due to strokes and dementing illnesses, such as Alzheimer's disease (US Congress, 1987; Cummings and Jarvik, 1990).[1] Accordingly, while the elderly are more likely to need medical services, they are also more likely to lack the capacity to make decisions about their own health care, and it is not an overstatement to maintain that 'decision-making under circumstances of mental incapacity is a particularly relevant issue in the care of elderly persons' (Uhlmann *et al.*, 1988, M115).

According to a 'patient-centred' model, when elderly patients are incompetent, health care decision-making should be based on their distinctive preferences, values and interests (President's Commission, 1982; Buchanan and Brock, 1989). Advance directives, especially instruction directives which provide more or less explicit expressions of a person's goals and treatment preferences, are often recommended as means to facilitate this objective. When elderly patients do not have an instruction directive, or when they do but it does not provide unambiguous guidance for the actual clinical situation, a patient-centred approach calls for decision-making by surrogates who are to decide on the basis of the substituted judgement and/or best interests standards. The former directs surrogates to decide as the incompetent patient herself would, and the latter instructs surrogates to decide on the basis of the incompetent patient's well-being. Both standards are *patient-centred* insofar as surrogates are to consider the *patient's* distinctive preferences, values and interests.

As a model for decision-making when elderly patients are incompetent, a patient-centred approach can be questioned on a number of grounds. One of these has to do with its practicality. With respect to advance directives, for some a cornerstone of patient-centred decision-making when patients are incompetent, studies in the United States suggest that only a small percentage of elderly Americans have one (Zweibel and Cassel, 1989; La Puma *et al.*, 1991; Gamble *et al.*, 1991; and High, 1988).[2] Moreover, standard instruction directives authorised by state living will statutes in the US typically are restricted to two conditions, terminal illness or persistent vegetative state (Meisel, 1995; Choice in Dying, 1994). Other types of instruction directives often use language, such as 'no significant chance of meaningful recovery', which fails to provide unambiguous guidance for actual clinical situations. Consequently, it is to be expected that patient-centred decision-making for incompetent elderly patients often will be impossible without surrogates.[3] Yet, several studies have raised serious doubts about the ability of surrogates to accurately identify patients' treatment preferences and goals (Emanuel and Emanuel, 1992; Finucane *et al.*, 1988; Lo *et al.*, 1986; Seckler *et al.*, 1991; Tomlinson *et al.*, 1990; Uhlmann *et al.*, 1988; and Zweibel and Cassel, 1989). There can also be considerable uncertainty about which decision will promote a patient's best interests as well as conflict among surrogates (e.g., family members). Finally, elderly patients sometimes have no known family or friends to serve as surrogates. Accordingly, there are a number of formidable obstacles to patient-centred decision-making for incompetent elderly patients.

The patient-centred model has also been challenged on ethical grounds, and doubts have been raised about its appropriateness as an *ideal*. For example, it is said to be inadequate because it disregards resource scarcity and justice. Suppose Mr A., a moderately demented 75-year-old patient in chronic renal failure, is likely to benefit from dialysis. Suppose also that he made it clear while he was still competent that he would want dialysis in the current circumstances. From a pure patient-centred perspective, it would be ethically inappropriate to withhold dialysis from Mr A. However, it might be claimed that when scarcity and justice are also considered, withholding dialysis may be justified (Veatch, 1979, 1988).[4] Unilateral futility judgements represent another alleged ethical constraint on patient-centred decision-making. Suppose Ms B., an 82-year-old ventilator dependent patient in a persistent vegetative state, is known to be a vitalist who would want to be kept alive on a ventilator in her current condition. From a pure patient-centred perspective, it would be ethically inappropriate to withdraw ventilator support. However, it might be claimed that if the physician concludes that continued life-sustaining treatment would be futile, it is ethically justified to discontinue mechanical ventilation (Blackhall, 1987; Tomlinson and Brody, 1988; Schneiderman *et al.*, 1990).[5]

Recently, the patient-centred model has also been subject to community-based challenges on the grounds that patient-centred decision-making is 'individualistic' or 'atomistic' and fails to recognise the ethical significance of communities. An important criticism along these lines focuses on the family, a paradigm community, claiming that the patient-centred model fails to take families seriously (Lindemann Nelson, 1992; Lindemann Nelson, H. and J., 1994 and 1995). In the first section, I will examine several respects in which it might be claimed that patient-centred decision-making fails to take families seriously. In the second and third sections, I will discuss two community-based models: a 'liberal communitarian' model (Emanuel, 1991) in the second section and a 'communities of patients' model (Emanuel and Emanuel, 1993) in the third section. Throughout, I will focus on health care decision-making for incompetent elderly patients.

The patient-centred model and the family

One respect in which it might be claimed that a patient-centred model does not take families seriously is an alleged failure to acknowledge the special importance of family members in relation to surrogate decision-making for incompetent elderly patients. However, this charge is unsustainable. From a patient-centred perspective, surrogate decision-making should be based on the patient's distinctive preferences, values and interests; and there are several reasons for adopting a presumption that family members are most qualified to serve as surrogates for incompetent elderly patients. First, elderly patients are likely to want family members, such as spouses and adult children, to make health care decisions for them when they are unable to do so. Indeed, at least one study suggests that elderly persons care more about having family members make medical decisions for them if they are unable to do so themselves than they care about the content of the decisions (High, 1994, 1989). Second, family members are generally more likely to have the knowledge about the patient's distinctive preferences and values that is required for substituted judgements (President's Commission, 1982; Buchanan and Brock, 1989). Third, family members generally are most likely to be concerned about the patient's well-being and to want to protect the patient's interests (President's Commission, 1982; Buchanan and Brock, 1989).

There are at least two reasons for claiming that the foregoing patient-centred account of the decision-making authority of family members fails to take families seriously. First, it fails to acknowledge the independent value of the family. Second, it derives the moral authority of family surrogates from the preferences, values and interests of individual patients. In effect, proponents of the patient-centred model acknowledge this criticism when they recognise an additional basis of the decision-making authority of family members. The family is said to be a valued social unit, and social recognition of its value is said to require a zone of privacy and autonomy which encompasses the authority of family members to make health care decisions for incompetent adult patients (President's Commission, 1982; Buchanan and Brock, 1989). Insofar as it is based on the alleged value of the family and not on the individual patient's presumed preferences, values and/or interests, this account of the decision-making authority of family members is not patient-centred. Nevertheless, insofar as family members who serve as surrogates are supposed to decide on the basis of the individual patient's preferences, values and/or interests, surrogate decision-making is patient-centred.

Another criticism of the patient-centred model is that it doesn't take families seriously because it excludes a consideration of the interests of the family.[6] This is a serious charge, and if it were correct, it might well deal a fatal blow to patient-centred decision-making. However, this charge is based on the untenable assumption that a patient's interests are only interests *in the self* or *self-centred* interests, such as an interest in good health, pain avoidance, longevity and so forth. People can have interests of the self that are not interests in the self. People can and do care about other family members and the family as a whole, and they are often willing to sacrifice some of their more self-centred interests for both. Patient-centred decision-making can and should be sensitive to the family in this respect. It would be inappropriate to tell patients to disregard the interests of their families, and no less inappropriate to instruct surrogates to consider only the patient's self-centred interests. Only a caricature of patient-centred decision-making would require patients or surrogates to disregard patients' interests in their families.

This response, it might be claimed, still fails to take families seriously because it does not ascribe *independent* ethical significance to families and their interests. It gives moral weight to the interests of the family only insofar as patients themselves do. To be sure, the patient-centred model would be unacceptable if it implied that patients' beliefs and values are the only basis for ascribing moral weight to the interests of families, but this is not an implication of that model.

Suppose Ms C. is a 79-year-old retired librarian who is severely disabled due to an arthritic hip. She lives with her 45-year-old son and his 32-year-old second wife and their two young children. Due to her hip condition, Ms C. is unable to help with the housework or the children, and her care is a significant burden on the family. Ms C.'s family would benefit substantially if she were to have hip replacement surgery. However, Ms C. has decided against surgery because of her unwillingness to risk death or serious cognitive impairment. It is consistent with the patient-centred model to hold that Ms C. is giving insufficient consideration to her family. It is also consistent with that model to encourage her to: (1) discuss her decision with her son and daughter-in-law, (2) consider the impact on the family of her refusal to undergo surgery, and (3) reconsider her decision for the sake of her family.[7] By contrast, it would be incompatible with that model to force her to undergo surgery against her will for the sake of her family, and there are good reasons for not doing so, including: (1) respect for Ms C.'s autonomy and moral agency, (2) respect for Ms C.'s bodily integrity, and (3) a recognition that even though her family is affected by the decision, it is primarily Ms C. who will have to live (or die) with the effects of the decision.[8]

It would be seriously mistaken to think that respect for autonomy, an important ethical foundation of the patient-centred model, implies that patients have no ethical obligations to their families or cannot be faulted ethically for disregarding such obligations. Respect for autonomy imposes constraints on unwanted interventions by others, including efforts to enforce ethical obligations against a patient's will, but it does not give patients a moral licence to make decisions without considering their obligations to family and others.

Suppose Ms C. suffers a mild stroke. She is no longer competent to decide whether to have hip replacement surgery, but her physical abilities have not been affected. Although the surgery will no longer enable her to perform housework and care for the children, increased mobility will make it less difficult and costly for her family to care for her. Would it be ethically justified for her son, acting as her surrogate, to disregard her prior wishes and consent to surgery for the sake of the family? Insofar as it would have been inappropriate to permit Ms C.'s son to override her refusal when she was competent, it seems appropriate to require him to consider whether his mother could have been persuaded to give up her opposition to surgery if she hadn't suffered the stroke, or whether she would not have opposed surgery if she had been presented with the current scenario. Such a requirement is suggested by a patient-centred approach, which does not allow family-surrogates to make treatment decisions for the sake of the family if they have good reason to believe that the patient would have objected.

Generally, although the patient-centred model allows family-surrogates to conclude that the best decision from an ethical perspective is not the one that is most consistent with a patient's preferences, values and/or interests, it requires them to nevertheless select the latter. In addition to the reasons already cited in relation to competent patients, there are two other reasons for accepting this conclusion. One is the controversial nature of the value judgements involved. In many cases, reasonable people might disagree about whether the family's interests ethically trump the interests of an individual patient. For example, reasonable people might well disagree about whether Ms C.'s interests are outweighed by her family's interests in either scenario (i.e., when she was competent or when she was incompetent).

A second reason for not authorising family-surrogates to decide whether their preferences and interests may trump those of the patient is a concern about conflicts of interest. Family members might be biased and deliberately or unintentionally give more weight to their interests simply because they are theirs. For example, if Ms C.'s son were authorised to determine whether the interests of the family trumped those of his mother from an ethical perspective, his judgement might be biased by his own stake in the outcome. To address this concern, it has been proposed that an independent 'patient advocate' represent incompetent patients before an 'ethics panel' (Lindemann Nelson, 1992). This proposal may prevent conflicts of interest, but it does not address other concerns cited previously, including the controversial nature of the ethical judgements that would be required. Further, the proposal would require incompetent elderly patients to be represented by third parties rather than their family, and setting up a more or less adversarial proceeding between a patient-advocate and family members hardly promotes the idea of the family as an association of intimates who are united by common goals and values.

Finally, from a communitarian perspective it might be claimed that the patient-centred model fails to take families seriously because it is associated with a faulty conception of the self and its relation to the family. Jeffrey Blustein nicely summarises this charge as follows:

> The patient is not, as this theory presupposes, an atomic entity, a free and rational chooser of ends unencumbered by communal and other allegiances. On the contrary, his or her identity is constituted by family relationships, and he or she is united with other family members through common ends and mutual understanding.
>
> (Blustein, 1993, 8)[9]

To take families seriously according to such a communitarian analysis would rule out requiring family-surrogates to decide on the basis of the patient's distinctive preferences, values and interests, for such a requirement would create an artificial separation between patients and their families. Instead, we should recognise that:

> even if we are no longer able to express ourselves through direct choice, families still serve as a home to those values that have helped make us who we are. It does not matter very much if other family members cannot duplicate the choices we might have made; they still speak out of a context that was in an important sense constitutive of us.
>
> (Lindemann Nelson, H. and J., 1994, S20)

This is not the place for a philosophical analysis of the communitarian theory of the self.[10] However, leaving aside an assessment of the theory itself, there are several problems with the conception of surrogate decision-making by families that communitarians derive from it. For one thing, some elderly persons who live in the community or in nursing homes either have no living relatives or have had no contact with them for decades. Accordingly, as noted previously in the context of discussing practical limitations of the patient-centred approach, in some cases there are no family members to act as surrogates for incompetent elderly patients. More importantly, even when elderly patients have living relatives and ongoing relations with them, not all families are even minimally functional, let alone tight-knit and cohesive. In contrast to the idealised portrait of the family that underlies the communitarian view, social realities include divorce, estrangement, abuse, assault, neglect and so forth. Indeed, Hilde and James Lindemann Nelson, two US medical ethicists who advocate taking families seriously, caution against a 'romantic' view of the family that idealises it and disregards social realities. However, they also warn against the other extreme, cynicism, which 'settles for individuation and separation, assuming competing interests among family members and distrusting the possibility of altruism' (Lindemann Nelson, H. and J., 1995, 34). To give a fair hearing to the communitarian perspective, let us try to steer a middle course between romanticism and cynicism and focus on families that are relatively tight-knit and cohesive.[11]

Even when families are relatively close-knit and cohesive, individual family members can have different values and goals (e.g., religious beliefs, political ideologies, life styles, etc.), and there can be significant generational differences between elderly persons and their adult children and grandchildren. In this respect, even relatively close-knit and cohesive families in pluralistic societies such as the United States and the United Kingdom can be a microcosm of the society as a whole. As an extreme, but not unrealistic example, consider the following: a 72-year-old woman is a Christian Scientist, her husband is a Methodist, their 37-year-old son is a Hari Krishna, their 40-year-old son married a Jew and converted, and their 43-year-old daughter is an atheist. Even if the parents and their adult children have maintained a close and caring relationship, their religious beliefs may support significantly different health care decisions. As a less extreme example, spouses of many years and elderly parents and their adult children who identify with the same religious denomination, usually vote for the same political candidates, enjoy many of the same leisure time activities, and have a close and caring relationship, can have widely differing health care preferences. The first example casts doubt on the assumption that if an incompetent elderly person is part of a relatively close-knit and cohesive family, then family-surrogates need not be required to decide on the basis of her distinctive preferences, values and interests because family surrogates 'speak out of a context that was in an important sense constitutive of [her]'. The second example suggests that even when family-surrogates do 'speak out of a context that was in an important sense constitutive of [the patient]', that context may be compatible with a wide range of health care decisions. Accordingly, that common 'context' may fail to provide a basis for deciding among treatment options, and/or it may be compatible with a decision that is contrary to the patient's preferences and values.

It does not take a cynic to realise that families, even relatively close-knit and cohesive ones, can perpetuate oppressive attitudes and practices. Ageism can shape roles and expectations and affect relations with elderly family members. In the case of elderly women, there may be sexism as well as ageism. Such attitudes can be so well ingrained within family tradition that they are also accepted by elderly family members. Only an extreme form of 'cultural relativism' would ascribe moral authority to ageist and sexist family traditions in the context of surrogate decision-making for incompetent elderly patients.

Families should be taken seriously, but to do so while at the same time adequately protecting vulnerable incompetent elderly patients, it is advisable to accept the patient-centred principle that directs family-surrogates to be guided by the patient's preferences, values and interests. There is another reason to direct patient-surrogates to adopt the patient's perspective. If family-surrogates are not explicitly instructed to focus on the patient's preferences and goals, they may feel that it is *their responsibility* to make life or death decisions. The result might be anxiety and stress that they would not have experienced if they thought that they were implementing the patient's preferences and goals. Another possible result is a reluctance to be responsible for the death of a loved one, and the 'default' position, continued treatment, may be contrary to the patient's preferences and interests and/or pointless and wasteful.

To take families seriously, a patient-centred approach should allow family-surrogates considerable discretion. However, to protect vulnerable incompetent elderly patients, the discretion of family-surrogates should not be unlimited. It may be helpful to consider discretion in relation to parents and their young children. Although parents have considerable decision-making discretion with respect to important aspects of their children's lives, such as health care, education, nutrition, life style, and so on, their decision-making authority is not unlimited. For example, although parents may choose among a variety of educational options for their children (including public schools, parochial schools and home schooling), they may not choose to forgo education altogether. Similarly, although family-surrogates may have more or less discretion in relation to health care decision-making for incompetent elderly patients, their authority is not unlimited.[12]

A liberal communitarian model

Whereas some communitarians have stressed the importance of the family in relation to decision-making for incompetent patients, others have focused on larger communities. An important contribution along the latter lines is Ezekiel Emanuel's 'liberal communitarian' proposal for 'community health plans' (CHPs) which, among other things, are supposed to facilitate decision-making for incompetent patients (Emanuel, 1991).

Two characteristics distinguish CHPs from typical health plans, such as health maintenance organisations (HMOs). First, a CHP is a genuine community in the sense that its members are united by common values.[13] Second, a CHP is a 'deliberative democracy', which is the core of Emanuel's conception of liberal communitarianism: 'The liberal communitarian ideal is one of deliberative democracy in which the citizens participate in formulating their own conception of the good life and policies' (240).

This communitarian ideal is 'liberal' insofar as it acknowledges the sociological fact of diversity and the ethical value of pluralism. In Western democratic societies, there are numerous religious and secular groups with significantly different conceptions of the good, and these differences reach into the domain of health care as well. CHPs are supposed to enable this diversity to flourish by providing a 'home' for individuals who share similar values related to health care. For example, one CHP might allow abortion on demand and another might forbid it; one CHP might embrace vitalism and another might reject it; and one CHP might deny chronic dialysis to the elderly while another might reject such rationing by age.

As Emanuel conceives CHPs, the members of each will agree on certain fundamental values and will 'articulate the broad outlines of their shared conception of the good life' (179), especially in relation to health care. If CHP members are all members of a particular religious community (e.g., Orthodox Jews, Amish or fundamentalist Christians), they may already have a well-articulated vision of the good life. However, when such prior ideological bonds are absent, it may be necessary to articulate a collective vision of the good life. Acknowledging the difficulty of doing so in the abstract, Emanuel recommends a case-based approach for generating general principles and common values.

Through a process of deliberative democracy, CHP members are also to reach agreement about specific policies and guidelines, including those pertaining to decision-making for incompetent patients. Accordingly, health care decisions for incompetent elderly patients can be determined by the values, guidelines and policies of their respective CHPs, and there will be little or no need to rely on advance directives and/or surrogates.

The liberal communitarian model is subject to challenge on a number of grounds. First, its practicality is highly questionable. One cannot reasonably expect genuine communities to thrive and deliberative democracy to take hold in relation to health care while the society as a whole remains 'community unfriendly' and deliberative democracy is not part of the general political culture. Accordingly, in the absence of pervasive social change, it is doubtful that CHPs offer a workable alternative to the standard tools of the patient-centred model (i.e., advance directives and surrogates).[14]

Second, there is legitimate concern about discrimination and bias. Might there be fundamentalist Christian or Muslim CHPs which exclude Jews, Catholics, Buddhists and atheists? Might there be Aryan Nation CHPs which exclude Blacks, Asians and all other non-whites? Does the liberal communitarian ideal require toleration of such intolerant CHPs? Emanuel addresses this question, but his treatment of it is neither consistent nor satisfactory.[15]

Third, one can question whether allowing patient-dominated CHPs to determine health care standards and policies jeopardises the integrity of the medical profession and relegates physicians to the status of technicians for hire. Emanuel responds to this problem by distinguishing between clinical and non-clinical issues and decisions, but the line is much less clear than this response assumes.[16]

Fourth, a concern can be raised about guaranteeing just access to health care in a system of CHPs. Some CHPs may have members who are rich, while others may have members who are poor; and some CHPs may have members with relatively spartan health care preferences, while others may have members with relatively expensive and unlimited desires related to health care. For example, whereas elderly members of one CHP may have no interest in transplants and costly experimental life-prolonging treatments, elderly members of another CHP might desire such procedures. What does justice require in such contexts? Emanuel's proposed solution is to provide health care vouchers to all CHP members. However, two problems are not adequately resolved. One is determining the *value* of vouchers. The other is the propriety of compelling people to support, through taxes, CHPs with values and policies they oppose.

Emanuel only addresses the former problem and his proposed solution is that 'the collection of medical services that cure or ameliorate diseases, permitting an individual to participate in communal deliberations and the community to perpetuate itself, should provide a basis for defining the value of the voucher' (237). This standard may produce a 'black hole' in relation to health care spending, since almost any treatment, no matter how expensive, might be justified by means of it. Moreover, Emanuel's proposed standard is unacceptable from the perspective of his liberal communitarian ideal. On the one hand, it might require vouchers to cover the cost of a variety of services that members of certain CHPs do not value (i.e., transplants and other expensive cutting-edge treatments that can restore a person's ability to participate in communal deliberations). On the other hand, it might fail to set the value of vouchers high enough to cover services that members of other CHPs value (e.g., life-prolonging treatment for patients who are no longer able to participate in communal deliberations because of irreversible conditions). Emanuel responds by stating that individuals could receive refunds for a portion of their vouchers, or CHPs could generate additional revenue by taxing members. However, this response fails to address the issue of setting the appropriate value of *vouchers*.

In addition to these limitations, and of most importance from the perspective of this chapter, the liberal communitarian model does not offer an alternative to patient-centred decision-making for incompetent elderly patients. From the perspective of that model, a CHP's standards have moral authority with respect to decision-making for an incompetent elderly patient only if the patient: (1) is a member of that CHP, and (2) explicitly acknowledged and accepted those standards while she still was competent. The second condition is also a requirement of the patient-centred model.

Suppose Ms D. is a 76-year-old 'pleasantly demented' resident of a long-term care facility. She can speak a few words but cannot engage in significant communication; she cannot identify her son and other family members by name, but her face lights up when they visit; and she smiles frequently and appears to be generally content. Ms D. develops pneumonia and is taken to a hospital. In the attending physician's judgement, Ms D. probably can be restored to her baseline condition if she receives mechanical ventilation for several days, but she is expected to die without it. Since her retirement twelve years ago, she has belonged to a CHP which has a policy that moderately to severely demented patients over 65 are not candidates for mechanical ventilation. From the perspective of the liberal communitarian ideal, the 'community standards' of Ms D.'s CHP do not suffice to justify withholding ventilator support in her case. An additional requirement, one that is essentially patient-centred, is that she *understood* and *accepted* the standard at issue while she still was competent. Emanuel sometimes suggests an even stronger patient-centred requirement, namely, the CHP's policy was adopted as a result of a deliberative democratic process, and Ms D. participated in that process and accepted its outcome. This condition may well be too strong, but the weaker patient-centred requirement that Ms D. understand and accept the relevant standard seems reasonable.

Since individuals might be members of CHPs and not understand and/or accept policies that could affect the kind of treatment they would and would not receive if and when they were to become incompetent, the liberal communitarian model does not eliminate the need to establish the preferences and values of particular patients. Advance directives and surrogates might help to determine which of a CHP's policies an incompetent elderly patient understood and accepted when he was competent. Consequently, the liberal communitarian model does not eliminate the need to rely on these key tools of the patient-centred model.

A communities of patients model

In an article published about two years after the book in which Ezekiel Emanuel explains and defends the liberal communitarian model, he and Linda Emanuel propose a more workable one (Emanuel and Emanuel, 1993). The heart of this proposal is the notion of a 'community of patients' (COP). The primary unit of COPs is the health care organisation (e.g., hospital, nursing home, or rehabilitation facility).[17] By virtue of being an in-patient or out-patient at a certain facility, a person is a member of the corresponding COP. In contrast to CHPs, then, members of COPs do not necessarily share a common conception of the good.

147

Each COP would have a 'local patient community medical directive' that would provide decision-making guidelines ('community default guidelines') for incompetent patients who do not have instruction and/or proxy directives. If an incompetent elderly patient did not execute either type of advance directive, the family would not be asked to determine what she might have wanted or what is in her best interests. Instead, decision-making would be based on the facility's community default guidelines.[18]

In contrast to the standards of CHPs, which require a deliberative democratic process, community default guidelines are rooted in empirical research:

> First, using rigorous and validated survey methodology, a random selection of patients enrolled in the health care facility would be surveyed to document their specific preferences for care in a full range of illness scenarios involving incompetence. Patients would select treatment goals and options as if they were completing their actual instructional directives.
>
> (10)

The Emanuels identify three additional steps for generating community default guidelines. First, 'an institutional committee representing physicians, nurses, social workers, the chaplaincy, administration, and the lay community would be convened to use the survey results to develop guidelines on life-sustaining treatments' (10). Second, 'this committee would convene a variety of open community meetings to present and discuss the proposed policies' (10). In contrast to CHPs, the meetings, which are open to all, 'would not be expected to constitute a thorough deliberative discussion; rather, they would provide an opportunity for voicing perspectives and considerations not captured by the patient survey process' (10). It would be up to the committee to 'assemble and analyse the comments and revise the policy proposal, always bearing in mind that patient preferences are the central focus' (10). Third, the final version of the guidelines and the results of the empirical survey would be publicised (e.g., at the time of admission, patients and families would receive a brochure summarising the hospital's policy), and the entire process would be repeated periodically.

The Emanuels offer several reasons to support community default guidelines. First, such guidelines are said to promote autonomy by facilitating decision-making that matches patient preferences. Second, autonomy is also said to be promoted by the open community forums. Third, decision-making for incompetent patients without advance directives based on community default guidelines is said to be more efficient than surrogate decision-making by family. Fourth, 'local patient community standards can revive and nourish the value of communal solidarity' (12). Fifth, 'a policy of local patient community standards could relieve much of the uncertainty and anxiety now associated with end-of-life decision-making for incompetent patients' (12).

Available empirical data is said to support the first reason by suggesting that 'community standards are probably very similar to instructional directives and proxy decision-making in their ability to match patients' preferences'. This claim is problematical in at least two respects. First, the reliability of instruction directives is unclear. The best the Emanuels can say is that 'living wills and other written instructional directives can be relied on to represent a patient's wishes accurately, *under good circumstances*, in 46 to 84 percent of decisions' (7; emphasis added). Second, from the perspective of 'reliability', the primary question is not whether community default guidelines would be as reliable as instruction directives, but whether they would be more reliable than decision-making by physician designated surrogates who were instructed to apply the substitute judgement and/or best interests standards. It is important to rec that some people are reported to care more about who will m health care decisions for them if and when they are incompe than they care about the content of those decisions (Lynn, 1 High, 1989, 1994). If such people have not executed directives, their most important preferences related to healtl decision-making may not be promoted by the use of comr default guidelines.

With respect to the second reason, it is doubtful th community forums will substantially enhance patient av People are often reluctant to attend such open forums wher healthy, let alone when they are sick and hospitalised. even among those who attend, only a small percentage m participate, and an even smaller percentage are likely to significant impact on the final guidelines.

More importantly from the perspective of this appeal to autonomy suggests that despite references t standards and *communal solidarity*, COPs are no centred than CHPs. An important aim of comr guidelines is to match the preferences of the individual members of a COP. When they are surveyed, patients are not asked to articulate *community* goals or values.[19] Rather, they are asked to express their individual preferences, and the committees that formulate guidelines are to select guidelines that satisfy the treatment preferences of most patients. For example, if it is determined that 65% of a COP's patients do not want tube feeding if they are severely demented, the default guideline would be to forgo tube feeding when patients are severely demented. The largely unsubstantiated claim on behalf of COPs and community default guidelines is that they will promote more reliable patient-centred decision-making for incompetent elderly patients without advance directives than decision-making by family and other physician-selected proxies.

The claims that community default guidelines will promote greater efficiency and less uncertainty and anxiety are also questionable. First, interpreting instruction directives and applying them to specific clinical situations can be difficult. Proxies may provide valuable guidance in these respects. Community default guidelines are also likely to require interpretation in specific clinical situations, and family members and other physician-appointed surrogates may be as valuable in this context as they are in relation to instruction directives.[20] Thus, it may not be feasible or desirable to replace proxy decision-making with community default guidelines. Second, communication and collaboration between physicians and family members can promote a number of important goals, such as responsible and informed decision-making and acceptance of the impending loss of a loved one. Consequently, there may be good reasons not to bypass families in order to eliminate 'the uncertainty and anxiety that physicians experience in calling together the family, educating them about the situations, delineating the treatment options, and adjudicating any family conflicts' (12). Third, as the Emanuels rightly observe, a significant source of family stress and anxiety can be the fear that they will be responsible for a loved one's death if they decide to forgo life-sustaining treatment. However, to prevent such stress and anxiety by denying family members a meaningful decision-making role is both paternalistic and unnecessary. A non-paternalistic alternative is to encourage families to think of themselves as representatives of the *patient* and his or her preferences, values and interests.

Finally, the ethical authority of advance directives for incompetent patients has been challenged on the grounds that decisions should be based on a consideration of the patient's current well-being rather than previously expressed preferences (Dresser, 1986; Dresser and Robertson, 1989; and Robertson, 1991).

Insofar as decision-making on the basis of community default guidelines would rule out any independent consideration of a patient's current best interests, the COP model is subject to a similar challenge. Consider again the case of Ms D. the 76-year-old 'pleasantly demented' nursing home resident who develops pneumonia. It might be argued that in view of her current situation, providing her with mechanical ventilation for a few days to restore her to her baseline would be a benefit to her. However, suppose 70 per cent of the competent residents in Ms D.'s nursing home indicated that they would not want even temporary ventilator support for pneumonia if they were to become 'pleasantly demented', and the nursing home adopted the corresponding community guideline. This guideline would not permit a consideration of Ms D.'s current best interests. In relation to residents whose preferences when competent corresponded to the guideline, it might be claimed that their prior preferences have more moral weight than any 'objective' best interests judgement. At best, this is a controversial claim, and its assessment may require a theory of personal identity.[21] However, there is another problem in relation to COPs. Ms D. may be among the 30 per cent whose preferences did not match the guideline. If she is, disregarding her current (objective) best interests cannot be justified by invoking preferences and values she had when she was competent.[22]

Conclusion

The patient-centred model has survived the community-based challenges examined in this chapter. Families often have an important role to play in relation to decision-making for incompetent elderly patients. However, it is possible to acknowledge the ethical importance of families within a patient-centred framework. The liberal communitarian model proved to be impractical. Moreover, although it proposes the formation of genuine communities to facilitate health care decision-making for incompetent elderly patients, decision-making according to that model is essentially patient-centred. The communities of patients model may be more workable than the liberal communitarian one, but in contrast to community health plans, communities of patients are not genuine communities. The latter's value is primarily instrumental, namely, to facilitate more efficient and effective patient-centred decision-making when incompetent patients do not have advance directives, and it is questionable that they accomplish this objective better than family and other physician-selected surrogates.

NOTES

1 One estimate is that 5–7 per cent of persons over 65, and 25 per cent of those over 84, suffer from severe dementia (US Congress, 1987, 15–16).
2 According to the studies cited by Zweibel and Cassel, from 4 per cent to 17.5 per cent of respondents had executed living wills. In the study by Gamble and colleagues of ambulatory elderly persons in a rural county in North Carolina, whereas 86 per cent only wanted basic medical care or comfort care in the event of a terminal illness, none of the 75 persons questioned had executed a living will. In High's study of non-institutionalised elderly persons, he reports that only 17.5 per cent executed a formal living will. Gamble and colleagues identify one possible source of a reticence to execute living wills: 'concerns about signing any legal document that [people] believe may limit their freedom and expose them to legal and societal forces that are beyond their control' (280).
3 Some advocates of a patient-centered approach have eschewed decision-making by means of instruction directives as a goal or ideal (Lynn, 1991). Some ethicists have questioned the moral authority of instruction directives (Dresser, 1986; Dresser and Robertson, 1989; and Robertson, 1991). This challenge to advance directives is discussed at the end of the third section.
4 For a communitarian defence of age-based health care rationing, see Callahan (1987). For a critical examination of age-rationing, see Wicclair, 1993, Chapter 3.
5 For a critical analysis of medical futility, see Wicclair, 1993, 22–29.
6 I will use the expression 'interests of the family' to refer to: (1) interests of other family members, and (2) interests of the family as a whole. Nelson provides the following example of the latter: a family with a long tradition of music-making has an interest in sustaining this tradition (part of its character). In his example, this tradition would be jeopardised if a family member were to enrol in a clinical trial to determine whether tamoxifen can prevent breast cancer because the drug may cause significant vocal changes (Lindemann Nelson, 1992, 10).
7 Illness can make people more vulnerable, and it would not be permissible to exploit Ms C.'s vulnerability.
8 Hardwig proposes mandatory patient-family conferences and joint decision-making as a means to give effect to family interests (Hardwig, 1990). However, due to the increased vulnerability of elderly persons who are ill, this proposal may fail to adequately protect them.
9 Blustein focuses on competent patients and rejects a communitarian-based 'family decision-making' model for them. Hilde and James Lindemann Nelson, who are communitarians, criticise 'a view of human selves which neglects the circumstances of their making, and portrays them as disengaged, unencumbered, characterless' (Lindemann Nelson, H. and J., 1994, S20).

10 For a communitarian conception of the self, see Sandel, 1982 and Taylor, 1979. For a critique of the communitarian theory of the self, see Kymlicka, 1990, Chapter 6.

11 The 'household' sense of family that the Nelsons identify appears to exclude dysfunctional 'families' (i.e., persons related genetically or by marriage). A ' household' is defined as 'an aggregate or group of actual (living) members, who are closely associated by living arrangement or by commitment, for better or worse' (Lindemann Nelson, H. and J., 1995, 35). To constitute a 'family' in this sense, persons would not have to be related genetically or by marriage. For example, depending on the quality of their relationship, unmarried gay or lesbian couples could qualify as a family.

12 For a discussion of proposed limits, see Wicclair, 1993, 57–58, 61.

13 Emanuel offers the following (partial) definition of a community: 'Formally, a community is defined by the people who are eligible to participate in the deliberations, where the primary, although not sufficient, requirement of eligibility is some commitment to recognising, elaborating, affirming, and abiding by the community's particular conception of the good life. There will be other requirements for eligibility, often specified by a community's particular conception of the good life, but this commitment is fundamental' (167).

14 At times it appears that Emanuel is more interested in promoting the 'liberal communitarian vision' than resolving problems specifically associated with health care, such as decision-making for incompetent patients and just access. He identifies three values associated with that vision and deliberative democracy: autonomy or self-rule, self-development and establishing a common life.

15 See pp. 238–240, 174–175, 184 and 196.

16 See pp. 228–229 and 233–235.

17 Although they focus on health care institutions, the Emanuels also identify an alternate unit that may be more suited to managed care: health care plans.

18 The Emanuels propose the following role for families: 'Family participation in discussions, albeit without formal proxy designation or action in that role, would be entirely possible and is usually desirable' (10). If a patient's family disagrees with the community default guidelines, the Emanuels recommend that an institutional ethics committee attempt to resolve the disagreement. If conflict persists, they recommend judicial adjudication.

19 The Emanuels admit that a 'community of patients bears only a mild resemblance to more commonly accepted notions of community' (9).

20 A similar point applies to the standards of CHPs.

21 For a communitarian approach to this problem, see Kuczewski, 1994.

22 As noted above, only a relatively low percentage of elderly persons with definite preferences concerning life-sustaining treatment have executed instruction directives. Consequently, it is unwarranted to conclude that a failure to execute such a directive indicates the absence of clear preferences. In the case of Ms D., then, her failure to execute a personal instruction directive documenting her dissent may not be sufficient grounds for concluding that she accepted the nursing home's guidelines.

9

POWER, LIES AND INJUSTICE

The exclusion of service users' voices

Vivien Lindow

Introduction

The discussion of ethical issues in mental health has been con-
ducted almost entirely by people on the powerful side of the divide
in the psychiatric system. The voices of the recipients of the services
of psychiatrists and their predecessors, the mad doctors and Poor
Law administrators, have seldom been heard.

The question of why our voices are not heard is an interesting
topic, which I hope to explore later. First, however, I should say that
I do not have a background in ethics or philosophy, so this chapter
is a challenge to write. What I shall try to do in it is to identify some
of the ethical issues that are discussed in mental health service
user/survivor groups, as well as to look at some of the reasons why
their conclusions are not heard and acted on.

There is no consensus about what people who receive mental
health services like to be called: 'service users', 'survivors',
'recipients', 'patients', 'loonies', 'mad people', 'clients', 'consumers'
and (in Japan) 'psychiatrically disabled people'. I have heard people
ask to be called all these things in the past three years, and here, I
shall interchange the most usual terms. The people who use the
mental health system are not, of course, a homogenous group.
Together, we discuss issues that affect us. Our discussions are seldom
about new styles of management, or changes in service organisations: I have heard little interest in the idea of a GP-led National
Health Service. There is, rather, much discussion of poverty,
employment, housing; about services that control and rob our
experiences of meaning and about dangerous treatments. One of the

most frequent refrains amongst service users remains 'They never listen.' Increasingly, we speak: but our voices are still not heard. In this chapter I shall explore some of the reasons for this.

Power and vested interests

Some functions of psychiatry

The general public and most media reporters assume that it is beneficial for psychiatrists to have control of mad people. There are some obvious advantages for us in this. The historical recategorising of psychotic experience as 'illness' rather than 'wickedness' clearly has had advantages in how both the public and service users understand these experiences. Medical treatment is preferable to the criminal justice system to many people. People are not expected to continue to work and can get state benefits if certified by doctors on the grounds of 'mental illness'. Many psychiatrists are genuinely motivated to relieve suffering: some of them do relieve suffering, particularly in the short term.

Psychiatry, of course, also brings benefits to others in society, not least of these are the numerous employees of the mental health industry and the workers and shareholders of pharmaceutical companies. These 'benefits' can frequently be seen to work against the civil liberties and other best interests of recipients of mental health services.

The mental health system performs a public function by controlling people who do not fit in. Recent press campaigns against people who use mental health services, suggesting that the public are in danger because of the closure of the asylums, have strengthened the controlling role of mental health services despite the Royal College of Psychiatrists' recent 'Report of the Confidential Inquiry into Homicides and Suicides by Mentally Ill People'[1] which found no evidence of an increase in killings by people diagnosed by psychiatrists in the last two decades. Psychiatry benefits from public and press belief to the contrary.

Nowhere is the control function of psychiatry more obvious than in the system of 'Special Hospitals'. One former ex-patient of two of these high-security hospitals, Kimberley Andrews,[2] has written:

> I will always maintain that I was never mad – bad, yes! And the longer I vegetated, I became very bad, sometimes out of sheer boredom. I could never be physically ill – it would be

interpreted as my being disturbed. I couldn't laugh....If I cried, I was liable to be a candidate for a jolt of ECT. It was impossible for me to display normal behaviour. The staff were not trained to recognise it.

Other mechanisms for social control are the programmes of 'education' of service users and their families into believing that psychiatry's theories are facts, and that their treatments represent medical science not behaviour control. A common form of 'information' by doctors and nurses attempting to persuade people to take medication is to say that their condition is like diabetes. This suggests a known chemical deficit and a known effective antidote, neither of which applies in psychiatry. Programmes of 'assertive outreach' to ensure that people take toxic drugs have burgeoned. New coercive laws, such as the Mental Health (Patients in the Community) Act 1995 which gives mental health workers powers to take and convey people to places of treatment and to tell people where to live have been passed.

There is no discussion of the ethics of these procedures with those affected most. Clearly, there are issues about finding a balance between the individual's civil rights and the rights of the community, but service users ought to be involved in the discussion of what constitutes the right balance. Other people have had much to say about this, for example Marjorie Wallace argues that, 'We have swung too far the other way and put far too much emphasis on the liberty of individuals and confidentiality, when knowledge could help prevent tragedies.'[3]

But this looks very different from the perspective of those who use mental health services. A woman who works full time in a demanding and responsible job in mental health, who had a diagnosis of manic depression, describes her experience as the mother of a 10-year-old boy:

> Social Services initiated adoption proceedings before he was born solely because of my psychiatric history. Yet for the past eight years I have worked, gained a good degree, and have had only one episode of illness.[4]

This suggests that if there is an imbalance it is in the direction opposite to that claimed by Wallace, for this is by no means an isolated experience, there are examples of oppression in all branches of mental health services. The balance seems to remain too far against civil rights from a less powerful perspective than Marjorie Wallace's.

The importance of the user view of this imbalance is endorsed by Liberty.[5] In its examination of the UK mental health system in relation to the International Covenant on Civil and Political Rights, to which the UK government has agreed to be bound, Liberty concludes that:

> People with 'mental disorder' are subject to arbitrary detentions and denied equal treatment before courts and tribunals. The Mental Health Act 1983 does not provide sufficient protections against wrongful detentions and neither the Mental Health Review Tribunals or the more recently introduced Code of Practice are adequate in preventing them.

Reliance on science

The question at the foundation of psychiatry, 'What, if anything, is mental illness?' is barely in the public awareness. Such is the power of the establishment, embodied in the Royal College of Psychiatrists and drug-company funded academic psychiatrists, that the views of those who question the current bio-medical orthodoxy have little effect on the delivery of medical mental health services. Such arguments appear to sink unnoticed.

Dishonesty is rife. Many people who use mental health services do not know, for example, that what they are told about their 'illnesses' and about their 'treatments' is highly speculative. Psychiatrists claim that theirs is a medical science, treating illnesses in a way which is similar to those used in the treatment of other illnesses. However, the symptoms of 'mental illness' are not physical, they are people's behaviour, speech and reported mental and emotional experiences and thus far, we have no unit of measurement (the inch, the nanosecond) for behaviour and speech, so how can psychiatry be the same as a natural science?

Our knowledge about links between the neural system and behaviour and experience remains in the dark ages. After millions of USA dollars and UK pounds, there is no identified physical pathology to match 'mental illnesses', and there are no physical diagnostic tests. Research takes place on people already subject to brain-damaging drugs. The most honest and useful debates on this subject are philosophical, not scientific. One service-user perspective on this is introduced by Peta Masters:[6] 'To write the manic experience off as a "chemical imbalance" at best mistakes the cause for the effect. It negates what in other circles would be deemed valuable.' This is a theme in much protest by people who have been diagnosed by psychiatrists: diagnosis robs us of the meaning of our experiences.

A thread of bio-medical research that is particularly threatening to mental health service users is genetic research. Periodic announcements that the gene for schizophrenia has been discovered are quietly refuted afterwards, leaving the impression that a genetic link has been discovered. Being diagnosed with schizophrenia undoubtedly runs in families. Being a doctor runs in families. Is being a doctor caused by genetic transmission?

Particularly alarming to service users are echoes in genetic research of the eugenics movement of the 1930s in the USA and Europe, and in particular of events in Nazi Germany in the 1930s and 1940s. The murder of people in mental hospitals who were deemed 'unworthy of life' was organised and executed by psychiatrists and other doctors.[7] If this episode was acknowledged in the discussion of the possibility of genetic transmission of 'mental illness', it would be less worrying. As it is, however, announcements of 'discoveries' are always couched in the heroic mould of doctors looking for cures. The desire to prevent us from existing, quite apart from the horrors of possible extermination, sends a strong message that people like me are not worthy of life.

Fundamental to bio-psychiatric research is the problematic nature of psychiatric diagnosis (and some medical diagnoses), amply demonstrated by Mary Boyle.[8] Boyle examines the history of the concept of schizophrenia and finds that it first identified a wholly different set of 'symptoms'. As one constellation of behaviour and psychological experiences is observed to have no meaningful pattern, the diagnosis has been 'refined' to describe something else. What is not generally understood is that these refinements of psychiatric diagnoses bear no relation to medical research in laboratories. They are made by committees of psychiatrists arriving at a consensus: psychiatry is still at the stage of 'armchair' theorising backed by prestigious pronouncements.

Research into 'mental illness' is based on the diagnostic categories arrived at by this method. Psychiatrists create wonderfully precise scientific methodologies for their research activities, without revealing that the assumption of the existence of 'illnesses' on which such research is based is controversial. This hides the dishonesty behind claims of scientific discovery and helps to exclude other forms of research. Claridge[9] having reviewed much of the non-neurological research on schizophrenia noted:

> A very recent multi-authored 'state of the art' review of schizophrenia research (Crow, 1987)[10] makes no mention of the kind of experimental data referred to here, and promotes the misleading conclusion that the psychoses are very near to being established as organic brain diseases, in the narrow neurological sense.

The type of non-biological research described by Claridge is difficult to mount. Establishment psychiatrists are in strategic positions on government committees distributing the public's research money, and resources are not made available while psychiatrists retain this control. Wealthy drug companies also have a great vested interest in psychiatry retaining control of mad people. A major proportion of research is carried out or funded by these companies, adding weight to the biological interpretations of mental and emotional distress.

Unequal opportunities

One way in which the mental health system's control function is manifested is in its relationship with the least powerful sections of society. It has long been documented that people who experience oppression and discrimination in society in other ways, generally fare worse in the white middle class institutions of the mental health system. People from minority ethnic groups[11], women[12], lesbians and gay men[13] and many other groups such as older people, disabled people, working class and unemployed people and people who are HIV positive have all reported unfair and discriminatory experiences in both hospital and community mental health services.

Liberty[14] cite evidence for example that women are disproportionately likely to be held in high security special hospitals (compared with women in prison) and gives other evidence of inequality of treatment of women. This leads them to conclude that the UK does not comply with Article 3 of the International Covenant on Civil and Political Rights. Next, citing some of the overwhelming evidence that black and Irish people are also discriminated against and the lack of race awareness training in mental health services, Liberty continues: 'The right to equal treatment is also contradicted by the experience of ethnic minorities in relation to mental health services.'[15]

Treatments

There are profound ethical questions to be discussed about the way in which the drug companies dictate what psychiatrists do and about the way psychiatrists fail to inform people of the dangers and discomforts of their products. The drug company representatives can now say more clearly which process of the brain their chemicals act upon. They, with the psychiatrists they support, imply that these neural processes are those known to be implicated in 'mental illness'.

These drug dealers have proved adept at marketing. For example, many people with the diagnosis 'manic depression' believe that their 'illness' is caused by a deficiency in a naturally occurring mineral, and that doses of lithium make good that lack. This is not the case: little is known about the mechanisms of extreme mood swings and lithium introduces quantities of a dangerous chemical found naturally only in traces in humans.

Another successful strategy used by drug companies has been to call one range of drugs 'anti-depressants', despite their variable efficacy. More recently, they have artfully also renamed 'neuroleptics' (or 'major tranquillisers') as 'anti-psychotics'. This despite the fact that they have limited effect on psychosis, sometimes causing it. They do, however, often stop people from talking about their psychotic experiences and this again raises the question of the ethical balance between the liberty of individuals and the protection of communities. These seductive names help to obscure the dangerous effects of most of these drugs. One of the hardest areas for service users to get their voices heard is when we say that these drugs make our lives intolerable.

The ill effects of psychiatric drugs has been the subject of recipients' protests since they were introduced. Peta Masters gives a graphic example:

> These are drugs which make you claustrophobic, make you shake, make you lose time, which open your mind to terrifying hallucinations – the only visual hallucinations I've ever had have been in hospital while taking 'curative' drugs. When a hospital patient tells you he's 'in hell', you'll probably find he's on Haloperidol.[16]

Betty Blaska, in the USA, writes similarly about the psychiatric drug side effects she has experienced:

> Nausea, diarrhoea, dizziness. Vision so bad you can't cross the street because you can't judge the cars' distances from you. Drug-induced psychosis so bad you can't leave your bed or look out the window for the terror you feel. Low blood pressure so bad you can't stand for very long, and your voice so weak you can't be heard across a telephone wire.[17]

I give two examples of the same thing because I feel sceptical that anyone will vigorously bring the discussion of this issue into the public arena, however often we say it (daily, world-wide).

These writers do not mention the permanent physical and mental impairment that millions of people suffer at the hands of psychiatric drugs: they also kill some people. One official publication has drawn attention to deaths where psychiatric drugs are implicated – *Deaths of Detained Patients: A Review of Reports to the Mental Health Act Commission* by Banerjee, Bingley and Murphy.[18] Such honesty is refreshing, but neither the government nor anyone else in a position of power has taken up the issue of such deaths, although they are known to be the tip of an iceberg of prescribed drug-implicated deaths nationwide.

One of psychiatry's best-known critics from within, R. D. Laing, characterised mainstream psychiatric treatment shortly before he died in 1989 thus: 'It was like they were simply pouring cement into someone's system to straighten them up, and zonk them with electric shocks and so forth.'[19] Psychiatrists often pretend that real opposition to what they do ended in the sixties, but there is an ongoing and current literature of protest by fellow professionals. Another psychiatrist who is a critic is Peter Breggin:[20]

> If neuroleptics were used to treat anyone other than mental patients, they would have been banned a long time ago. If their use wasn't supported by powerful interest groups, such as the pharmaceutical industry and organised psychiatry, they would be rarely used at all. Meanwhile, the neuroleptics have produced the worst epidemic of neurological disease in history.[21]

Another doctor, M. P. Dumont, concludes of psychiatry's complicity with big business:

> The difference between the criminal drug abuse and legal medication is often as thin as the piece of paper on which the prescription is written, the law and the media treat one as a felony and the other as sacred.[22]

If those within medicine have no impact on the behaviour of their colleagues, it is not surprising that those of us with experience of the drugs but also the stigma of being diagnosed are not heard.

People have also been protesting about electroconvulsive therapy (ECT) since its first experimental application in Italy.[23] The response of psychiatrists to people's testimony against the experience of ECT has often been that this is 'anecdotal evidence', although their evidence that it saves lives is equally anecdotal and second person. Generations of people who have experienced ECT have protested, some spending the rest of their lives campaigning against the practice,[24] but, after a decrease in its use in the 1970s, it has been increasing ever since.

Informed consent is of central importance here. Psychiatrists often say: 'If we told people about the side effects they would not take the drugs.' Quite. Psychiatrist-devised information leaflets for drugs and ECT look like drug- and ECT-company advertisements. People diagnosed by psychiatrists cannot fight in the courts for damages from treatment because the courts treat them as non-competent, and even clinicians often seem unaware that many ill effects are caused by their treatments: they tend to regard such effects as further symptoms of 'mental illness'.

In addition to physical harm from treatments, the notion of mental and emotional harm seems to have been lost in the system. When people are seen as bunches of bio-chemical imbalance, it allows mental health professionals to ignore the psychological harm they do. The psychological effects of electric shocks to the head and of seclusion, two practices condemned when used by torturers and kidnappers, are denied within the mental health system. The subjective experience of having one's liberty taken away by detention under the Mental Health Act is identical to kidnapping. Where is the post-traumatic counselling that kidnapping victims are routinely given? The very idea comes as a surprise to most mental health professionals.

One psychiatric system survivor, Patricia Deegan, titled her article 'Spirit Breaking: When the Helping Professionals Hurt'.[25] She describes how, when she changed role from being a clinician to receiving psychiatric services, she was not allowed to comfort a fellow patient who was in seclusion (solitary confinement), even to bring him a glass of water. In the system:

> If you respond humanly and with compassion, you get punished. That is, if you are a patient in a mental hospital and you try to go in and comfort a person who is crying out from the seclusion room, you get an initial warning from the staff and, if you repeat the violation, you get your 'privileges' revoked for the day.[26]

Not only was the man abandoned in seclusion, but Deegan herself was psychologically harmed by this inhumane practice. Deegan's term 'spirit breaking' has resonance for many psychiatric system survivors.

As well as toxic drugs and psychologically harmful procedures, disrespectful 'community care' services result from professional dishonesty about the scientific/medical nature of psychiatric knowledge. Other professions also rob our experiences of personal meaning, ignoring past history and current pressures. There are psychologists who respond to calls from residential staff by devising a behavioural programme for the resident to ease the staff's problem before meeting the person concerned. This continues alongside the rhetoric about 'user-led' services.

Many other aspects of 'community care' are also experienced as no such thing by its recipients. Diana Rose's study of mental health service users quotes a user who says that: 'They think they can come into my flat without my permission. They think they can do that to everybody here because we have been in hospital.'[27] Nor is talking therapy free from controlling aspects, for the minority who are able to access it. The issues about psychotherapy that come up most frequently in user groups are related to the oppression of the therapist always being right about what we know about ourselves (who is the expert here?) and that of sexual abuse in therapy.

There is some advantage in the number and diversity of alternative and complementary therapies available, in that they provide choice. But two obvious weaknesses of this for mental health service users are first, that most complementary treatments are outside the National Health Service, and so inaccessible to all but a minority, and second, that accountability to clients or the public is even more difficult to establish in relation to such treatments than in the NHS. Even though some associations and societies of therapists and counsellors do have ethical committees and disciplinary procedures, as Milan Ghosh (a service user) has written: 'counsellors investigating counsellors is like the police investigating the police, not credible'.[28] The inclusion of a few, outnumbered, recipients of therapy on panels does not answer the case.

Mad people trying to be heard

People who have received psychiatric treatment have a long and largely hidden history. Most of the protests of earlier survivors have been lost. We hear rumours of attendants and patients protesting about the conditions in the early asylums. John Perceval wrote an account of his experiences in the madhouses of the last century and of the Alleged Lunatics' Friend Society which he founded with lawyers to advocate for people trapped in the madhouse system.[29] His actions and writings reflect the same sense of outrage that colours the current mental health system survivor movement.

Ways of not listening in individual encounters with professionals

When people are not listened to, they cease to talk. Those mental health system survivors who see themselves as part of a liberation movement would agree with survivor Kate Millett[30] when she writes that 'All systems of oppression depend finally upon the surrender and even the collusion of the oppressed. This collusion has been secured through our silence.' Two common methods which are used to get service users to comply are the threats by mental health workers either to detain someone under the Mental Health Act or to withdraw all services. There are also less obvious mechanisms at work in the mental health system.

Now that consumerism and the market have come to the National Health Service, one might expect psychiatric system survivor voices to have some effect. It is certainly true to say that we are being given permission to speak but in this, as in other aspects of mental health services, dishonesty and inequality prevail. As a consequence of this and other factors service users' voices are still not being heard.

Some of the forces that work against service users' voices being heard when talking about individual needs are:

- Selective listening: only those who have been educated successfully into believing that they have a neuro-chemical imbalance are heard by workers.
- Historical stigma has reasserted itself with community care and public scare: mental health workers have to cover their backs and adopt the most controlling option. They cannot 'afford' to hear what we say.
- Historical assessments of mad people as being without any capacity for rational thought and speech die hard.
- Diagnoses: medics listen to our words as symptoms, not for their meaning. Once diagnosed, everyone discredits our ability to know what is best for ourselves.
- Analysis: the ideas of psychoanalysis have pervaded the mental health system. A justifiably angry demand for rights is seen as a symptom of mental illness or 'acting out'. Attempting to get one's rights by other means are described as 'denial' or 'manipulative'. Our words are not taken at face value.

Debates about people's rights being balanced by responsibilities seem irrelevant in a system where mental patients are seen as irrational and unable to be responsible. These factors also apply in situations where service users' voices are currently supposed to be specially privileged, the much discussed collective 'user involvement'.

Strategies for discrediting the user voice in 'user involvement'

The prevalence of a market ideology particularly in the period of Conservative government in the 1980s and early 1990s might perhaps have been expected to have given the opportunity for service users' voices to be heard in decisions about how services will be provided and run. However, the market has tended to lead to increased competition between professions, leading them to assert even more often that they know what is best for us. When they feel the need to justify their positions, they are hardly going to concede that service users are also experts in the system.

Workers have also adopted some strategies to discredit user voices during consultation and 'involvement'. One such strategy is to suggest that when groups of service users talk about their experiences this has the status of 'anecdotal evidence' rather than human testimony (as mentioned earlier). This invalidation happens with topics we know are universal: wherever there is Westernised psychiatry issues such as drug misuse by psychiatrists, lack of humane responses to our experiences and the wish to live independent lives arise. Many workers get upset and are often rude when relating to service users as equals on committees and planning groups. Indeed, when workers find what we say challenging, the most usual strategy to discredit service user voices is to suggest we are not to be listened to because we are too articulate, and not representative.[31] Workers seem to be looking for someone, the 'typical' patient, who is so passive and/or drugged that they comply with their plans.

We are developing our own strategies to respond to these challenges in an attempt to reveal to such workers their double standards:

- We ask how representative are they, and the others on the committee? We point out that as they are selected for their expertise and experience, so are we. Indeed, we are more likely to have been selected by a group than they are.
- We ask, would workers send their least articulate colleague to represent their views, or the least confident nurse to negotiate for a change in conditions?
- We ask, if a person's criticisms are valid, what relevance has representativeness?
- We point out that it is very rude to suggest that someone is not a 'proper' service user (that is, so disempowered and/or medicated that they cannot speak). We could ask, but do not, that the challenger produce his or her credentials, their certificates of qualification.

The situation is more complex than this, of course. User representatives do want to be representative and to consult other service users. But to do this our self-advocacy groups need to be properly funded so that they are able to reach out to as many people who use mental health services as possible and so that we can inform 'user consultations' in a more representative way. Jane Thompson suggests further reasons why user voices are not being heard:

The gulf between service users' concerns on the one hand, and professional and managerial concerns on the other, is perhaps not as clearly understood as one might imagine. Equally, the implications of different ethical stances amongst different groups of service users may not be fully appreciated.[32]

The differences between service user and worker agendas, in particular the major control function of the services, and influence from government imperatives and drug company finances are seldom brought out when service users are being consulted. No wonder there is growing frustration about 'user involvement' taking much time and energy and achieving little. Once again, we are not treated honestly.

Advocacy

Some good intentions can be seen among the people providing mental health services in the 1990s. Nowhere is this more evident than in the provision of advocacy for people who use mental health services. Or is it? If a surgical specialty was found consistently to damage a large proportion of its most needful patients, the surgeons would be required to reform. Surgical advocacy services are not a burgeoning industry.

I have doubts about the many poorly funded, provider-dependent 'mental health' advocacy schemes being set up like sticking plasters on malignant melanoma. The phenomenon has been referred to by Tracy Stein[33] as the tomato sauce approach to advocacy, a little bit on everything will make it better.

In the independent local psychiatric system survivor group I belong to, two of our most active members have recently been back in the local psychiatric institution, where even giving an asked-for opinion at a ward meeting was seen as trouble making. If they made a complaint, there would be reprisals from ward staff, as one of them observed happening to a fellow patient. There was nowhere else for them to go, we have no non-medical day or crisis alternatives. The under-funded Patients' Council was barely visible, its support group dominated by mental health workers. Yet the managers there believe that advocacy is alive and well, and have been heard at conferences boasting about 'their' Patients' Council. Worse, in Wiltshire a Patients' Council was forced to close because psychiatrists wielded their power to remove all independent advocacy functions from the group.[34]

This pattern is repeated in many places. While some service users are empowered and invigorated by advocacy schemes, at least as many feel burnt out and exploited in their work. Time shows that ultimately such schemes do not change what most psychiatrists do. Even when Patients' Councils and individual advocacy have legal status and statutory funding, as in The Netherlands, they remain limited in their effects.[35]

Ethical questions for the future

Peter Campbell,[36] a leader in the organisation 'Survivors Speak Out'[37] wrote in 1991: 'A feature of the user movement in the last five years has been the consistency with which groups across the country have called for 24-hour crisis houses.' That call continues, while safe houses remain like hen's teeth. Will this still be so when the organised user movement is not five or ten but twenty years old? At the current rate of progress, this seems likely.

Much is being written about safe houses designed by people who experience mental health crises.[38] Almost every user group has discussions and some make plans, yet funding is not forthcoming. The question is, will those who control resources – statutory commissioners or charitable trusts – release funds for development projects to enable new providers including service users to provide some substantial, not marginal, non-medical services? So far, funds have been given grudgingly, often a one-year part-time worker to develop something that needs two workers for two years to develop and then ongoing funding. We need a real shift of funding away from unpopular services that can only be filled compulsorily, to user-led alternatives.

Some user initiatives require more modest funds and struggle on with great success. Survivors' Poetry[39] and the Hearing Voices Network[40] are two such national initiatives. The effect of taking part in such self-help initiatives can be transforming. Colin Hambrook[41] describes joining Survivors' Poetry:

> It was a new and vital experience to have the opportunity to share with others who are also struggling to find some meaning in lives which the world looks on at best as failed, and at worst as a burden to society.

One of the most positive aspects of Survivors' Poetry for Hambrook is working with 'people that recognise and appreciate the pain behind your experience, people who value your expression as poetry and who are prepared to help refine that expression and appreciate it'.

When mental health system survivors talk about user-controlled initiatives, the issue of having the meaning of our experiences recognised is central. There are initiatives that specifically explore personal meanings and helpful responses to various manifestations of mental and emotional distress. The Hearing Voices Network is one such initiative involving specialist groups of people who meet and collect first-hand information about helpful and unhelpful responses to their troubles. Other specialist groups focus on self-harm, eating distress, surviving incest, 'manic depression', 'schizophrenia', experiencing sexual abuse by therapists and experiencing ECT.

Will anyone with power and resources hear mental health service users' hard-lived experience of what helps, and what does not, in their lives? Will professional people colonise this information, taking what does not threaten them and cornering available resources? There are signs of this happening to the ideas of the Hearing Voices movement. Why is self-help expected to take place amongst the poorest people in society without adequate resources?

Many people who use mental health services do aspire to seeing those services improved. Their voices are barely heard. When they are, Melba Wilson warns of the danger that, for example, 'the experiences of white survivors are automatically assumed to hold true for black survivors of incest and child sexual abuse'.[42] This holds true for all mental health service users from minority ethnic and other oppressed groups.

In conclusion, some major ethical questions that service users want addressed are: Will mental health professionals be honest with us about their lack of knowledge, about the toxic nature of their procedures and the inequalities within the mental health system? Will the government take steps to comply with the International Covenant on Civil and Political Rights, to which it has nominally agreed? Will the training of mental health workers include discussion of all the issues raised in this chapter, making sure that a cross-section of people who use mental health services take part in the debate? Lastly, will people who take part in ethical debates please include sufficient numbers of mental health service users in their discussions?

VIVIEN LINDOW

NOTES

1 Steering Committee of the Confidential Inquiry into Homicides and Suicides by Mentally Ill People, *Report of the Confidential Inquiry into Homicides and Suicides by Mentally Ill People*, London, Royal College of Psychiatrists, 1996.
2 Andrews, K., 'Overdosing on Freedom' *OPENMIND*, 54, 1992, p. 10.
3 Thompson, A., 'Bound to Secrecy', *Community Care*, 11–17, April 1996, p. 16.
4 An anonymous letter in *Community Care*, 1–7, August 1996, p. 10.
5 Liberty, *People With Mental Health Problems and Learning Difficulty*, Human Rights Convention Report 1, London: National Council for Civil Liberties/MIND, 1993, p. 266.
6 Masters, P., 'Brainstorm' *OPENMIND*, no. 49, 1991, p. 15.
7 Burleigh, M., 'Death in the Community', *Asylum*, vol. 9, no. 2, 1995, pp. 11–12.
8 Boyle, M., 'Schizophrenia: The Fallacy of Diagnosis', *Changes: An International Journal of Psychology and Psychotherapy*, 1996, vol. 14, no. 1, pp. 5–13. Boyle, M., *Schizophrenia: A Scientific Delusion?*, London: Fontana, 1990.
9 Claridge, G., 'Can a Disease Model Survive?', in Bentall, R. (ed.), *Reconstructing Schizophrenia*, London: Routledge, 1990, p. 178.
10 Crow, T. J., (ed.), 'Recurrent and Chronic Psychoses', Edinburgh: Churchill Livingstone, 1987, cited in Claridge, 'Can a Disease Model Survive?'.
11 Beliappa, J., *Illness or Distress? Alternative Models of Mental Distress*, London: Confederation of Indian Organisations, 5 Westminster Bridge Road, London SW1 7XW, 1991. Butler, R., 'Forgotten Figures: Mental Health and the Irish in Britain', *OPENMIND*, 70, 1994, pp. 16–17. Fernando, S., *Mental Health, Race and Culture*, Basingstoke, Macmillan/MIND, 1991.
12 Darton, K., Gorman, J. and Sayce, L., *Eve Fights Back: The Successes of MIND's Stress on Women Campaign*, London: MIND Publications, 1994. Showalter, E., *The Female Malady: Women, Madness and Culture 1830–1980*, London: Virago, 1985.
13 Kitzinger, C. and Perkins, R., *Changing Our Minds: Lesbian Feminism and Psychology*, London: Only Women Press, 1993. Sayce, L., *Breaking the Link Between Homosexuality and Mental Illness*, London: MIND, 1995.
14 Liberty, *People With Mental Health Problems and Learning Difficulty*, Human Rights Convention Report 1, London: National Council for Civil Liberties/ MIND, 1993, p. 9.
15 Ibid., p. 12.
16 Masters, P., 'Brainstorm', *OPENMIND*, no. 49, 1991, p. 15.
17 Blaska, B., 'What it Feels Like to be Treated Like a CMI – and Prevailing Over It', *Changes*, 10, 4, 1992, p. 284.
18 Banerjee, S., Bingley, W. and Murphy, E., *Deaths of Detained Patients*, London: The Mental Health Foundation, 1995.
19 Mullan, B., *Mad to be Normal: Conversations with R. D. Laing*, London: Free Association Books, 1995.

20 Breggin, P., *Toxic Psychiatry: Drugs and Electroconvulsive Therapy: The Truth and the Better Alternatives*, London: Fontana Paperback, 1993.

21 Breggin, P., 'Should the Use of Neuroleptics be Severely Limited?', *Changes: An International Journal of Psychology and Psychotherapy*, vol. 14, no. 1, 1996, pp. 62–66.

22 Dumont, M.P., 'In Bed Together at the Market: Psychiatry and the Pharmaceutical Industry' *American Journal of Orthopsychiatry*, vol. 60, no. 4, 1990, pp. 484–485.

23 Described in Baruch, G. and Treacher, A., *Psychiatry Observed*, London: Routledge and Kegan Paul, 1978, p. 42.

24 Frank, L. R., 'Electroshock: Death, Brain Damage, Memory Loss and Brainwashing' in Cohen, D. (ed.), *Challenging the Therapeutic State: Critical Perspectives on Psychiatry and the Mental Health System*, New York: The Journal of Mind and Behaviour, 1990, pp. 219–242. Morgan, R. F., *Electroshock: The Case Against*, Toronto: IPI Publishing, 1991.

25 Deegan, P. E., 'Spirit Breaking: When the Helping Professionals Hurt', *The Humanistic Psychologist*, vol. 18, no. 3, 1990, pp. 301–313.

26 Ibid., p. 304.

27 Rose, D., *Living in the Community*, London: The Sainsbury Centre for Mental Health, 1996.

28 Ghosh, M., letter published in *Cahoots*, 52, April–June 1995, p. 2.

29 Podvoll, E. M., *The Seduction of Madness: A Compassionate Approach to Recovery at Home*, London: Century, 1990.

30 Cooper, C., 'The Loony Bin Trip', *OPENMIND*, 52, 1991, p. 13.

31 Lindow, V., 'Experts, Lies and Stereotypes', *Health Service Journal*, vol. 101, no. 5,267, 1991, pp. 18–19.

32 Thompson, J., *User Involvement in Mental Health Services: The Limits of Consumerism, the Risks of Marginalisation and the Need for a Critical Approach*, Hull: Research Memorandum No. 8, Centre for Systems Studies, University of Hull, 1995, p. 41.

33 Stein, T., 'A Voice in the Wilderness', *Health Service Journal*, 4 March 1993, p. 30.

34 Wiltshire Users' Network, Fourth Annual Report, 1996, p. 39.

35 Glasman, D., 'The Challenge of Patient Power', *Health Service Journal*, 5 September 1991, pp. 16–17 and 'Divided Opinions', *Health Service Journal*, 12 September 1991, p. 20.

36 Campbell, P., 'In Times of Crisis', *OPENMIND*, 52, 1991, p. 15.

37 Survivors Speak Out, 34 Osnaburgh Street, London NW1 3ND.

38 See for example, Lindow, V., *A Special Place for People in a Special State of Being*, Bristol: Bristol Survivors' Network, 1996.

39 Survivors' Poetry, 34 Osnaburgh Street, London NW1 3ND, Tel.: 0171 916 5317 encourages the development of groups nationally, and has published two anthologies of survivors' poetry.

40 The Hearing Voices Network, Creative Support, Fourways House, 16 Tariff Street, Manchester, Tel.: 0161 228 3896; the initial ideas in Romme, M. and Escher, S. *Accepting Voices*, MIND, 1993.

41 Hambrook, C., 'Healing Through Creativity', *OPENMIND*, 62, 1993, p. 23.

42 Wilson, M., *Crossing the Boundary: Black Women Survive Incest*, London: Virago, 1993, p. 169.

10

ETHICAL CODES

The protection of patients or practitioners?

J. Stuart Horner

The Hippocratic *Oath* is often thought to mark the beginning of ethical practice among doctors. This is, however, largely a modern invention. As Nutton (1993) points out, 'no other document from the ancient world, save for the Bible has undergone so many transformations and yet retains authority today'. Part of the reason for this authority is that the *Oath*, like much of the Hippocratic corpus, is consistent with Christian values, so that it quickly became assimilated into the early Christian church (Temkin, 1991). Indeed, as Nutton (1993) also points out, the *Oath* is frequently cited by those who perceive that Christian values are ebbing and that any given community may be experiencing a decline in ethical standards. Such perceptions were evident in Germany (1960s), Italy (1970s) and Russia (1990s). The decision of the British Medical Association to press for a commitment by all new graduates to an 'updated Hippocratic Oath' in 1995 may reflect similar concerns. Nevertheless, the *Oath* was by no means the only ethical code for doctors, either in antiquity, or since. Nor should it be assumed that the adoption of an ethical code was motivated by purely altruistic considerations. The various Hippocratic writings clearly assert 'that the morality they were advocating was a useful weapon in the struggle for patients' (Nutton, 1993). Similarly, Jonsen (1990) has argued that the *Oath* was almost certainly motivated by professional self-interest and designed to ensure a plentiful supply of patients.

Perhaps, Hippocrates' greatest gift to medicine was the concept of self-regulation. In other times and places, state codes of practice have been used to regulate medical practice. One of the earliest was the Hammurabi stela in Babylonia which, in 1727 BC became 'the first attempt in any culture to protect patients from incompetent doctors' (Carrick, 1985). It covered a wide range of health care professionals, including wet nurses. Following the collapse of Roman civilisation in Western Europe, both the Germanic law codes, and perhaps a similar code in the Ostrogoth Kingdom in Italy, sought to exercise state control over the practice of health care (MacKinney, 1952). In China, South America, India and Egypt the practice of medicine was for long periods under the religious control of priests (McIlrath, 1959) and some detect religious undertones in the Hippocratic *Oath* itself.

Modern professional ethics may be dated to the writings of Thomas Percival, a physician in Manchester, who was asked to adjudicate in a dispute between doctors at the Manchester Royal Infirmary (Leake, 1927). He was much influenced by his contemporary, Thomas Gisborne, a leading Church of England writer who vigorously opposed the utilitarian philosophies of Jeremy Bentham. Gisborne was concerned that medical professionalism should not subvert common fellowship and Christian charity. Although Porter (1993) concludes that Gisborne's text did not have much impact on the subsequent development of medical ethics, Thomas Percival cites him as one who provided helpful criticism on earlier drafts of his *Medical Ethics* (1803). He also acknowledges the contribution of John Gregory, who has been described as 'the first modern figure in Anglo-American medical ethics' (McCullough, 1993). John Gregory published his *Lectures on the duties and qualifications of a physician* in 1772, a year before his death. It is in effect an ethical code, dealing with such subjects as confidentiality; truthfulness, especially if the prognosis is doubtful; taking seriously the suggestions of patients; and not abandoning hopeless or dying cases. It does seem to have been genuinely concerned with the needs of patients, rather than the advancement of doctors. It owed much to the philosopher David Hume's concept of sympathy as a motive which 'activates in us the very same feeling as another person has' (McCullough, 1993).

John Gregory's contribution to medical ethics is overshadowed by the work of Thomas Percival, whose major work *Medical Ethics* was published in 1803, a year before his death. Although suffering from poor eyesight, Percival was a prolific writer, much of it originally intended for his children (Percival, 1779). Indeed on 24 February 1794 he wrote, 'the prosecution of this work [an earlier version of *Medical Ethics*] has been suspended by the death of a beloved son, for whose use it was peculiarly designed' (Percival, 1794). His published work runs to four volumes and many of his conclusions have a striking contemporary relevance two centuries later. Significantly his definitive work on medical ethics (Percival, 1803) also includes a sermon preached by his son at Liverpool in May 1791.

In this sermon the younger Thomas shows the same far-sighted vision as his father and urges the virtues of community care. Even the quaint language cannot conceal the unmistakable meaning.

> It is wisdom therefore and duty not to frustrate the benevolent constitutions of Heaven by dissolving the salutary connections of sickness and transporting into a public asylum those who may, with little aid, enjoy in their own homes, benefits and consolations which, elsewhere, it is in the power of no-one to confer.
>
> (Percival, T. B., 1794)

The importance of Percival's work on ethics cannot be overstated. It led directly to an ethical code adopted by the American Medical Association in 1847 (Leake, 1927). Percival's code includes items we would recognise as ethical in nature, e.g. the importance of confidentiality and truth telling, but it also includes advice about how doctors should relate to one another, i.e. matters of professional etiquette. Leake's assertion that Percival confused the two is however easily dismissed. Not only did Percival clearly distinguish between them, but he also makes it clear that whenever the two are in conflict, ethics always has the primary claim over etiquette. The distinction is a timely reminder in our own day that professional ethics has always had a wider canvas than what is now called 'bioethics'. The issues change over time, a fact which can be well illustrated by reference to the development of medical ethics in the British Medical Association.

Development of ethics within the British Medical Association

The official history of the British Medical Association states that its first ethics committee was established in 1849, just seventeen years after its foundation (Little, 1932). Indeed this was the first of three attempts during the following decade to establish a code of ethics for British doctors. Unlike their American counterparts and most other health care professionals, British doctors have consistently resisted the production of an ethical code (Report of Committee of Inquiry, 1975), although there may be some evidence that the situation is changing. The General Medical Council has now produced 'guidance' under the title *Duties of a Doctor*. Three attractive booklets comprehensively review a wide range of issues affecting all aspects of medical practice. It is difficult to believe that these publications will not be used as a yardstick against which the performance of individual doctors will be assessed. If so, they will have become a *de facto* code.

After its failure to produce an ethical code by 1858, the British Medical Association seemed actively to resist discussion of ethical matters, although there is a tantalising reference to a matter of etiquette (as we would now define it) in the historical record. It was not until 1895 that the Association acceded to requests to include an ethical section at its annual meeting. The resolutions passed were a curious mixture of matters of medical registration; ethical concerns; matters of etiquette; and issues more appropriate to a trade union (BMA Council, 1895).

The Central Ethical Committee was finally established in 1902 and has continued to the present day, although it changed its name and constitution in 1988 to allow members of other professions to join it. Over the years its business has gradually changed. Initially preoccupied with concerns about unqualified practitioners, its agenda quickly became dominated by consideration of relationships between doctors. Indeed a complex machinery was built up to deal with the many problems which arose. Between the two world wars its major concern moved to disputes between doctors and the friendly societies with whom many were in contract. It seems strange that such trade union matters were considered to be the chief concern of an ethical committee, but Percival (1794) gave advice on fees as part of his ethical discourses. The BMA continued to discuss such problems in its ethical committee until at least 1965. Thereafter modern ethical concerns assumed an increasing importance, until by 1980 they had begun to dominate the agenda. The reason is not hard to discover.

Modern ethical concerns

In Seattle on 9 March 1960, Dr Belding Scribner began to dialyse a patient, Clyde Shields. Albert Jonsen (1990) considered that, 'this event marks a suitable inauguration of the era of bioethics'. As the technology became increasingly available, demand quickly exceeded supply, prompting the question which has plagued health services world-wide ever since – 'who should decide which patients should first benefit?' Ramsey (1970) considered that, 'larger questions of ordering medical and social priorities are almost, if not altogether, incorrigible to moral reasoning'. Howard Hiatt (1975) was among the first to argue that rationing was inevitable, although he felt that it should be done by policy makers, not by individual medical practitioners. John Kilner (1990, 230) has put forward an interesting approach to the rationing of scarce medical services. Providing that certain preliminary criteria are met, he suggests that all the remaining facilities should be allocated by lottery.

Campbell (1977) discussed the ethics of medicine in a state health service. In a conclusion pregnant with political overtones in the light of subsequent events, he wrote:

> what is required is a genuinely national health service. Such a service must be national in two senses; firstly, the provision of medical services must become a function of government for all groups in Society; but secondly, in order to control the power of such centralisation, there must be structures at community level that can guide the decisions of priorities that are to be made – in a phrase, decentralised democracy in health care provision.

This stress on the local community has been weakened by recent organisational changes in the National Health Service. Effective health care depends on the commitment of local communities. It cannot be imposed from outside by some national agency unable to relate to the community it serves. Present proposals to abolish the 'internal market' stress the need for active involvement of local communities (Dept of Health, 1997).

Surgical advances, particularly in children, led to new ethical dilemmas (Lorber, 1971), whilst advances in resuscitation led to a new definition of death (BMA, 1980). A special panel was set up by the Association to consider euthanasia (BMA, 1971), following a flurry of parliamentary interest in the matter. The modern era of medical ethics had unquestionably arrived. Pellagrino (1993) has reviewed developments during this period and rather gloomily concludes that: 'Medical ethics is now increasingly a branch of moral philosophy more and more responsive to shifts in philosophical opinion and fashion.' Rather more encouragingly he points out, however, that relativism is less relevant in medicine because the experience of illness and care for the sick are common to us all.

Are, then, matters of professional etiquette a thing of the past? A powerful factor influencing medical ethics historically has been the organisation of health care services. The development of the modern hospital in the eighteenth century brought doctors into close proximity with one another. In an age of manners this created a number of problems which Thomas Percival sought to address. In particular he established the concept of 'the grand round', in which each member of the faculty gave his opinion on the case in a strictly hierarchical fashion, from the most junior to the most senior, and from the surgeons to the physicians. Similarly, careful rules were established at the newly created hospitals to allow the patient to resume care under a former physician, if the latter did not happen to be on duty on the day of the patient's emergency admission (Anderson, 1995).

This trend towards hospital development has now been reversed and the last decade has witnessed a dramatic increase in the pace of change. Large mental hospitals have been closed, often with little thought to the needs of that small but important group of patients who require long term 'asylum'. Services have been totally reorganised to provide 'care in the community'. This is an umbrella term, including any form of care provided outside a hospital; the provision of small residential units often providing 24-hour nursing care near to the patient's perceived 'home'; the accommodation of patients in homes of their own; and the development of a whole variety of day hospitals and day care centres.

It would be extremely surprising if these changes did not cause strains on professional relationships, at least as great as those which occurred during the concentration of patients in large hospitals. In the wider community throughout the history of the National Health Service, the general medical practitioner has been the supreme final authority responsible for the patient's care. A system of specialist referral, painfully worked out ninety years ago, determined the general practitioner's relationship with the hospital consultant. Indeed, if the latter saw patients in their own homes, it was considered good practice to do so only in the presence of the general practitioner. Now, however, consultants may be called in by other health care professionals and see the patient without the general practitioner even being aware of it. Modern primary health care teams provide a wide range of services and a nursing – or other – member of the team may decide he or she requires specialist help. The patient may then be seen by, for example, a community psychiatric nurse, who may accept – or recommend – referral to the day hospital, where the patient is in the care of the specialist psychiatric team, usually led by a consultant. Indeed the patient may simply 'drop in' to a mental health centre without reference to any health care professional. Responsibility is assumed by the consultant and/or the specialist team, without the primary health care team even being aware of the problem. This is not just a matter of professional etiquette. Potentially it may have profound consequences for the safety of the patient. Usually medication can be checked by telephone (although raising the important issue of releasing confidential medical information to an unknown caller).

However, who is now responsible for the patient's care? What happens if a further exacerbation in the patient's condition occurs at a time when the specialist team is no longer on duty? Should the patient be admitted to hospital, or should the general practitioner, who was not involved in the original episode, be contacted? What about the ambulance services, which are increasingly offering 'pre-arrival advice'? Many professional relationships within primary health care teams have still to be resolved – most notably the doctors' automatic assumption of the leadership role. The introduction of specialist health care teams into the community complicates the issues still further. At present, there appears to be no professional forum in which such issues are even being debated, much less resolved. Bioethics tend to dismiss them as merely 'boundary issues between separate professionals'. This approach ignores the practical consequences for patients, which are potentially very serious. Similarly, the increasing interchange of roles between members of the health care team raises issues of training and quality audit.

Developments in other health care professions

Other health care professions have generally followed the pattern of the medical profession. The first task has been to establish a register of suitably qualified practitioners. The General Medical Council was established in 1858 after a long and sometimes bitter struggle. The then Chief Medical Officer (Sir John Simon) seems quickly to have lost patience with it (Lambert, 1963) and a wider concern about its limited powers led to the establishment of a Royal Commission to enquire in the widest sense into its activities (Heseltine, 1949). A General Nursing Council was established in 1919 and under a later Act of 1943 even the title 'nurse', unlike that of 'doctor', became statutorily protected. A wide range of professions supplementary to medicine was able to be registered through an Act passed in 1960, which is currently under review. In recent sessions Parliament has legislated to register the practices of chiropractic and osteopathy, whilst The Royal College of Speech and Language Therapists has set up a system of voluntary registration, including disciplinary procedures, with a view to ultimate statutory recognition. It is customary to assume that these efforts are an altruistic attempt by professionals to put patients before themselves. Waddington (1984) is less certain. He points out that 'the [medical] profession derived significant monopolistic advantages from registration', and claims that the medical profession clearly recognised these advantages 'from the very beginning of the campaign for registration'. Hart (1985) considered that registration is 'a monopoly granted by the state, giving the profession exclusive occupational rights, freedom to control the process of recruitment, training and practise, and control over the conduct of individual members'. Porter (1987) believes that registration is an 'ingenious compromise', whilst Stacey (1992) also believes that 'the interests of the public were a secondary, not a primary, consideration'. Similarly, Weatherall (1996) points out that registration conveniently excluded competing practitioners who used methods which the profession considered 'unscientific'.

The second stage is to secure control of training and professional standards. Registration is a step along this process, but not necessarily related to it. In the last thirty years health care professions have increasingly turned away from doctors for training purposes and gradually assumed total control over their own training requirements. This 'balkanisation' of health care training is potentially damaging in the field of medical ethics, since there are surely some core values to which all health care professionals should seek to aspire.

Relationships between practitioners

A third stage concerns the relationships between qualified practitioners. In a profession like medicine, in which individual practitioners were essentially independent, this involved a process which evolved over many years. In 1908, after three years of consultation and discussion, the British Medical Association produced the Rules of Consultation, which set out when and how a second opinion should be sought. It laid down detailed rules of etiquette affecting a domiciliary consultation between the general practitioner and the hospital-based consultant. This was necessary since many consultants, then, were part time and also engaged in general practice in the same community.

The last twenty years have seen a largely successful campaign to force other groups of doctors practising outside hospitals in very different ways and in different settings into this rigid and inflexible relational pattern. Community health doctors and occupational health doctors have both suffered as a result of these changes. There is little evidence to suggest that the changes are beneficial, either to children and other vulnerable groups, or to employees.

In a hierarchical profession like nursing, intra-professional relationships seemed easier, but are now being exposed to increasing tensions. Should a nurse follow the instructions of her manager (as etiquette requires), or the requirements of her code of conduct (as ethics demands)? In a cash constrained, politically motivated service in which truth telling has become relative (Bruggen 1997, 99), such dilemmas are no longer academic.

Relationships with employers

Health care workers working in a market-based National Health Service are likely to face conflicts of loyalty between the ethical demands of their professions and the commercial requirements of their employers. The advice of the Department of Health (1993) about so-called 'whistle blowing' makes it unambiguously clear that the contractual requirement of confidentiality to the NHS employer overrides any ethical obligations to one's profession or to patients although the current Government's White Paper (Dept of Health, 1997) considerably softens this approach. The price of conscience for a health care worker can be one's professional career and salary. Increasingly discussions are taking place on issues such as the individual ethical responsibilities of health care workers, which arise when staffing levels are poor or inadequate.

There is some evidence that ethical standards are being subtly eroded. A survey of neuroleptic drug use in residential homes (McGrath and Jackson, 1996) showed that 24 per cent of residents were receiving the drugs and 88 per cent of these were being prescribed outside American guidelines for their use. This finding strongly implies that the drugs were being used inappropriately to make patients more compliant and so allow lower staffing levels. Stout (1988) considers that market economics constitute the greatest threat to ethical standards at the present time. It has already been demonstrated that registration is part of an often undisclosed and tacit agreement with the state employer.

For some health care professions it seems inevitable that these stages in the development of ethical codes will be telescoped. The advances in technology over the last twenty years have placed modern ethical concerns at the top of everyone's ethical agenda. Speech therapists working on dysphagia are increasingly being drawn into the debate about advance directives. If they should decide that teaching a patient to eat by normal means creates too great a risk of choking, they may precipitate a decision to offer parenteral nutrition. If the patient has expressed a previous wish not to be fed in this way, the speech therapist's clinical decision may have signed the patient's death warrant. Midwives and gynaecology nurses are daily confronted with the issue of where life begins. Each profession is moving through the stages at its own pace, but each must now deal with the central issues confronting medical ethics today.

Supervisory mechanisms

Few of the health professions appear to have adequate machinery in place to address these modern ethical concerns. The medical and nursing professions each has a registration council established, with an ethics committee in place. Each has a well-defined disciplinary procedure. How then could both professions react so inadequately and inappropriately in two recent cases of euthanasia? In each case society had registered its disapproval through the judicial process. There was therefore no requirement to prove the facts. In the case of Doctor Cox, for example, it was his employers who elected to provide the training and supervision to remedy the deficiencies they considered that they had identified. In a similar case involving nurses an enraged community was reported to be exploring whether it had any options for judicial redress. Self-regulation of the professions is under extreme criticism and, since the Bristol paediatric surgery case, not just from the political right. Such cases do little to reassure either the professions or the public that the registration authorities are regulating adequately the actions of the professionals concerned. The registration authorities must demonstrate that their primary concern is for the protection of patients. Every decision that makes them look like bodies concerned to protect the reputation and livelihood of practitioners makes their long-term survival less likely. Their replacement by some form of state-controlled body, however, would do nothing to protect patients in the longer term. The only solution is some form of internal reform of the present arrangements to provide a greater emphasis upon the patients whom the registration councils exist to protect. In the case of the General Medical Council, Stacey (1992) seems optimistic that such a change in emphasis will be achieved. The response of some senior councillors to her gentle and friendly criticisms is not, however, encouraging. In a paper to the second international conference on medical registration (Stacey, 1996) she outlined six requirements before self-regulation can work well. At least three, and possibly four, of these criteria are not met in the United Kingdom.

Other writers are more forthright. Duncan Campbell (1997) concluded that most doctors who behave unethically are escaping exposure or sanction. The problem is one of the level of proof required. Ever since the GMC was required to reinstate the first doctor it erased from the register, it has demanded levels of proof which it is beyond the ability and competence of many patients to provide. It is right that if draconian measures are being taken against the doctor's livelihood, the profession should be protected against malicious and frivolous complaints. Nevertheless Campbell's conclusion that special methods are needed to support valid complaints must be endorsed if patients are to be protected. Far too few complaints about doctors' unethical behaviour get past the GMC's preliminary procedures. Moreover is the punishment so draconian? Most people assume that erasure from the register (which only takes place for the most serious disciplinary offences) effectively marks the end of the doctor's medical career. It comes as something of a shock to learn that application for reinstatement can be made after only ten months and is usually successful. Figures collected by Smith (1994) appear to show that of those who have actively sought reinstatement, no less than 83.5 per cent have eventually been successful. Thereafter, no mechanisms appear to exist which might warn patients or employers of what may have been an extremely serious breach of trust in the doctor–patient relationship. Moreover, there is some evidence to suggest that reasons for disciplinary action change over time (Smith, 1994, 10) giving the impression that the GMC seeks to draw attention to particular aspects of ethical conduct at different times. Smith (1994) concludes that 'there are, however, important flaws in the operation of the existing structures' and that 'at present, the quality of justice and procedure in relation to the hearing of cases is placed in jeopardy by the under-financing of the jurisdiction' (22).

Approaches to ethical issues

There is nothing in the practice of health care professionals, and even less in their training, which makes them inherently more capable of solving ethical dilemmas although the common 'healing ethos' (Campbell *et al.* 1997) which they all share is a valuable contribution to ethical debate. Brewin (1993) has questioned the value of teaching medical students a smattering of ethical terms. Professional practice undoubtedly allows the ethical problem to be delineated more clearly and ethical training may allow it to be discussed more logically and dispassionately. The so-called four principles (autonomy, benefi-cence, justice, non-malificence) however are soon found to be inadequate. Moody (1992) points out that they are almost entirely inadequate to deal with the problems of geriatric practice. Others have questioned their relevance in paediatric care (Gamston, 1993). Even in acute adult medical practice they are often in conflict with one another, so that a judgement must be made between them.

Equity in health care requires positive action by a health care system which seeks to be comprehensive and usually involves positive discrimination on the side of those most in need of care in a particular community, or even on behalf of whole communities. Yet Whitehead (1994) notes a steady withering of the concept of equity in the National Health Service in the last fifteen years and Hutton (1995) believes that the political consensus on which it was built has now collapsed. Pollock (1995) showed that the private finance initiative is producing damaging effects on the public purse and public account-ability, as well as the founding principles of the NHS – equity, comprehensiveness and universality, whilst a *Lancet* editorial (1995) believes that the NHS has been betrayed. Campbell (1977) points out that public participation in policy decisions is not enough. It can only lead to what John Stuart Mill described as the 'despotism of the majority'. It was Aristotle who pointed out that injustice consists as much in treating unequals equally as treating equals unequally (Lloyd, 1968). Both children and old people need more health care than the rest of the population. Moody (1992) also discusses the dangers of intergenerational inequity in, for example, state pension schemes.

Value systems

The truth is that our ethics are determined by our personal value systems. Percival's ethics were deeply rooted in a belief in God and the nature of man. A survey of members of the Medical Ethics Committee of the British Medical Association revealed that a significant majority believed that the Committee's decision-making was strongly influenced by religious factors. In fact it was by far the most influential of the factors identified. Neuberger (1992) reported a similar finding among members of local research ethics committees. Once again, religious criteria were among the few factors in regular and consistent use. The rise of secularism in the two hundred years since Percival has brought a new group of philosophers to provide their own solutions to these value judgements. Paul Johnson (1988) has tested the performance of some of the leading secular intellectuals in the moral judgements they have made in their personal lives and has found it sadly wanting. The decline in religious belief, although less dramatic in the health care professions than in society at large, means that many younger members now have no personal value system, other than some poorly digested deist or humanist ideas. When confronted with such everyday dilemmas as 'should I always tell the patient the truth?'; 'is it ever right to kill a patient?'; 'is this conceptus a living human being?', they have neither training nor value system to guide them. It should surprise no-one if they crumple under the strain, adopting either a position of moral indifference, or exhibiting obvious stress-related symptoms. Respect for teachers (a feature of most ethical codes) is no guide if what the teacher is doing may be technically right, but is morally wrong.

Nurses in particular face such problems in many practical situations. Confronted with the legal emphasis on autonomy, they are often left to ensure that the patient's consent is 'informed'. Pressure of time or the instructions of an unhelpful manager may lead them to suppose, erroneously, that the legal requirement is satisfied by a freely given signature on a piece of paper. The doctor's refusal to write 'do not resuscitate' in the medical notes requires them to resuscitate a lovely elderly lady, exactly like their own grandmothers, who has repeatedly told them that she wants no heroics and to be left to die quietly. The nurse sees tiny babies denied food and given drugs to keep them drowsy. Should she protest? She sees a doctor or a senior nursing colleague apparently break patient confidence for reasons she assumes to be valid but which are never explained to her. Is confidentiality now relative for the patient and only absolute for the employer?

It is interesting that the reluctance of doctors to record a 'do not resuscitate decision' often arises from a perception that it is inappropriate to discuss with a patient who has been admitted for a procedure carrying relatively little risk, the possibility that the patient may die of something else. It does not seem to be appreciated that the very fact of hospital admission has inadvertently given the patient a greater degree of protection from the normal risks of life in the community. If cardiac arrest occurs outside hospital a 'crash team' will not be immediately available. Percival (1794, 6) had no such scruples. He concluded that where there was any risk that the patient might die during a hospital admission, he should be encouraged to make a will. He also thought the discussion should be initiated by the one in closest contact with the patient – in his case the house surgeon.

Most importantly of all, each of the health care professions is trying to grapple with the same ethical problems, but independently of one another. There are praiseworthy exceptions, such as the two sets of guidelines issued by the BMA and the RCN (1993). There seem to be no mechanisms, however, where the professions can jointly discuss the urgent ethical dilemmas of euthanasia, human fertilisation and embryology, and the new genetics.

A co-ordinated approach

A possible solution might be a single professional ethics body, incorporating all the health care professions. There are, however, formidable problems with the creation of such a body. The Nuffield Foundation has established a national bioethics committee to look at the impact of scientific advance and its possible ethical implications. There are a number of organisations, such as the Institute of Medical Ethics, which offer a multi-disciplinary forum for the discussion of ethical problems. Like members of the Appleton Consensus on aspects of euthanasia (Stanley, 1992), they are largely self-selected and their views do not necessarily carry the support of other organisations to which they belong, or by whom they may be sponsored. Neither do they achieve the purpose of this chapter. A working group of the Institute of Medical Ethics considered the problems associated with medical research in children (Nicholson, 1986). The group was certainly composed of representatives of a wide range of professional disciplines. Yet of the nineteen members, although eight list a medical qualification, only one records a nursing qualification (and she is known to have been out of active nursing practice for many years, although she writes extensively on nursing matters). None lists a qualification supplementary to medicine within the meaning of the Act.

The most appropriate way forward would seem to be the use of existing ethical structures within the professions themselves. In 1988 the British Medical Association changed the constitution of its Medical Ethics Committee to allow the participation of other professions. A distinguished professor of nursing used to sit on the Committee and was also involved in the General Medical Council (GMC). The chair of the BMA Medical Ethics Committee is invited to contribute to the work of the GMC's Professional Standards Committee. The UKCC sought nominations from other professions to sit on the Standards and Ethics Committee which it has now disbanded. A number of smaller health care professions meet together from time to time to discuss ethical matters, although they have lately been finding difficulty in identifying a sufficiently comprehensive agenda to attract the various groups involved. One needs some ethical training even to recognise a potential ethical problem.

The health care professions need to recognise that they are part of a single community. Berwick *et al.* (1997) have argued in a **BMJ** editorial that there should be a single ethical code to which everyone in health care could subscribe by developing common structures and cross representation they can begin to act in a communitarian way, rather than in a traditional isolationist one. If such cross fertilisation between the health care professions could be fostered and widened, a broad consensus might also begin to emerge on these difficult ethical dilemmas. Such a consensus would be more likely to command respect and acceptance among all the professions, since they would have a greater sense of ownership from their participation, than if one profession alone were consistently seen to be taking the lead. Cross representation would help to reduce, but not eliminate, the risk that the individual professions reached different conclusions on the same ethical issue. Moreover, if all the professions were working to a common agenda, there might be less antagonism when, at the level of an individual patient, one health care professional challenged or reported the actions of a colleague in a different discipline. In the absence of a formal code of conduct, the medical profession has always endorsed the principle laid down by Dr W. H. Michael in 1853, namely that ethical recommendations are a guide to which all should aspire, but which not everyone will attain (Report, 1853). In the teamwork characteristic of the best of current clinical practice it is essential that those who believe the particular circumstances of an individual case warrant an exception from the general rule, should share those insights with those who are likely to be closely involved in the implementation of the decision.

Such an approach would also demonstrate a commitment by all health care professions to the best interests of patients. This commitment would be further confirmed by the inclusion of distinguished representatives from moral philosophy and from theological and legally qualified members. By broadening the membership of individual ethics committees in this way, and allowing the mutual exchange of helpful insights, professional ethics will be seen to be designed for the best interests of the patient, rather than as a mechanism for the protection of the practitioner.

REFERENCES

Achterhuis, H., *Het rijk van de schaarste van Thomas Hobbes tot Michel Foucault*, Baarn: Ambo, 1988.

Airaksinen, T., *Ethics of Coercion and Authority: A Philosophical Study of Social Life*, Pittsburgh: Pittsburgh University Press, 1988a.

—— 'An Analysis of Coercion', *Journal of Peace Research*, 25, 1988b, pp. 213–227.

Alexander. J., *Fin de Siècle Social Theory*, London: Verso, 1995.

Alford, C. F., *The Self in Social Theory*, New Haven: Yale University Press, 1991.

Anderson, G. H., 'Lancaster's House of Recovery', *Lancaster and Westmoreland Medical Journal*, 2, 1995, p. 84.

Andrews, K., 'Overdosing on Freedom', *OPENMIND*, 54, 1992, p. 10.

Aquinas, T., *Summa Theologiae*, vol. 28, London: Blackfriars, Eyre and Spottiswoode; New York: McGraw-Hill, 1966.

Aristotle, *The Metaphysics I–IX* [Loeb ed.], London: Heinemann; Cambridge: Harvard University Press, 1932/1967.

—— *Politics*, London: Heinemann; Cambridge: Harvard University Press. 1933/1967.

—— *The Nicomachean Ethics*, London: Heinemann; Cambridge: Harvard University Press, 1926/1967.

Avineri, S. and de Shalit, A., *Communitarianism and Individualism*, Oxford: Oxford University Press, 1992.

Banerjee, S., Bingley, W. and Murphy, E., *Deaths of Detained Patients*, London: The Mental Health Foundation, 1995.

Barham, P., *Schizophrenia and Human Value*, London: FAB, 1993.

Baruch, G. and Treacher, A., *Psychiatry Observed*, London: Routledge and Kegan Paul, 1978, p. 42.

Bauman, Z., *Postmodern Ethics*, Oxford: Blackwell, 1993.

Beauchamp, T. and Childress, J., *Principles of Biomedical Ethics*, second edition, New York: Oxford University Press, 1983.

Beck, U., *Ecological Enlightenment*, New Jersey: Humanities Press, 1995.

Beck, U. and Beck-Gernsheim, E.,*The Normal Chaos of Love*, translated by Ritter, M. and Wiebel, J., Cambridge: Polity Press, 1995.

REFERENCES

Beliappa, J., *Illness or Distress? Alternative Models of Mental Distress*, London: Confederation of Indian Organisations, 1991.

Bell, D., *Communitarianism and its Critics*, Oxford: Oxford University Press, 1993.

Berlin, I., 'Two Concepts of Liberty', in *Four Essays on Liberty*, London: Oxford University Press, 1969.

Berwick, D., Hiatt, H., Janeway, P. and Smith, R., 'An Ethical Code for Everybody in Health Care', *British Medical Journal*, 315, 1997, pp. 1633–1634:

Blackhall, L. J., 'Must We Always Use CPR?', *New England Journal of Medicine*, 317, 20, 1987, pp. 1,281–1,285.

Blackstone, W., *Commentaries on the Laws of England in Four Books*, fourth edition, ed. Thomas Colley in two volumes, Chicago, 1899.

Blaska, B., 'What it Feels Like to be Treated Like a CMI – and Prevailing Over It', *Changes* 10, 4, 1992, p. 284.

Blum, L., 'Vocation, Friendship and Community', in Blum, L., *Moral Perception and Particularity*, Cambridge: Harvard University Press, 1994.

Blustein, J., 'The Family in Medical Decision Making', *Hastings Center Report*, 23, 3, 1993, pp. 6–13.

Boyle, M., 'Schizophrenia: The Fallacy of Diagnosis', *Changes*, 14, 1, 1996, pp. 5–13.

—— *Schizophrenia: A Scientific Delusion?*, London: Fontana, 1990.

Breggin, P., *Toxic Psychiatry: Drugs and Electroconvulsive Therapy: The Truth and the Better Alternatives*, London: Fontana Paperback, 1993.

—— 'Should the Use of Neuroleptics be Severely Limited?', *Changes*, 14, 1, 1996, pp. 62–66.

Brewin, T. B., 'How Much Ethics is Needed to Make a Good Doctor?, *Lancet*, 341, 1993, pp. 161–163.

British Medical Association, *The Problem of Euthanasia*, a report by a special panel appointed by the Board of Science and Education, London: BMA, 1971.

—— *Handbook of Medical Ethics*, London, BMA, 1980, p. 31.

—— *Euthanasia*, Report of a Working Party, London: BMA, 1988.

—— *Medical Ethics Today: Its Practice and Philosophy*, London, BMA, 1993, p. 285.

British Medical Association and Royal College of Nursing, *Tracheal Intubation of Recently Deceased Patients for Teaching Purposes*, London: BMA, 1993.

—— *Decisions Relating to Cardiopulmonary Resuscitation*, London: BMA, 1993.

British Medical Association Council, *Minute 3322*, 23 October 1895.

Bruggen, P., *Who Cares? True Stories of the NHS Reforms,* Charlebury, Oxfordshire: Jon Carpenter Publishing, 1997.

189

REFERENCES

Buchanan, A. E. and Brock, D. W., *Deciding for Others: The Ethics of Surrogate Decision Making*, Cambridge: Cambridge University Press, 1989.

Burleigh, M., 'Death in the Community', *Asylum*, 9, 2, 1995, pp. 11–12.

Butler, R., 'Forgotten Figures: Mental Health and the Irish in Britain', *OPENMIND*, 70, 1994, pp. 16–17.

Butler, M. A., 'Early Liberal Roots of Feminism: John Locke and the Attack on Patriarchy', in Shanley, M. C. and Pateman, C. (eds), *Feminist Interpretations and Political Theory*, Cambridge: Polity, 1991, pp. 74–94.

Callahan, D., *The Tyranny of Survival*, New York: MacMillan, 1973.

—— 'On Defining a "Natural Death". An Ideal for Public Policy', *Hastings Center Report*, 7, 6, 1977, pp. 32–36.

—— *Setting Limits: Medical Goals in an Ageing Society*, New York and London: Simon and Schuster, 1987.

—— 'Afterword: Daniel Callahan Responds to his Critics', in Homer, P. and Holstein, M. (eds) *A Good Old Age? The Paradox of Setting Limits*, New York: Simon and Schuster, 1990.

—— *The Troubled Dream of Life*, New York: Simon and Schuster, 1993.

Campbell, A., Charlesworth, M., Gillett, G. and Jones, G., *Medical Ethics*, Oxford: Oxford University Press, 1997.

Campbell, A. V., 'Establishing Ethical Priorities in Medicine', *British Medical Journal*, 1, 1977, pp. 818–821.

Campbell, D., 'Medicine Needs Its MI5', *British Medical Journal*, 315, 1997, pp. 1,677–1,680.

Campbell, P., 'In Times of Crisis', *OPENMIND*, 52, 1991, p. 15.

Campbell, T., *Justice*, Basingstoke: MacMillan, 1990.

Carrick, P., *Medical Ethics in Antiquity*, Dordrecht, Holland: D. Reidel Publishing Company, 1985.

Choice in Dying, *Refusal of Treatment Legislation*, New York: Choice in Dying, 1994.

Claridge, G., 'Can a Disease Model Survive?', in Bentall, R. (ed.), *Reconstructing Schizophrenia*, London: Routledge, 1990, p. 178.

Cocks, J., *The Oppositional Imagination: Feminism, Critique and Political Theory*, London: Routledge, 1989, pp. 128–135.

Commentary, *Medical Law Review*, 1, 2 , 1993, pp. 271–273.

Cooper, C., 'The Loony Bin Trip', *OPENMIND*, 52, 1991, p. 13.

Crow, T. J. (ed.), 'Recurrent and Chronic Psychoses', Edinburgh: Churchill Livingstone, 1987, cited in Claridge, *Can a Disease Model Survive?*.

Cummings, J. L. and Jarvik, L. F., 'Dementia', in C. K. Cassel *et al.* (eds), *Geriatric Medicine*, second edition, New York: Springer-Verlag, 1990, pp. 428–448.

Cusk, R., 'How We Turn Children into our Battlefield', *The Guardian*, 3 December 1996.

Danley, J., 'Liberalism, Aboriginal Rights and Cultural Minorities', *Philosophy and Public Affairs*, 20, 2, 1993, pp. 168–185.

REFERENCES

Darton, K., Gorman, J. and Sayce, L., *Eve Fights Back: The Successes of MIND's Stress on Women Campaign*, London: MIND Publications, 1994.

Deegan, P. E., 'Spirit Breaking: When the Helping Professionals Hurt', *The Humanistic Psychologist*, 18, 3, 1990, pp. 301–313.

Delphy, C., *Close to Home: A Materialist Analysis of Women's Oppression*, translated and edited by Diana Leonard, London: Hutchinson, in association with the Explorations in Feminism Collective, 1984.

Department of Health, *Guidance for Staff on Relations with the Public and Media*, Annex to EL(93)51, Leeds: NHS Management Executive, 1993.

—— *The New NHS*, Cm. 3807, London: HMSO, 1997.

Devereux, J. A., Jones, D. P. H. and Dickenson, D. L., 'Can Children Refuse Consent to Treatment?', *British Medical Journal*, 306, 29 May 1993, pp. 459–461.

De Vries, K., *Organisational Paradoxes*, London: Routledge, 1995.

Dickenson, D. and Jones, D., 'True Wishes: The Philosophy and Developmental Psychology of Children's Informed Consent', *Philosophy, Psychiatry and Psychology*, 2, 4, December 1995, pp. 287–303.

Dickenson, D., *Property, Women and Politics: Subjects or Objects?*, Cambridge: Polity Press, 1997.

Dobson. R., 'On the Cheap', *Community Care*, 2–8 March 1995a.

—— 'Social Nightmare', *Community Care*, Supplement, 27April–3 May 1995b.

Downie, R. and Calman, K., *Healthy Respect: Ethics in Health Care*, London: Faber and Faber, 1987, p. 61.

Dresser, R., 'Life, Death, and Incompetent Patients: Conceptual Infirmities and Hidden Values in the Law', *Arizona Law Review*, 28, 1986, pp. 373–405.

Dresser, R. and Robertson, J. A., 'Quality of Life and Non-Treatment Decisions for Incompetent Patients: A Critique of the Orthodox Approach', *Law, Medicine, and Health Care*, 17, 1989, pp. 234–244.

Dumont, M. P., 'In Bed Together at the Market: Psychiatry and the Pharmaceutical Industry', *American Journal of Orthopsychiatry*, 60, 4, 1990, pp. 484–485.

Durkheim E., *Suicide: A Study in Society*, London: Routledge, 1950.

Dworkin, R., *Taking Rights Seriously*, London: Duckworth, 1977.

Editorial, 'Betrayal of the NHS', *Lancet*, 346, 1995, p. 651.

Eekelaar, J., 'Commentary on "True Wishes" ', *Philosophy, Psychiatry and Psychology*, 2, 4, December 1995, pp. 304–306.

Eisenstein, Z., *The Radical Future of Liberal Feminism*, New York: Longman, 1981.

Elshtain, J. B., *Public Man, Private Woman: Women in Social and Political Thought*, Oxford: Martin Robertson, 1984, pp. 108–146.

Emanuel, E. J., *The Ends of Human Life: Medical Ethics in a Liberal Polity*, Cambridge, Mass. and London: Harvard University Press, 1991.

REFERENCES

Emanuel, E. J. and Emanuel, L. L., 'Proxy Decision Making for Incompetent Patients: An Ethical and Empirical Analysis', *Journal of the American Medical Association*, 267, 15, 1992, pp. 2,067–2,071.

Emanuel, L. L. and Emanuel, E. J., 'Decisions at the End of Life: Guided by Communities of Patients', *Hastings Center Report*, 23, 5, 1993, pp. 6–14.

Enthoven, A. C., *Reflections on the Management of the National Health Service: An American Looks at Incentives to Efficiency in Health Services Management in the UK*, London: Nuffield Provincial Hospitals Trust, 1985.

Etzioni, A., *The Moral Dimension: Towards a New Economics*, New York: MacMillan, 1988.

—— *The Spirit of Community*, Fontana: London, 1993.

—— *The London Times*, 20 February 1995.

—— *The Guardian*, 13 March 1995.

Feinberg, J., *Social Philosophy*, New Jersey, Englewood Cliffs: Prentice-Hall, 1973.

Fernando, S., *Mental Health, Race and Culture*, Basingstoke, Macmillan/MIND, 1991.

Filmer, R., *Patriarcha*, ed. P. Laslett, Oxford: Blackwell, 1949.

Finucane, T. E. *et al.*, 'Planning with Elderly Outpatients for Contingencies of Severe Illness: A Survey and Clinical Trial', *Journal of General Internal Medicine*, 3, 4, 1988, pp. 322–325.

Fleck, L. M., 'Justice, HMOs, and the Invisible Rationing of Health Care Resources', *Bioethics*, 4, 2, 1990, pp. 97–120.

Flew, A., *Thinking About Social Thinking*, second edition, London: Fontana Press, Harper Collins, 1991.

Foucault, M., *Naissance de la clinique. Une archeologie du regard medical*, Paris: Presses Universitaires de France, 1963.

—— *Resumé des cours 1970–1982*, Paris: Julliard, 1989.

Frank, L. R., 'Electroshock: Death, Brain Damage, Memory Loss and Brainwashing', in Cohen, D. (ed.), *Challenging the Therapeutic State: Critical Perspectives on Psychiatry and the Mental Health System*, New York: The Journal of Mind and Behaviour, 1990, pp. 219–242.

Fried, C., *Right and Wrong*, Cambridge, Massachusetts: Harvard University Press, 1978, pp. 9ff.

Gamble, E. R., McDonald, P. J. and Lichstein, P. R., 'Knowledge, Attitudes, and Behavior of Elderly Persons Regarding Living Wills', *Archives of Internal Medicine*, 151, 2, 1991, pp. 277–280.

Gamston, F. E. and Horner, J. S., *Innovative Therapy and Research in Children: A More Realistic Approach to Consent*, Occasional Paper Number 1, University of Central Lancashire: Centre for Professional Ethics, 1996.

Gatens, M., *Feminism and Philosophy*, Oxford: Polity Press, 1991.

Ghosh, M., letter published in *Cahoots* 52, April–June 1995, p. 2.

REFERENCES

Gilligan, C., *In a Different Voice*, Cambridge, Mass. and London: Harvard University Press, 1982.

Glasman, D., 'The Challenge of Patient Power', *Health Service Journal*, 5 September 1991, pp. 16–17.

—— 'Divided Opinions', *Health Service Journal*, 12 September 1991, p. 20.

Glendinning, C. and Millar, J., (eds), *Women and Poverty in Britain: The 1990s*, Hemel Hempstead: Harvester Wheatsheaf, 1992.

Green, L., 'Internal Minorities and Their Rights', in *The Rights of Minority Cultures*, ed. Will Kymlicka, Oxford: Oxford University Press, 1995.

Gutman, A., 'Communitarian Critics of Liberalism' in *Communitarianism and Individualism*, ed. Avineri, S. and de Shalit, A., Oxford: Oxford University Press, 1992.

Habermas, J., *Justification and Application: Remarks on Discourse Ethics*, Oxford: Polity, 1993.

Haldane, J., 'Identity, Community and the Limits of Multiculture', *Public Affairs Quarterly*, 7, 3, 1993, pp. 199–214.

Hambrook, C., 'Healing Through Creativity', *OPENMIND*, 62, 1993, p. 23.

Hardwig, J., 'What About the Family?' *Hastings Center Report*, 20, 2, 1990, pp. 5–10.

Harre, R. and Gillett, G., *The Discursive Mind*, London: Sage, 1994.

Hart, N., *The Sociology of Health and Medicine*, Causeway Books, 1985, p. 112.

Häyry, H., *The Limits of Medical Paternalism*, London: Routledge, 1991.

Häyry, M., 'Moral Relativism and the Philosophical Criticism of Other Cultures', *Science Studies*, 5, 1, 1992, pp. 53–56.

Heginbotham, C., *Return to Community*, London, Bedford Square, 1990.

Heseltine, M., 'The Early History of the General Medical Council 1858–1886', *The Medical Press*, 222, 1949, pp. 3–52.

Hewlett, S. A., *A Lesser Life: The Myth of Women's Liberation*, London: Michael Joseph, 1987.

Hiatt, H., 'Protecting the Medical Commons: Who is Responsible?', *New England Journal of Medicine*, 235, 1975, pp. 235–240.

High, C., 'All in the Family: Extended Autonomy and Expectations in Surrogate Health Care Decision-Making', *The Gerontologist*, 28 (Supplement), 1988, pp. 46–51.

—— 'Standards for Surrogate Decision-Making: What the Elderly Want', *Journal of Long Term Care Administration*, 17, 1989, pp. 8–13.

—— 'Families' Roles in Advance Directives', *Hastings Center Report* 24, 6 (Special Supplement), 1994, S16–18.

Hirschmann, N. J., *Rethinking Obligation: A Feminist Method for Political Theory*, Ithaca and London: Cornell, 1992, pp. 55ff.

Holmes C., 'Attachment Theory: A Secure Base for Policy', in Kraemer, S. and Roberts J. (eds), *The Politics of Attachment*, London: Free Assoc. Books, 1996.

REFERENCES

Howard, R., 'Cultural Absolutism and the Nostalgia for Community', *Human Rights Quarterly*, 15, 2, 1993, pp. 315–338.

Hutton, W., *The State We're In*, London: Vintage, 1995.

Johnson, P., *Intellectuals*, London: Weidenfeld and Nicholson, 1988.

Jonsen, A. R., *The New Medicine and the Old Ethics*, Cambridge, Massachussetts: Harvard University Press, 1990, p. 171.

Kant, I., 'Social Contract as an Idea of Reason', in Lessnoff, M., *Social Contract Theory*, Oxford: Basil Blackwell, 1990.

Kilner, J. F., *Who Lives? Who Dies? Ethical Criteria in Patient Selection*, Newhaven and London: Yale University Press, 1990.

Kitzinger, C. and Perkins, R., *Changing Our Minds: Lesbian Feminism and Psychology*, London: Only Women Press, 1993.

Kuczewski, M. G., 'Whose Will is it Anyway? A Discussion of Advance Directives, Personal Identity, and Consensus in Medical Ethics', *Bioethics*, 8, 1, 1994, pp. 27–48.

Kukathas, C., 'Are There Any Cultural Rights?', *Political Theory*, 20, 1, 1992, pp. 105–139.

Kymlicka, W., *Liberalism, Community and Culture*, Oxford: Clarendon Press, 1989.

—— *Contemporary Political Philosophy: An Introduction*, Oxford: Clarendon Press, 1990.

—— 'Response to Kukathas', *Political Theory*, 20, 1, 1992, pp. 140–146.

—— 'Some Questions about Justice and Community', in Bell, D., *Communitarianism and its Critics*.

—— (ed.), *The Rights of Minority Cultures*, Oxford: Oxford University Press, 1995.

Lambert, R., *Sir John Simon 1816–1904 and English Social Administration*, London, MacGibbon and Kee, 1963, pp. 324–325.

La Puma, J., Orentlicher, D. and Moss, R. J., 'Advance Directives on Admission: Clinical Implications and Analysis of the Patient Self-Determination Act of 1990', *Journal of the American Medical Association*, 266, 3, 1991, pp. 402–405.

Leake, C. D., *Percival's Medical Ethics*, Baltimore: Williams and Wilkins Co., 1927.

Liberty, *People with Mental Health Problems and Learning Difficulty*, Human Rights Convention Report 1, London: National Council for Civil Liberties/MIND, 1993, p. 266.

Lindemann Nelson, H. and J., 'Preferences and Other Moral Sources', *Hastings Center Report*, 24, 6 (Special Supplement), 1995, S19–21.

—— *The Patient in the Family: An Ethics of Medicine and Families*, New York and London: Routledge, 1994.

Lindemann Nelson, J., 'Taking Families Seriously', *Hastings Center Report*, 22, 4, 1992, pp. 6–12.

Lindow, V., *A Special Place for People in a Special State of Being*, Bristol: Bristol Survivors' Network, 1996.

REFERENCES

—— 'Experts, Lies and Stereotypes', *Health Service Journal*, 101, 5,267, 1991, pp. 18–19.

Lister, R., *Women's Economic Dependency and Social Security*, Manchester: Equal Opportunities Commission, 1992.

Little, E. M., *History of the British Medical Association 1832–1932*, London: British Medical Association, 1932.

Lloyd, G. E. R., *Aristotle : The Growth and Structure of his Thought*, Cambridge: Cambridge University Press, 1968, p. 261.

Lo, B., McLeod, G. A. and Saika, G., 'Patient Attitudes to Discussing Life-Sustaining Treatment', *Archives of Internal Medicine*, 146, 8, 1986, pp. 1,613–1,615.

Locke, J., *Two Treatises on Government*, Cambridge: Cambridge University Press, 1967.

Lorber, J., 'Results of Treatment of Myelomeningocele', *Developmental Medicine and Child Neurology*, 13, 1971, p. 279.

Lynn, J., 'Why I Don't Have a Living Will', *Law, Medicine and Health Care*, 19, 1–2, 1991, pp. 101–104.

MacIntyre, A., *After Virtue*, London: Duckworth, 1984.

—— 'The Spectre of Communitarianism', *Radical Philosophy*, 70, March/April 1995, p. 35.

MacKinney, L. C., 'Medical Ethics and Etiquette in the Early Middle Ages: The Persistence of Hippocratic Ideals', *Bulletin of the History of Medicine* , 18, 1952, pp. 371–412.

MacLean, M., *Surviving Divorce: Women's Resources after Separation*, London: Macmillan, 1991.

McCullough, L. B., 'John Gregory's Medical Ethics and Humean Sympathy', in *The Codification of Medical Morality*, Baker, R., Porter, D. and Porter, R. (eds), Dordrecht/Boston/London: Kluwer Academic Publishers, 1993.

McGrath, A. M. and Jackson, A., 'Survey of Neuroleptic Prescribing in Residents of Nursing Homes in Glasgow', *British Medical Journal*, 312, 1996, p. 611.

McIlrath, M. B., 'History of Medical Ethics in the Non-Christian World Before the Rise of Modern Medicine', MD Thesis in the University of Sydney, 1959.

Manoledakes, I., 'Scientific and Legal Problems Concerning the Phenomenon of AIDS', *Bulletin* (Quarterly Edition of the Hellenic Centre for the Control of AIDS and STDs), 2, 1996, p. 7.

Masters, P., 'Brainstorm', *OPENMIND*, 49, 1991, p. 15.

Meisel, A., *The Right to Die*, second edition, New York and Chichester: John Wiley and Sons, Inc, 1995.

Mendus, S., 'Strangers and Brothers', in Milligan, D. and Watts-Miller, W., *Liberalism, Citizenship and Autonomy*, Aldershot: Avebury, 1992.

Mill, J. S. *On Liberty*, New York: Prometheus Books, 1986.

Moody, H. R., *Ethics in an Ageing Society*, Baltimore: John Hopkins University Press, 1992.

REFERENCES

Morgan, R. F., *Electroshock: The Case Against*, Toronto: IPI Publishing, 1991.

Mount, F., *The Subversive Family: An Alternative History of Love and Marriage*, New York: Free Press, 1982.

Mulberg, J., *Social Limits to Economic Theory*, London: Routledge, 1995.

Mullan, B., *Mad to be Normal: Conversations with R.D. Laing*, London: Free Association Books, 1995.

Neuberger, J., *Ethics and Health Care – The Role of Research Committees in the United Kingdom*, Research Report no. 13, London: King's Fund Institute, 1992.

Neugarten, B. L., 'Social and Psychological Characteristics of Older Persons', in Cassel, C. K. *et al.* (eds) *Geriatric Medicine*, second edition, New York: Springer-Verlag, 1990, pp. 28–37.

Nicholson, R. H., *Medical Research with Children: Ethics, Law and Practice*, Oxford: Oxford University Press, 1986.

Nussbaum, M., *Nature, Function, and Capability: Aristotle on Political Distribution*, WIDER Working Paper 31, Helsinki: UNU/WIDER Publications, 1987.

—— 'Non-Relative Virtues. An Aristotelian Approach', in Nussbaum, M. and Sen, A. (eds), *The Quality of Life*, Oxford: Clarendon Press, 1993.

Nutton, V., 'Beyond the Hippocratic Oath', in Wear, A., Geyer-Kordesh, J. and French, R. (eds), *Doctors and Ethics*, Amsterdam/Atlanta: G. A., Rodopi, 1993.

Oakeshott, M., *On Human Conduct*, Oxford: Clarendon Press, 1975.

—— 'The Rule of Law', in his *On History and Other Essays*, Oxford: Blackwell, 1983.

—— 'Introduction to Leviathan', in his *Rationalism in Politics and Other Essays*, expanded edition, Indianapolis: Liberty Press, 1991.

Okin, S. M., *Women in Western Political Thought*, Princeton: Princeton University Press, 1980, pp. 200–201.

O'Neill, O., 'Justice, Gender and International Boundaries', in Nussbaum, M. and Sen, A. (eds), *The Quality of Life*, Oxford: Clarendon Press, 1993.

Pahl, J., *Money and Marriage*, London and Basingstoke: Macmillan, 1989.

Parker, M. *The Growth of Understanding*, Aldershot: Avebury, 1995.

—— 'Liberalism and Its Problems', *Cogito*, July 1996.

—— 'Communitarianism and Its Problems', *Cogito*, November 1996.

—— 'What is Communitarianism?', Paper for Riverside Mental Health Trust, Ethics Committee, unpublished, 1995.

Pateman, C., *The Sexual Contract*, Cambridge: Polity Press, 1988.

Pellagrino, E. D., 'The Metamorphosis of Medical Ethics: A Thirty-Year Perspective', *Journal of the American Medical Association*, 269, 1993, pp. 1,158–1,162.

Percival, T., *A Father's Instructions Consisting of Moral Tales, Fables and Reflections*, London: J. Johnson, 1779.

—— *Medical Jurisprudence*, Manchester: Nicholson and Co., 1794.

—— *Medical Ethics; or a Code of Institutes and Precepts Adapted to the Professional Conduct of Physicians and Surgeons*, London: J. Johnson, 1803.

Percival, T. B., *A Discourse Addressed to the Faculty, Officers and Clergy at Liverpool Infirmary*, Manchester: Nicholson and Co., 1794, p. 11.

Podvoll, E. M., *The Seduction of Madness: A Compassionate Approach to Recovery at Home*, London: Century, 1990.

Pollock, A. M., 'The NHS Goes Private', *Lancet*, 346, 1995, pp. 683–684.

Porter, R., *Disease, Medicine and Society in England 1550–1860*, London: MacMillan, 1987, p. 51.

—— *Thomas Gisborne;* Physicians, Christians and Gentlemen in *Doctors and Ethics*, Amsterdam and Atlanta: G. A. Rodopi, 1993.

President's Commission for the Study of Ethical Problems in Medicine and Biomedical and Behavioral Research, *Making Health Care Decisions*, Volume 1: Report, Washington, DC: US Government Printing Office, 1982.

Ramsey, P., *Patient as a Person*, New Haven: Yale University Press, 1970, p. 240.

Rawls, J., *Theory of Justice*, Cambridge, Mass.: Harvard University Press, 1971.

—— *Political Liberalism*, New York: Columbia University Press, 1993.

Reeve, T., *The Law of Baron and Feme, of Parent and Child, of Guardian and Ward, of Master and Servant, and of the Powers of Courts of Chancery*, New Haven, 1816.

Report of the Committee of Inquiry into the Medical Profession London, HMSO, Cmnd 6018, 1975, pp. 91–92.

Report of the Twenty-First Anniversary Meeting, *British Medical Journal*, 1853, pp. 738–740.

Richardson, W. J., 'Lacanian Theory', in Rothstein, A. (ed.), *Models of the Mind*, Madison, London: American Psychoanalytic Association (IUP), 1985.

Roberts, M., 'Beyond Revisionism', London: *Radical Philosophy*, 73, 1991.

Robertson, J. A., 'Second Thoughts on Living Wills', *Hastings Center Report*, 21, 6, 1991, pp. 6–9.

Romme, M. and Escher, S., *Accepting Voices*, MIND, 1993.

Rorty, R., *Contingency, Irony, and Solidarity*, Cambridge: Cambridge University Press, 1989.

Rose, C. M., 'Women and Property: Gaining and Losing Ground', in *Property and Persuasion: Essays on the History, Theory and Rhetoric of Ownership*, Boulder, Colorado: Westview Press, 1994, pp. 233–263.

Rose, D., *Living in the Community*, London: The Sainsbury Centre for Mental Health, 1996.

Rustin, M., 'Incomplete Modernity: Ulrich Beck's Risk Society', *Radical Philosophy*, 67, 1994, p. 5.

Salmon, M., *Women and the Law of Property in Early America*, Chapel Hill and London: University of North Carolina Press, 1986.

REFERENCES

Sandel, M., *Liberalism and the Limits of Justice*, Cambridge: Cambridge University Press, 1982.

Sayce, L., *Breaking the Link Between Homosexuality and Mental Illness*, London: MIND, 1995.

Sayers, S., 'The Value of Community', London, *Radical Philosophy*, 69, Jan/Feb 1995.

Schneiderman, L. J., Jecker, N. S. and Jonsen, A. R., 'Medical Futility: Its Meaning and Ethical Implications', *Annals of Internal Medicine*, 112, 12, 1990, pp. 949–954.

Seckler, A. B., Meier, D. E., Mulvihill, M. and Cammer Paris, B. E., 'Substituted Judgment: How Accurate are Proxy Predictions?', *Annals of Internal Medicine*, 115, 2, 1991, pp. 92–98.

Seedhouse, D., *Health: The Foundations for Achievement*, Chichester: John Wiley, 1986.

Sen, A., *On Ethics and Economics*, Oxford: Blackwell, 1987.

—— 'Capability and Well-Being', in *The Quality of Life*, Nussbaum, M. and Sen, A. (eds), Oxford: Clarendon, 1993.

Showalter, E., *The Female Malady: Women, Madness and Culture 1830–1980*, London: Virago, 1985.

Smith, R. G., *Medical Discipline*, Oxford: Clarendon Press, 1994.

Sokolov, M., 'Marriage Contracts for Support and Services: Constitutionality Begins at Home', *New York University Law Review*, 49, December 1974, pp. 1,195ff.

Soros, G., 'Capital Crimes', *The Guardian*, London, 18 January 1997.

Sournia, J-C., *The Illustrated History of Medicine*, London: Harold Starke Publishers Ltd, 1992, p. 38.

Stacey, M., *Regulating British Medicine – The General Medical Council*, Chichester: John Wiley, 1992.

—— 'The Case for and Against Self-Regulation', Paper presented at the Second International Conference on Medical Regulation, 1996.

Stanley, J. M., (eds) 'Developing Guidelines for Decisions to Forego Life Prolonging Medical Treatment', The Appleton International Conference, *Journal of Medical Ethics*, 18 supplement, 1992.

Steering Committee of the Confidential Inquiry into Homicides and Suicides by Mentally Ill People, *Report of the Confidential Inquiry into Homicides and Suicides by Mentally Ill People*, London: Royal College of Psychiatrists, 1996.

Stein, T., 'A Voice in the Wilderness', *Health Service Journal*, 4 March 1993, p. 30.

Stock, F., 'Commentary: Time to Revisit the Child in All of Us', *The Guardian*, 24 April 1996.

Stout, J., *Ethics after Babel*, Cambridge: James Clarke and Co., 1988.

Tam, H., 'Towards a Communitarian Philosophy', *Philosophy Today*, 19 May 1995.

Taylor, C., *Hegel and Modern Society*, Cambridge: Cambridge University Press, 1979.

REFERENCES

—— *Sources of the Self: The Making of Moral Identity*, Cambridge: Cambridge University Press, 1989.

—— *Multi-culturalism and the 'Politics of Recognition'*, Princeton: Princeton University Press, 1992.

Temkin, O., *Hippocrates in a World of Pagans and Christians*, Baltimore and London: The John Hopkins University Press, 1991.

Thompson, A., 'Bound to Secrecy', *Community Care*, 11–17 April 1996, p. 16.

Thompson, J., *User Involvement in Mental Health Services: The Limits of Consumerism, the Risks of Marginalisation and the Need for a Critical Approach*, Hull: Research Memorandum no. 8, Centre for Systems Studies, University of Hull, 1995, p. 41.

Tomlinson, T. and Brody, H., 'Ethics and Communication in Do-Not-Resuscitate Orders', *New England Journal of Medicine*, 318, 1, 1988, pp. 43–46.

Tomlinson, T., Howe, K., Notman, M. and Rossmiller, D., 'An Empirical Study of Proxy Consent for Elderly Persons', *Gerontologist*, 30, 1, 1990, pp. 54–64.

Uhlmann, R. F., Pearlman, R. A. and Cain, K. C., 'Physicians' and Spouses' Predictions of Elderly Patients' Resuscitation Preferences', *Journal of Gerontology*, 43, 5, 1988, M115–121.

US Congress Office of Technology Assessment, *Losing a Million Minds: Confronting the Tragedy of Alzheimer's Disease and Other Dementias*, Washington, DC: US Government Printing Office, 1987.

Veatch, R. M., 1979, 'Justice and Valuing Lives', in Veatch, R. M. (ed.) *Life Span: Values and Life-Extending Technologies*, New York: Harper and Row, 1988.

—— 'Justice and the Economics of Terminal Illness', *Hastings Center Report*, 18, 4, 1988, pp. 34–40.

Waddington, I., *The Medical Profession in the Industrial Revolution*, Dublin: Gill and MacMillan, 1984.

Walzer, M., *Spheres of Justice*, Oxford: Blackwell, 1983.

—— 'The Communitarian Critique of Liberalism', *Political Theory*, 18, 1, February 1990, pp. 6–23.

—— *Interpretation and Social Criticism*, Cambridge: Harvard University Press, 1987.

Watson, D. (ed.), *Ethics for Social Work*, London: RKP, 1995.

Weatherall, M. W., 'Making Medicine Scientific: Empiricism, Rationality and Quakery in Mid-Victorian Britain', *Journal of Social History of Medicine*, 9, 1996, pp. 175–194.

Weatherill, R., *Cultural Collapse*, London: FAB, 1994.

Weinstein, L., *The Marriage Contract*, New York: Free Press, 1981.

Whitehead, A., 'I'm Hungry, Mum: The Politics of Domestic Budgeting', in Young, K., Wolkowitz, C. and McCullagh, R. (eds), *Of Marriage and the Market*, London: CSE Books, 1981, pp. 49–68.

REFERENCES

Whitehead, M., 'Who Cares About Equity in the NHS?', *British Medical Journal*, 308, 1994, pp. 1,284–1,287.

WHO, 'A Traditional Practice that Threatens Health – Female Circumcision', *WHO Chronicle (1986)*, 40, 1, pp. 31–36.

Wicclair, M. R., *Ethics and the Elderly*, New York and Oxford: Oxford University Press, 1993.

Williams, B., *Morality*, Cambridge: Cambridge University Press, 1972.

Williams, J., *HIV/AIDS and Community Care – A Struggle for Survival*, research study published by National Network of Body Positive Groups, 1995.

Williams, M. S., 'Justice Toward Groups', *Political Theory*, 23, 1, 1995, pp. 67–91.

Wilson, M., *Crossing the Boundary: Black Women Survive Incest*, London: Virago, 1993, p. 169.

Wolfensberger, W., *Normalisation*, Toronto: National Institute on Mental Retardation, 1972.

Zwart, H., 'Rationing in the Netherlands: The Liberal and the Communitarian Perspective', *Health Care Analysis*, 1, 1993, pp. 53–56.

——— 'De morele betekenis van onze biologische natuur: ethische aspecten van postmenopauzaal moederschap', *Tijdschrift voor Geneeskunde en Ethiek*, 4, 2, 1994, pp. 39–42.

Zweibel, N. R. and Cassel, C. K., 'Treatment Choices at the End of Life: A Comparison of Decisions by Older Patients and Their Physician-Selected Proxies', *The Gerontologist*, 29, 5, 1989, pp. 615–621.

INDEX